D0722362

Something's Wrong with My Child

Something's Wrong with My Child

A Parents' Book about Children with Learning Disabilities

Milton Brutten, Ph.D.
Sylvia O. Richardson, M.D.
Charles Mangel

Harcourt Brace Jovanovich, Inc.
NEW YORK

Copyright © 1973 by Charles Mangel, Milton Brutten, and
Sylvia O. Richardson

All rights reserved. No part of this publication may be reproduced or
transmitted in any form or by any means, electronic or mechanical,
including photocopy, recording, or any information storage and retrieval
system, without permission in writing from the publisher.

Printed in the United States of America

Library of Congress Catalog Card Number: 73-5876

ISBN 0-15-183737-6

E

For every child
who needed only intelligent understanding—
and never received it

When one considers in its length and in its breadth the importance of this question of the education of a nation's young, the broken lives, the defeated hopes, the national failures which result from the frivolous inertia with which it is treated, it is difficult to restrain within oneself a savage rage.

—ALFRED NORTH WHITEHEAD
The Aims of Education

If a human right exists at all, it is the right to be born with normal body and mind, with the prospect of developing further to fulfillment. If this is to be denied, then life and conscience are a mockery.

—N. J. BERRILL
The Person in the Womb

I don't know what's the matter with me. I think I'm broken.

—ARTHUR, *twelve years old*

Contents

1 / Bright but Dumb

Many children, in this era of space exploration, are judged to be emotionally disturbed—but are not.

Many children are said to be low in intellectual ability—even mentally retarded—but are not.

Many children are given life sentences to institutions—but don't belong there.

No one knows how many of these mislabeled boys and girls there are or how they developed the problems they have.

But the most vital information is in hand: experts can identify most of them and, with proper treatment, save perhaps nine out of ten from wasted lives.

If they are diagnosed early enough. And if they are cared for properly.

These children are among an estimated 7.5 million boys and girls under the age of eighteen in this country who suffer from a little-understood group of related *physiological* problems called learning disabilities. These disabilities are believed to be primarily neurologic in origin. They make it difficult or impossible for these youngsters to learn normally and to behave well.

The disabilities do not impair intelligence. Rather, they affect specific areas of learning and behavior. Some of these children, though they perform well in other ways, cannot learn to read or write or spell or do arithmetic. Some cannot speak in organized sentences. Others are so clumsy they can hardly hold a pencil. Many are unmanageable. A number have been expelled from school for incorrigible behavior. Some have run away from home. Others have been in trouble with the police. They come from good families and bad ones. Alert and competent in some ways, inept, ineffectual, and foolish in others, these children often have been called "bright but dumb." "They are so smart, but just so—whacked up," one parent comments.

The outward characteristics or symptoms of many learning-disabled children frequently are mistaken for those of mental retardation or emotional disturbance. *Learning disabilities are neither of these.*

The mentally retarded child is permanently limited in his intellectual ability. He needs and can benefit from education, but he can never do schoolwork as well as a normal child of the same age. The learning-disabled child has an intellectual potential that is usually normal or better. But he *functions* at a lower level because of the specific impairments this book will discuss. Special teaching techniques can help most learning-disabled youngsters considerably, and can narrow the gap between them and children who have no learning handicaps. The retarded child doesn't catch up. He will always function at a lower level.

Learning-disabled children also differ from boys and girls who have solely emotional problems. Emotionally disturbed youngsters might have difficulties with school adjustment and behavior that, on the surface, bear a resemblance to the problems of learning-disabled children. But the difficulties of the emotionally disturbed child stem from disturbances in his feelings, his attitudes, his ideas of his own worth, his motivations, his aspirations. He is inhibited in learning—his energies are so tied up in maintaining inner stability that he has little left over to devote to education. The learning-disabled boy or girl may have some of these same disordered feelings; but in his case they are *a result* of his inability to learn and to function well. It is not hard to see that a child who cannot learn or behave like other children might develop emotional disorders. But, as will be seen, they are secondary to his basic problem; the learning disability was there first.

The learning-disabled child is frequently misdiagnosed. "Nationwide, there are thousands of [retardates], 'behavior problems' and 'slow learners' in residential facilities for the retarded who should not be in these institutions," the President's Committee on Mental Retardation stated, in its report in 1968. "Many 'mentally retarded' persons are not mentally retarded at all," said the U.S. Commissioner of Education, Harold E. Howe II, in a speech in 1968. "They have learning disabilities."

How does one recognize a learning-disabled youngster? Here are some of the common signs. All of these and others are discussed in greater detail in later chapters.

The learning-disabled child may find school hard from the very first day. He can't cut with scissors, can't color inside lines, has difficulty matching shapes and sizes. He may have trouble grasping abstract concepts (are jets and buses both means of transportation?) or relating what he has learned in one context to another. He may have difficulty expressing his ideas coherently. His schoolwork may be erratic: good in some areas, very poor in others.

He may appear to be in perpetual motion, spending more time under his seat than in it. He may be easily distracted, walking away from a teacher in midsentence to watch a classmate sharpen a pencil. His attention may dart about without apparent reason, and his concentration may last only minutes or seconds.

He may seem emotionally unstable. These children's moods often change from one extreme to another with stunning swiftness. Disappointment, frustration, unexpected variations in simple routine—realities a normal child copes with daily—can cause riotous tantrums, crying spells, hostility, or, for some, total withdrawal.

More than three of every four youngsters with learning disabilties appear to be clumsy and awkward. Catching a ball, walking along a chalked line, throwing a beanbag to someone five feet away may be impossible for them. (A parent says, "I don't care if Steve never catches a ball." His doctor replies, "If he can't move his hands to the ball, he can't move his hands to reproduce what he sees on the blackboard.")

Although symptoms of most disabilities are present and detectable during the preschool years, the typical learning-disabled child does not begin to show severe characteristics until he starts to attend school. Then pressures begin. The young student must now perform certain tasks in specified ways at definite times. Hampered by his deficiencies, the learning-disabled youngster begins to fall behind, possibly in kindergarten or first grade, sometimes later as school demands increase. If his behavior doesn't disrupt the class routine, he may be allowed to drift, gain "social" promotions, and thus "graduate." He sits, undiscovered and unaided, until he is old enough to leave school and enter an employment market in which he has little chance of success.

If his behavior or his academic handicaps are severe enough, the child may be held back a year or two, dismissed from school, or assigned to a catchall class with children who have *totally nonrelated* learning problems—such as the mentally retarded or the emotionally disturbed.

Much of what the learning-disabled child does is not willful or intentional on his part. He is not in control of his behavior or his inadequate learning performance. His physiological impairment seems to "short-circuit" what would be normal behavior and learning.

Now he begins to develop emotional problems on top of his learning difficulties. He learns about social rejection. Children can be cruel to the youngster who still uses baby talk, who can't climb the monkey bars, catch a ball, or swing a bat. Adults dismiss him as unruly, spoiled, or, worse, neurotic. Because he is intelligent, the learning-disabled youngster is acutely aware of his failures. He becomes frustrated, assumes he is worthless, and gives up on himself and school. His total inability to succeed in anything causes true psychological problems to begin. The damage to a child's ego often is more difficult to correct than the learning inadequacies themselves.

The agony is unnecessary. By a combination of techniques, a group of qualified professionals—chiefly in psychology, medicine, and education—can find most of these children. If the diagnosis is positive, education—in the form of tutorial assistance or, for children with more than mild impairment, special classes—becomes the key to improvement. This remedial training consists of finding the area in which the learning-disabled child is weak and then giving him exercises designed to improve his skills in that area. No one knows why such exercises work or what happens inside the child's brain. Educators have a number of ideas concerning the learning-disabled child, how his areas of weakness can be found and how special methods and teaching materials can be used to help overcome them. Their approach is pragmatic; in much the same way, a headache sufferer takes aspirin, although science has no sure knowledge of how aspirin functions to reduce the pain.

There is no cure for a learning disability in the sense that a disease has a cure. For example, antibiotics can end an infection. The learning-disabled child is considered "cured" if he begins to learn in accordance with what specialists believe to be his abilities, if he can, in essence, function as would a normal child without handicaps of any sort.

How long can this take? The time required to achieve a "cure"—where it can be achieved—varies according to the severity of each child's problems, his intelligence and emotional make-up, the co-operation of his family, the age at which a diagnosis is made, and the effectiveness of the special teaching he gets. One study of learning-disabled children who were put into special classes—their problems were too severe to allow them to remain in a regular classroom—found that 80 per cent of those with average or higher intelligence ultimately went back to regular classes. Children for whom help was started before the age of eight needed, on the average, two and a half years before they could return.

What is wrong with a learning-disabled child? Science doesn't know. To the best of current understanding, the central nervous system apparently is not working adequately, for one of two broad reasons.*

1. Disease or injury may have damaged the central nervous system. This can happen before or at birth or during a child's early years.

2. There may be delayed *or* improper development of the central nervous system. This is usually termed maturational delay or lag (or, sometimes, developmental deviation). Maturational lag in effect means that the child's nervous system is not developing at the same rate as those of other children his age. Therefore elements of his behavior or learning will not be normal. Most learning disabilities, researchers believe, fall into this category.

There are children with learning problems who might be confused with youngsters in these two categories. They are the boys and girls who are simply at the bottom of the normal range of development. They are normal, but are not quite as intelligent as others—perhaps slower in thinking and communicating.

Until recent years, child-development experts—chiefly educators, psychologists, and pediatricians—commonly believed that children who did not learn or behave appropriately had purely psychological problems. They blamed *all* childhood difficulties on misguided handling by parents. The battle is far from over. Many child-guidance professionals still scoff when they hear the term learning disability. Fortunately, they are decreasing in number.

The usual medical examination, for example, looks for disease in a child. The boy or girl who has none is judged to be normal. But little or no attention is paid to the way the child performs outside the doctor's office. Is he a terror at home? Does he "climb walls" at school? Is he excessively withdrawn and timid? He can't learn to read, spell, write? Too many

---

* The central nervous system supervises and co-ordinates the activity of the body's entire nervous system. It is the part of the nervous system that consists of the brain and the spinal cord. Sensory information is transmitted to the central nervous system; motor impulses pass from it to govern body movements.

physicians ignore—or do not elicit—this kind of information.

Just what does maturational lag mean to the developing child?

A child's growth ordinarily follows a well-timed developmental course. But nature can break down. For a variety of reasons that are not fully understood, development can be slowed or distorted. Maturational lag puts the child into immediate conflict with his society. Society is always striving to create order. So it makes demands of children according to their age levels.

Five-year-old children, for example, are expected to be ready for kindergarten. When a child's development—his maturation—is equal to the demands of this new situation, everyone is pleased. But when his development lags—a five-year-old child can have the maturation of a three-year-old *in some of the things he does*—the child will not meet the expectations placed on him.

He may draw like a three-year-old. He may be restless. He may be unable to pay attention. He may disturb. He may roam the room. He may have temper tantrums. He may wet his pants. He may seek constant attention from the teacher. None of this is intentional in a learning-disabled youngster. The child just is not able to cope with the first significant demands of the environment outside his family. This is why most cases of "problem" children surface when school begins, and why they increase in severity as school requirements escalate. The problem probably has been there since birth. But lesser stress and family love have muffled it.

A child of two years might have the maturation of a twelve-month-old—and would perform in part like a twelve-month-old. He could be slow in walking, in talking, in obeying. A child of ten years might have the maturation of a six-year-old. Should he be put into a fourth-grade social-studies class or on the baseball field? A child of fifteen might have the maturation of an eleven-year-old. Should he try to do geometry or keep up with adolescent social demands?

Everything children learn—academic, social, anything—is determined by how and what they experience with their basic physical and intellectual equipment—their bodies, in great part their nervous systems. They learn by trying, eventually succeeding. As a baby moves away from his need for complete care, he begins to establish a sense of initiative and exploration. As his parents allow him to explore while they still guide and control, he moves toward greater and greater autonomy. Gradually the child learns what he can do by himself. With that sureness comes self-esteem. After learning how to deal with others through his experiences with members of his family, he emerges from the home. He expands his range of activities and his knowledge of the world.

A child who is delayed or deviant in development doesn't socialize properly. Inept in play, he is soon abandoned by other children. This youngster is denied the successful accomplishments that would spur him to further effort and achievement. Trouble increases when he gets to school. He wants to do what the other children do, learn as well as they do. But he lacks the basic skills. If he can't express himself adequately, he can't take part in classroom discussion. If he can't run or catch a ball, he can't take part in play. It is not long before the self-confidence that will even let him try vanishes.

Most professionals concerned with children—physicians, psychologists—ignore slow maturation. They say the child will catch up: the slow-to-speak child will speak; the clumsy child will gain better control of his body. Many slow maturers do catch up—and many do not. But the key point— the point that is ignored—is the effect on the slow-maturing child of his continuing failure in school and in social activities, the increasing criticism, scorn, rejection, by teachers, family, and agemates. The extreme damage to the ego, to a child's image of himself, can be devastating. If the basic learning disabilities go undetected and unremedied too long, the damage to a child's ego will be difficult or impossible to correct (see the discussion of emotional and social development in chapter 3).

The explorations of early investigators who suspected that

neurologic dysfunction might be a cause for the failure of the intelligent child to function well, to keep up with the challenges of his expanding environment, received significant reinforcement from two actions of the federal government.

In 1964, the Department of Health, Education, and Welfare and the National Easter Seal Society for Crippled Children and Adults brought together a group of experts in various specialties to sum up current knowledge about the learning-disabled child. That was the first official and interdisciplinary panel to say flatly that there are children "with certain learning or behavioral disabilities associated with deviations of function of the central nervous system." These children, reported the experts, have problems in speaking, understanding, and thinking—skills vital to good learning. Some of these boys and girls, the panel added, also may have difficulty in controlling their impulsiveness or their attention span, and they may have poor physical co-ordination. This study group acknowledged the wide range of opinion concerning learning-disabled children and the cause or causes of their disabilities, but it emphasized, "We cannot afford the luxury of waiting until causes [of learning and behavior problems] can be unquestionably established by techniques yet to be developed. We cannot postpone [helping] as effectively and honestly as possible [this] large number of children."

The following year, another group of advisers to the Department of Health, Education, and Welfare confirmed the report of the earlier panel. This second collection of specialists spelled matters out a bit more: "[These] children . . . exhibit a disorder . . . in understanding or in using spoken or written language [such as] listening, thinking, reading, writing, spelling, or arithmetic."

The primary message in both findings: growing agreement among professionals in medicine and education that there is a physiological origin to many childhood learning and behavior problems.

Many of the symptoms noted here can occur in mild form in children who are *not* learning-disabled. A symptom is significant only if it exists to a serious degree—if, for example, the child is not just clumsy, but cannot walk without stumbling repeatedly. Or if it persists for a long time—length of time depends upon the particular symptom; one of the specialists described in later chapters must decide how long is "too long."

Learning disability is the most common of the more than fifty names that experts have attached to this collection of impairments. Some of the other names most commonly heard are: minimal brain dysfunction, minimal brain damage, cerebral dysfunction, neurological impairment, psychoneurological learning disorder, perceptual impairment, conceptual handicap, attention disorder, hyperkinetic (or hyperactive), hypokinetic, impulse-ridden child, specific reading disability, dyslexia, aphasia, and dyscalculia.

How many children is this book talking about? One specialist calls learning disabilities "the most common and pervasive neurological problem among children." But no one has any idea of the exact number. Estimates range from 1 to 40 per cent of all children in the United States. Language disabilities alone—taking in reading, writing, and speaking, just one part of the problem—are believed to involve 7 to 15 per cent of all children.

Some investigators go further. One out of every four students cannot read well; virtually every child who has normal intelligence and is seriously behind in reading has a specific language disability, Dr. Archie Silver, a New York child psychiatrist, told an interviewer in 1969. "In the majority of cases, [inability to read] is a result of minimal cerebral dysfunction," Dr. Maurice H. Charlton, chief of neurology clinics at New York's Columbia-Presbyterian Medical Center, said, at a medical society symposium in 1971.

Many researchers speculate conservatively that 10 per cent of all boys and girls under the age of eighteen have a learning disability. The authors agree. The figure of 7.5 million used here is based on 10 per cent of the boys and girls in this age group.

Learning disability is a mystifying handicap in so many ways. It encompasses an incredible variety of problems gathered under the same umbrella. (How can an aggressive child and a shy, withdrawn child suffer from the same organic problem? But they do.) Far more boys are affected than girls, for reasons that are not known. Many physicians, psychologists, and school personnel who come in contact with this child fail to diagnose him properly, thus delaying aid—many times until it is too late to do significant good. A child with a learning disability can't complain of it to his parents or teacher as he would with stomach cramps; he doesn't realize he *has* a problem. Professionals have yet to agree on the cause, or causes, of learning disabilities. They are not even sure why certain kinds of treatment work; no one knows, for example, why some of the medication used with these children is effective.

But one thing is extraordinarily clear: most of these boys and girls have the potential to lead fulfilling, productive lives. They are intellectually competent youngsters. With skilled and compassionate handling by parents and professionals, most of them can overcome much or all of their handicaps.

They *need* help. Without it, many will fail in their lives. The following chapters will discuss how to identify learning-disabled children, how to find sources of diagnosis and treatment for them, how to live with them and help them at home, and how to assist them in preparing for successful adult lives.

2 / Four Children

These are the true stories of four learning-disabled young-sters. They illustrate the great variety of ways this handicap can affect children.

The child is obviously quick and bright, but he shreds the hearts of his parents. His explosions have pushed him beyond the endurance of his family and his teacher. School routine is impossible when he is in the room. Unable to work at his classmates' first-grade level, he allows no one else to work. Four doctors, one a psychiatrist, have said he is emotionally disturbed, but a year of expensive therapy has not helped. Guilt-ridden and desperate to the point of sleeplessness, his parents are leaning to the advice of one of the physicians, who has said, "There's nothing more you can do. Put him in a home."

The day after that counsel, the mother, Theresa Anderson, waited until her husband had left for work, took his pistol from the bedroom closet shelf, loaded it, and called her three young children into the living room. She lined them up in front of the fireplace—Tim, eight, Bobby, six, Susan, three—and prepared to kill each of them and then herself.

Mrs. Anderson, intelligent, well educated, and to all appearances a good mother, could take no more of Bobby. "It got to the point where I began to doubt my own sanity."

The boy's supercharged behavior was destroying his family. His parents were on the verge of separation. His school, in a large suburb of New York City, was threatening to have him committed—at the age of six—to a reformatory, for "incorrigibility." He roamed around his classroom, disturbing children near him, ignoring his teacher's requests. He shrieked when irritated, regardless of time or place. He bit and hit without provocation. Mrs. Anderson had been called repeatedly to the principal's office. During one visit, the principal said, "I hope you realize how much of a problem your family has been to us. We just don't have time for a child like yours." "The impression was clear," said Mrs. Anderson later. "I was too ignorant to raise a child; if I used some discipline on my son, he might behave."

The children waited obediently. Mrs. Anderson, pistol held behind her back, stood in front of them. She finally turned and ran upstairs, the children still in an orderly row before the living-room fireplace.

The following week, the Andersons placed Bobby in a state-run home for the emotionally disturbed. He was to remain there for four years.

Bobby had kicked out the slats of his crib at eleven months and had been in constant motion ever since. "Every night I had to make fifteen or twenty trips upstairs to get him back into his crib," says Mrs. Anderson. "Finally, in frustration, I tied him spread-eagled to his crib with my husband's belts. I sat downstairs and cried, and he cried upstairs. Just to get dinner on the table for the other children, I had to tie him to the living-room railing each night with rope."

Housework was done around midnight, when Bobby would doze for a couple of hours. He never slept through the night. Mrs. Anderson "crept around" quietly washing the floors, doing laundry and her other chores, fearful the noise would wake Bobby.

Mr. Anderson simply fled from the problem. To escape his home, he worked almost constantly. He and his wife never went out. Bobby's parents refused all invitations to other people's homes. ("If I didn't go, I would not have to return the invitation.") Their daughter "developed a deep hatred for Bobby and for me," Mrs. Anderson said. "She deliberately belittled him."

At the age of two, Bobby hurled toys at his mother whenever anything frustrated him. He could not be left alone. "One day he went out to ride his bike," his mother said. "I found out by hearing car after car screech to a halt to avoid this little kid riding his tricycle in the busy street in front of our home. He just seemed to have no common sense. He never seemed to look ahead, to realize the consequences of his actions."

He once took a garden hose lying in front of a neighbor's home, turned it on, and sprayed water through the front door of the neighbor's house. A little girl who lived nearby came out one day, wearing a party dress, to wait for her parents. Bobby jumped with both feet into a mud puddle right next to the girl. His sister had a newly born kitten. His mother once caught him playing with the kitten by throwing it up in the air and letting it fall on the concrete basement floor. Bobby didn't seem to realize that he was hurting the kitten.

"I don't understand how this boy is alive today," his mother said. "We put him to bed one night at eight, and he kept getting up and wandering around bothering his sister. Finally, at eleven, my husband had reached the end of his patience. He raced up to Bobby in his sister's room, grabbed him by the neck of his pajamas, and threw him into his bed. He almost strangled him accidentally. He did do some damage to the neck cartilages."

Bobby had no fear. The day of a televised moon launch, his mother found him playing astronaut. He was about to jump out of a second-floor window. His parents put bars on his windows and a lock and chain on his bedroom door to keep him from roaming at night. He had had forty stitches in his head by the age of three, because he kept climbing and falling—out of trees, off roofs. At six, he came home from school by walking along the roofs of houses.

It was virtually impossible to ride with Bobby in the car. He would lean halfway out an open window or climb all over the driver. He could not be controlled in such public places as restaurants or supermarkets.

"All I wanted was someone to help this child," said Mrs.

Anderson. "All I seemed to do was take him to the hospital emergency room or go to the school humiliated to apologize for something he had done. The principal said, 'Smack him on the rear.' She didn't know we had beaten this boy practically unconscious. The teacher said, 'Make him do his homework.' I sat with him for two or three hours every night, slapping him most of the time because he couldn't do the work. One evening I found myself about to slam his head against the wall.

"School personnel said Bobby was disturbed or retarded. His first-grade teacher once asked me, 'Wouldn't you be satisfied if he could just learn to recognize that exit sign over there?'"

Bobby never finished his beginning reader. The first signs of pressure caused him to fall apart. He would not recite in front of the class. He crawled under his desk in school one morning and told his teacher, "Call the policemen and the firemen. Me not gonna read."

"I reached the point where I could no longer control my rages," said Mrs. Anderson. "I had total feelings of failure. He upset our whole life. While talking to my husband one night I found myself jumping out of the chair and screaming, 'I hate him! I hate him!'"

When Bobby entered the state institution for the emotionally disturbed, at the age of six, his family felt "overwhelming relief" at his removal from their care—and then immediate guilt for feeling good. Yet four years there brought only regression. He still could not read or write. His temper tantrums had increased markedly. Then a new psychologist at the institution suggested that Bobby be taken for testing at a private school designed for children with learning disabilities. That was where, at the age of ten, his disability was discovered.

Bobby's handicap, believed to have been caused by momentary deprivation of oxygen during birth, made it extremely difficult for him to translate his thoughts into words. He had a limited stock of words to choose from, and those were words that referred only to things he could see or feel.

He had virtually no vocabulary with which to express his desires and emotions. He burned with rage because he could not say what he was thinking. It was so much easier for him to do things than to speak that he used whirlwind activity to make up for his skimpy vocabulary. Asked why he played with matches, he said, "Don't make me. Shut up! I'll kill you dead!"

Bobby was enrolled in the private school. He was given intensive training to expand his vocabulary and help him express his thoughts in organized language. Medication calmed his behavior and allowed him to concentrate on his schoolwork. He began to learn, to climb past the second-grade level at which he had been mired. In six months, aided by the medication and the fact that he was learning at last, Bobby's gross misbehavior eased. He started to read for pleasure for the first time in his life. He enjoyed school and became a good student. He learned to accept and use constructive criticism, instead of exploding whenever it was offered.

In three years of hard work, he pulled up to his proper grade level. His IQ, which had been in the dull-normal area, moved well into the normal range. Bobby graduated from twelfth grade in the private school. He is now in a regular junior college studying accounting and will probably transfer to a four-year college.

Bobby overcame most of his learning disabilities, far beyond his parents' expectations. He illustrates how many learning-disabled children can be helped to virtual normality.

"Each gain that Bobby makes is measured from the last step," his mother told the authors. "He is always surprising us in being able to accomplish tasks or reach levels we would never have expected of him. Our attitude toward him is almost the same now as toward our normal children. Our goal, of course, is to help him be self-sufficient and employable and married. And why not? We never thought he'd ride a two-wheeler, or be able to travel confidently to and from New York City alone, or even be able to multiply numbers. That last took him ten years to accomplish."

Mike's parents became aware early that he was different.

He never liked the toys most children gravitate to. He showed very little curiosity. As he grew, he remained listless and played aimlessly if he played at all. When Mike was thirteen months old, his pediatrician suggested a neurological examination. The neurologist looked at Mike quickly ("Who can evaluate a human being in twenty minutes?" his mother was later to ask) and said, "Madam, you have a severely retarded son. He belongs in an institution for the rest of his life." In panic, the family consulted another neurologist; he told them Mike was mildly retarded. A third neurologist said nothing at all was wrong. Repeated physical examinations found him healthy.

Mike remained listless through his preschool years. When he was five, he entered a public-school kindergarten for retarded children. The next three years changed a quiet, sweet boy into a cranky, irritable child. He did nothing that first year but scribble endlessly with crayons. His attention span was dreadfully short. Was he in fact retarded? His parents began to wonder.

Midway through the year, a school psychologist told Mike's mother that her son was emotionally disturbed, not retarded, and should be transferred to a class for the emotionally disturbed. The psychologist also suggested counseling for Mike and his parents at a mental-health clinic in their rural eastern community. But a year of therapy achieved nothing.

Mike could not learn the alphabet in first grade, but he memorized a hundred words in his reading book and "read" to his teacher. He refused to try anything he did not think he could do. The other children were soon calling him "retard," and he began to balk at going to school. Yet his teacher passed him in every subject. "There seems to be a tendency in the schools when you get a child like this to just slide him through," Mike's mother said later. "Don't make waves."

Mike drifted through the first grades. Periodically he became so frustrated that he would pick fights in the classroom. He began to lie and to play with matches.

"No one gave us any help," Mike's mother recalled. "No one even tried. Who *was* he? What kind of child? Was he retarded? Was he disturbed? The professionals dumped the questions in our lap and walked away. They don't seem to care or to want to commit themselves. Unless the child disrupts the class. Then *you* fix him or take him out."

When Mike was eleven, his father was transferred to a large city in a mid-Atlantic state, and Mike was placed with his age group in a regular fifth-grade class. His new teacher immediately realized he could not work at that level. She suggested an examination by a pediatric neurologist, a specialist in neurological disorders of children.

This specialist was the first doctor to identify Mike's problem as learning disabilities combined with petit-mal episodes. Petit mal is a form of epilepsy in which the person who has it blanks out for a few seconds at a time. This accounted for Mike's lack of curiosity, his listlessness, and his seeming to tune people out.

Mike's learning disabilities were varied. He had a perceptual problem. All printed material was a blur to him, in spite of his normal vision; everything also appeared upside down or reversed. So he could not decipher a printed page. Basic number concepts threw him. He could not tell if the number of blocks in one pile was more or less than the number of blocks in another pile. He could not hold up two fingers when asked, or say how many pieces he would have if he cut an apple in half. Mike could not work well with his hands. A relative lack of control over his small muscles hampered his ability to draw and to write.

"Obviously, being unable to learn in an ordinary fashion, school provided a very frustrating situation for him and this would account for some of his behavior problems in school," the physician's report noted. "The only way Mike can be helped is to have intensive teaching assistance given by a person specially trained in working with learning-impaired children. If this help cannot be obtained for him, he cannot be expected to make any further progress in school."

Mike, too, was enrolled in a private school for learnin-disabled children. His education began again at the beginning, with much of his time spent in individual training with specialists in perception and co-ordination. They helped untangle the scrambled way he saw letters and numbers. Work with concrete teaching aids, like rods of various lengths and colors, dramatically improved his ideas about quantity, and hence his arithmetic ability. He had to learn the difference between up and down, between near and far, in relation to his own body. He was given carefully guided exercises to develop efficient co-ordination between his hands and his eyes. Medication ended his petit-mal seizures.

"For the first time, things were explained to us," his father said. "Now we could work together. When he reverses letters on his homework, I don't holler, 'Concentrate!' I know it's not his fault. The rural school never told us he had a special problem. I had seen his letter reversals, but I didn't know what they meant."

In two years, Mike was up to fifth-grade work, and eventually he reached a level only one year behind children his own age. His chronic frustration and irritability disappeared. He became alive and alert.

Mike is a success—academically, emotionally, and socially. His IQ has more than doubled, jumping from what is considered to be retardation into the high-normal area. He has made his greatest gains in mathematics, mastering all the basic number concepts that had once baffled him. He has changed from a passive, tightly inhibited child into an outgoing and spontaneous teen-ager.

"Problems still exist," his mother reports. "Understanding his offbeat thinking. He is fascinated with matches; he seems to have enough sense to light them in the bathroom or in an open field, but still not enough not to light them at all. He is still not able to think all things out—lack of logic and common sense in so many areas, and yet so clever. But the progress! My Lord, he's a whole boy now, and the problems are slowly falling away.

"I keep wondering what if we hadn't moved? Would he still be shuttling between classes for the retarded and the disturbed?"

Maureen was the kind of child teachers tend to overlook

because "they don't cause trouble." She was so well behaved that no one at her school noticed she wasn't learning.

She had developed slowly during her nursery-school years, a tiny, demure child who always seemed younger than she was. She clung to her mother and seemed to feel unsafe and insecure when asked to do something by herself.

Her parents, disturbed at her shyness in kindergarten and her seemingly paradoxic temper tantrums at home, took her to a psychiatrist for evaluation. His diagnosis: severe emotional problems. Maureen and her parents went into therapy for a year. They were then discharged with the comment "We can do nothing more for you." Nothing *had* been done.

Maureen was in trouble from the very first months in kindergarten. School became a lonely, often frightening experience for this little girl. Anything new threatened her. She refused to seek the company of other children. She spent recess and lunch periods sitting alone on the schoolyard steps. "She never had a happy look on her face," her mother said. "She rarely smiled, rarely got excited about anything."

Her parents kept telling school authorities that something was wrong. People "spent a great deal of time and energy attempting to reassure us," her mother said. Teachers insisted she was just a quiet child doing her best. Maureen's pediatrician believed she was a "slow developer." "We just didn't know where to turn for help," her mother said. "In hindsight, it's obvious that even people who work with young children and who have experts on hand still don't know enough about handling children who have any but 'normal' variations of behavior."

If school personnel were not "aware" of Maureen's learning problems, her classmates were. They imitated the halting, broken way she spoke. Every time she was called on to read (she never volunteered), the other children laughed at her. "Her life was a hell in school," her mother told the authors. "She came out of there crying almost every day. Kids find someone like Maureen a prime target. She continued to be a victim of ridicule. She was hurt and rejected so many times that even when she had invitations [to social occasions] she held back and missed out on them."

Maureen's younger sister and brother—he was five years younger than Maureen—taught her much of her lessons. "She would ask me how to spell a word, and her brother, who had just learned the alphabet, would shout it out," her mother said. "This made her furious. Maureen had a hard time with her academically gifted brother and sister. They were cruel. She was called 'idiot,' 'imbecile,' 'retard,' 'stupid' repeatedly."

There were thirty-nine children in Maureen's class. She kept getting B's and C's. When she "graduated" from sixth grade, she was awarded a plaque for making "the most improvement." She still could not read.

"We felt so helpless," her mother said. She continually asked the school psychologist to test Maureen. He didn't see the need.

Maureen's seventh-grade teacher was the first to recognize the girl was out of her level. She told Maureen's mother, "I wish she'd throw an eraser at someone. She's behaving in class, so I can't get her tested. Troublemakers get tested fast." This teacher began to grade Maureen honestly. For the first time in her school career, the girl got failing marks.

"Until then, teachers all through her schooling seemed to have no concept of the struggle Maureen was having," her mother said. "To them, she was a nice, quiet child who tried her best (and should be rewarded for that) and didn't cause trouble. The fact that she was learning very little and not reacting socially to anyone didn't seem a matter of great concern."

Maureen's teacher proved that the child was working at second-grade level. She was placed in a remedial-reading class. This teacher, when she found she was unable to help, recommended testing at a nearby medical center. Now thirteen years old, Maureen finally was discovered to have a learning disability.

She was so low in energy that she couldn't work as fast and as long as other children. She became exhausted quickly and found it easier just to sit passively. She didn't have the stamina to pay attention consistently enough to learn. In a self-defensive kind of maneuver, she ignored teachers and classmates. She had just sat there—for eight years. "When we tried to discuss the problem of her newly discovered learning disability with the principal, the school psychologist, and the teachers," her mother said, "we found them totally unaware of learning disabilities and of resources available in our area for dealing with them."

Maureen was enrolled in a private school. She could now work at her own pace. No one pushed her. But teachers encouraged her with lessons in small, concentrated doses at her level. Tiny learning triumphs—composition of one perfect paragraph about a trip to the zoo—catapulted the teen-ager into larger challenges. This new success in school made her understand she could accomplish something and made her like herself more. As a result, both her home outbursts and her school timidity waned.

"This special school changed her life," her mother said. "Her self-image and her sense of personal strength have improved immeasurably. She feels far less 'different.' She's made some friends. Her schoolwork has improved, although there are still gaps and inconsistencies. But she now has the opportunity to build on accomplishments, where previously everything was failure."

Maureen, at twenty, is still in a special school. She will never earn a high-school diploma. But she is progressing slowly, doing well in home economics and typing. If she continues her improvement, she will leave with a certificate of completion. She plans to enter secretarial school.

Maureen was diagnosed and begun on a special program too late for it to be an unqualified success. She remains unduly afraid of making mistakes; this apprehensiveness keeps her from attempting too many new things, in or out of school. Her academic work is better, but her vocabulary and abstract-thinking ability probably will remain deficient. She is still shy and inhibited, a lonely young woman ignored by most of her classmates. She will become self-sufficient, perhaps in an office job that puts little stress on her, but she is likely to be highly passive and fearful all her life.

Jeannie had always seemed different from her brother, Dan.

He was a placid boy, easy to raise and care for. She fussed and fumed and was miserably unhappy just about all the time. She seemed healthy, and her pediatrician couldn't be sure why she was such an uneasy child.

By the time Jeannie was two and a half, she was wild and uncontrollable. Her mother's nerves were worn trying to keep up with her and keep her out of trouble. Jeannie interfered with any kind of normal family routine. She fought with her brother because she wanted everything he played with. There seemed to be no way to make her content. She acted on every impulse, running, handling, grabbing, shouting. Neither parent could discipline her effectively. Patience simply seemed to stimulate Jeannie to even more outrageous behavior—demanding, crying, insisting on her own way. Spanking and yelling whipped the child into a frenzy of screams, kicks, and wild thrashing.

Life was torment for Jeannie's parents and obviously yielded no satisfaction to the child, either. Her parents were sensible enough to recognize that Jeannie was not deliberately bringing grief upon herself. They asked their pediatrician to check her closely. But he could not explain her uncontrollable behavior and referred Jeannie to a specialist, a pediatric neurologist at a nearby metropolitan medical center. The pediatric neurologist, Dr. Nathan, spent a lot of time with Jeannie. He saw her twice and then met with her parents. He told them that Jeannie had a neurologic impairment.

"It really doesn't matter too much what caused her condition," he explained to the parents. "The important thing is to understand that Jeannie has it, and that because of the impairment she can't control her behavior, or act and develop like other children.

"She's been so uncontrolled and impulsive that you probably aren't aware that her muscular co-ordination is not what it should be. Her speech development also is delayed. I'm going to set up a program to help Jeannie with her development. I will follow her on a regular basis until she is well along in school. I can't predict if she will have learning problems in school, but it seems likely. If we work carefully, we can help prevent learning problems from being too great, or from occurring at all. I'm pleased that you are meeting this problem early. It's much easier to help children like Jeannie —and the outcome is much more satisfactory—if we can find them while they are quite young."

Dr. Nathan wanted to calm Jeannie. He prescribed a mild medication. The medication did not "drug" her in any way. She reacted favorably within two weeks by seeming more calm and satisfied. She stopped charging around the house and became far less impulsive. She improved to the point where she was able to enter nursery school at the age of four. She did well, although her nursery-school teacher said Jeannie had a low frustration tolerance and became angry under any kind of stress. Jeannie also had a difficult time making her hands do what she wanted them to. It was hard for her to work on puzzles, to color within lines, to handle a pair of scissors.

Dr. Nathan recommended training with a co-ordination specialist, in this case an occupational therapist who specialized in working with children who had some form of mild neurological handicap. Jeannie enjoyed going to the co-ordination specialist for perceptual-motor training. She thought it was all a game and was delighted by her growing ability to handle crayons and pencils and to make things like scissors work properly.

The pediatric neurologist then suggested a psychological examination. A number of tests (described in chapter 6) revealed that Jeannie had better-than-average intelligence, but confirmed a mild neurological impairment that was interfering with her development of muscular skills and language. Other children seemed to understand what Jeannie was saying; but she did not make her sounds distinctly. The psychologist and Dr. Nathan suggested speech therapy, to try to avoid problems in kindergarten and beyond. A speech clinician began to see Jeannie and worked with her all through her kindergarten year.

By the age of six, Jeannie had improved so much with her co-ordination that the occupational therapist said no further perceptual-motor exercises were necessary. Jeannie's personality was changing as well. She was social and out-going in kindergarten. She co-operated with the speech thera-pist and did all the exercises at home that were intended to overcome her improper pronunciation of some sounds.

Jeannie's kindergarten teacher thought she was still behind her classmates in some activities and wondered if Jeannie was ready for first grade at the age of six. Fortunately her birth-day was in January, so Jeannie was older than most entering first-graders.

By now, Dr. Nathan was sure Jeannie could control herself without the need for medication. He first reduced the dosage and then eliminated the medication as Jeannie continued to show normal behavior and self-control. The speech clinician reported that Jeannie seemed to be making many of her sounds correctly, but thought she should continue with the child through first grade.

In first grade, Jeannie had minor problems starting to write, because her muscular control was not yet what it should have been. She had trouble staying within lines and making neat, legible letters. She was lucky that an expert itinerant learning-disability specialist (see chapter 7) was available in her public-school district. Jeannie's first-grade teacher asked this specialist to test the girl in visual perception and co-ordination and to prescribe a writing program for her. This worked, and Jeannie began to make progress.

She also had difficulty with beginning numbers work. The itinerant specialist thought that Jeannie needed help there as well. She took Jeannie out of class and worked with her alone for one period each week. Jeannie had trouble visualizing what numbers on a printed page meant. When she could *see* and *hold* a half-dozen pegs, she was aware that they meant *six*, which was one more than five but one less than seven and a lot less than ten. She could handle and manipulate these pegs and see for herself that two piles of six pegs made a total of twelve. She quickly learned that this meant the same thing as a dozen. After four months, Jeannie passed the need for concrete number aids and began to learn to use numerical principles.

School became a source of satisfaction to Jeannie. Bright

and ambitious, she was eager to learn. She took advantage of all the help given her. Near the end of first grade, the speech clinician found that Jeannie was fairly normal in her speech and that there was no interference with her reading. The itinerant learning-disability specialist said Jeannie was up to grade level in arithmetic and writing. Dr. Nathan re-evaluated her, and saw for himself that she had had a successful first year in school and seemed to need no further attention from him or the psychologist.

Jeannie was promoted. She was among the brightest pupils in second grade—with no sign that she had had difficulty or had made a slow beginning. She developed self-confidence. By the time she was ten, there wasn't the slightest trace of the difficulties that had made her early life a nightmare. Early attention from learning-disability specialists had solved her problems.

3 / How to Recognize the Learning-Disabled Child

No learning-disabled child is exactly like another. Learning disability is not like measles or the whooping cough. There is no one symptom. Symptoms occur in clusters. These clusters vary from child to child. Rebecca has a hard time reading, principally because she can't tell the differences in the letters of the alphabet. Milt reads well, but at the age of ten he still has not learned to subtract, because he can't grasp the concept that one number is more or less than another.

Specialists must determine whether a symptom is important or not. Tim has a problem cutting with play scissors in kindergarten, but his muscular control is likely to improve so that he will be able to learn to write in first grade. Some symptoms can be mild *now* but critical when the youngster meets a challenge for which he needs the particular skill affected. Patricia is bright, but she has a difficult time picking up the sounds and rhythmic flow of language. She was able to learn adequately in the early grades, but could not master any foreign language once she reached junior high school.

Symptoms often can be masked. It is hard to discover the especially bright child who has learning disabilities. These boys and girls, so clever, intuitively devise maneuvers to compensate for their handicaps. They use their superior abilities to work at an average level. Who looks for problems in students keeping pace with their class? Yet they meet the definition of learning disability because they are not working up to the potential that can be measured on tests—if anyone bothers to look. Jack had a consistent C+/B− average all through school. Until he reached eighth grade, no one wondered why this obviously bright boy read so laboriously. His eighth-grade teacher asked that he be tested. Finding: Jack saw everything he held at a normal reading distance as if it were double. Exercises eliminated the problems. At graduation, his high-school average was A. "I didn't know what I saw was different from anyone else," Jack said.

What are the major symptom-clusters?

Activity Levels and Attention

Some children seem to be born with their motors running. From earliest infancy, this kind of child is charged up, restless, fidgety. He may thrash about, scream, spit up, stiffen, pull away. It's hard to hold him, comfort him. This hyperactive child—he was soon dubbed that, and the name stuck—discourages and irritates baffled family members who try to soothe him with affection.

In the crib, the hyperactive child moves about with such explosive energy that he bruises himself against the bars. He can't wait to get out. Soon he *is* out and on his own. Then there is no stopping him. This awesome bundle of energy flits from one thing to another. He topples, disarranges, or pulverizes everything in his path. His prying fingers move restlessly over and around everything that comes into his grasp. He might have trouble sleeping and roam the house until the early hours of the morning, finally falling asleep utterly exhausted. This juggernaut, ironically called a toddler, invades neighboring apartments or houses before his parents know he is out of reach. The energy he expends is grotesquely out of proportion to what the particular activity he is involved in requires.

He doesn't seem to care where he is—visiting relatives or friends, in church or supermarket, in school or play group. Because he can't stay put, it is virtually impossible to involve him in everyday family living, such as mealtime. He is constantly getting up and running off, dropping cutlery, upsetting milk. His jagged, spasmodic movements carry over into his thought and speech. His ideas and words may dart about or pour out in a jumble. He talks in a rapid-fire manner, embarrassingly loud, without inhibition, out of keeping with what most children understand as acceptable socially. He may blurt out to a stranger, "How come you're so big and fat?" or "Why do you have such an ugly face?"

Not only is he always moving, but he may also appear clumsy, ungainly. He lurches when he walks. He has no orthopedic handicap or significant physical impairment. He moves with such vigor that it may not immediately be seen that these movements are awkward as well as impulsive. One doctor wryly noted of these children, "Who can tell how the hummingbird's wings flap?"

A learning-disabled child may respond immediately, totally, to every little thing he sees, feels, hears, no matter how trivial. If there is a strange sound outside the classroom—a truck rumbling by, a low jet overhead—he must run to the window. He is unable to block out irrelevant stimuli. So he is at the mercy of his environment.

This reaction is at the core of his inadequate impulse control. He does not have the ability to say no to his impulses. The average child learns as he grows to filter out the irrelevant things that occur around him all day, to react only to what is important. This child must respond to every stimulus. He must run across the street without looking, because there is something on the other side that attracts him; so he is prone to accidents. He must grab an object that attracts his attention, and it may break; so he is called destructive. He must shout an answer to a question in school without forethought (and without being called on); so he is often in error. He must blurt out a remark that is ill-considered; so he is called unmannerly.

So many learning-disabled children are fired up that people tend to call all of them hyperactive. This is not so. A large number are not hyperactive. Many have normal behavior. Their disabilities primarily affect the way they learn.

Others are just the opposite of the hyperactive child. They are "good babies," easygoing and placid. They may sleep a lot as infants and they generally develop slowly. At the age of two or three, they show little energy or drive. These slow-moving, slow-thinking children are called hypoactive.

Hypoactivity is a less-common form of learning disability. While quite different from hyperactive children, hypoactive boys and girls share so many characteristics with other learning-disabled children that they are placed in the learning-disabled category. But they are not impulsive, excitable, distractible. Instead of being restless, they are sluggish and apathetic. They are not as active as normal children. Emotionally, they are good-natured; they rarely vent temper or anger. They are not impulsive; they are comparatively lacking in impulse. They are not curious, eager, independent. Their over-all activity level is low: They just don't do much. Their responses are diminished, sort of flattened out. They are inhibited, impassive, stoical. It is difficult to excite them.

In school, it is hard to stimulate them. Their motivation to learn is slight. Their attention span is short. Not, as in the hyperactive child, because it flits about, but, rather, because their interest is hard to capture and hold. Hypoactive children tend to be rather solemn youngsters who have a low opinion of themselves and take little pleasure in anything. They lack sparkle, zest, spontaneity. They don't have the drive to be strong-minded and eager, so they tend to be dependent; they just go along without thinking for themselves very much. The aura of immaturity clings to them, and they tend to be rejected by their agemates. They learn little in school and little from social experiences. They enter the teen years "out of it," socially inept, shy, and withdrawn. They may look or act mentally retarded, but they are not.

Movement and Perceptual Development

The child with learning disabilities often is a clumsy child. He bumps into things, spills his milk, trips over a thread in the carpet. This lack of control, of refinement, in walking and in using his hands is directly related to the way this child will be able to play and learn. Awkwardness can show in either or both of two ways. He might not be able to synchronize his "large" muscles—so he will seem off balance as he moves around. He could have problems walking, hopping, skipping, running, riding a bike, playing ball. Or he might be unable to co-ordinate the "fine," or small-muscle, groups, particularly in his hands. He would have great difficulty using a crayon, scissors, or knife and fork, buttoning his clothes, and, at school, writing and drawing.

In some children, inaccurate and poorly controlled movements are associated with a *perceptual* disorder, a defect in the way they see or hear what is around them. Perceptual distortion can take many forms and, with a number of children, more than one form. Some youngsters have *visual*-perceptual problems, difficulties in their interpretation of what they see. Others have *auditory*-perceptual impairments, disturbances in grasping what they hear. These children *do* see and *do* hear. Their vision and hearing acuity are normal.

Everyone is linked to his environment, his own little world, by sensory information, or stimuli—all those things he sees, hears, touches, smells, and tastes during his waking hours. These stimuli bombard his senses; the sensory pathways carry them to the brain, the body's control center, or switchboard. Each person reacts to stimuli according to his interpretation of what he receives. This is his behavior. If the world is not delivered correctly to his brain over the sensory pathways, his behavior reflects this. In the perceptually handicapped child, visual and auditory signals may not be reaching the brain accurately.

Some children with visual-perceptual problems can't judge the relationship of objects to each other and to themselves in a reliable and predictable way. Anyone who has ever been in a carnival house of mirrors knows how those mirrors highly distort a person's sense of his own body and everything around him. Such confusion leads to dizziness, nausea, often fear if prolonged. The child with a visual-perceptual problem is locked up in that house of mirrors until diagnosis and remedial training let him out. Mario, nine, shrieked hysterically with fear every time he had to cross a street. He did not know if he could reach the other side before oncoming cars hit him. His brain said, "Look, you really don't know how far it is to the other side. So you don't know how long it's going to take you to get there from this curb. It might take so long that those cars coming will run you down." Most children learn easily from experience to measure the distance between curbs and to judge the time necessary to cross in relation to moving cars. Countless Marios cannot do this.

Many children with visual-perceptual problems like Mario's learn they can't trust their eyes to deliver factual information. One five-year-old couldn't tell what was happening across the room. He had to leave his seat and almost feel his way across the room to reach what he wanted to see. This boy, so confused in his awareness of space, had a hard time getting around even in familiar surroundings: house, yard, especially his neighborhood.

"I can merely try to explain what seeing was like in my worst days," writes television writer-producer Jess Oppenheimer, who suffered unknowingly from perceptual problems until he was an adult. "Describing the whole world as moving, or seeing double, is meaningless; because with the inner feelings of confusion, lack of equilibrium, nausea, strain and incompetence, a normal person can no more begin to sense it . . . than a congenitally blind person can begin to understand what the color red is," Oppenheimer continues, in "All about Me," an article in the *Journal of Learning Disabilities* of January, 1968. ". . . The confusion [was] inside, with mental impressions all disoriented. The way I saw things was something like two still pictures out of register with each other, with this lack of register continually changing, but super-imposed on this was the lack of ability to . . . tell where up and down really were and whether you were going to fall over the next minute or not."

The growing child's organization of his environment—everything around him—is based on the vantage point of his own being. From this center, he becomes aware of how things are related to him: whether they are near or far away, whether they are in front of him or behind him, whether they are larger than he or smaller, whether they are to the left or to the right. Any child who is unable to sort out his sensory impressions, who cannot create out of them an awareness of —and security in—a stable external world, will make blunders as he moves around.

If he is not sure how far away something is, he will not be able to grasp it; either he will not reach far enough for it or he will overreach. If he cannot make an accurate estimate of an object's size, height, or shape, he will have countless practical difficulties. He will not know how low to duck to get under an overhanging branch, whether he must turn his body sideways to sidle through a narrow doorway, how high to lift his foot to go up some steps. "I was never able to . . . ride a bike between the uprights of a basketball back-board," writes Oppenheimer. "These uprights were almost four feet apart, but nine times out of 10 I ran into them instead of going through. In a much more complex and con-fused manner than can possibly be told, [I saw] four uprights instead of two, which made three possible passageways, and I had no ability to choose the right one since they constantly moved in relation to each other."

Terror lies in wait for the child whose experience will not let him make an instant, accurate estimate of space and time.

The child with visual-perceptual impairment lives in a world in which objects, events, and persons are constantly changing. Oppenheimer again, this time on learning to play the piano: "When I looked from one part of the keyboard to another, the entire keyboard shifted laterally [and] in a very confused manner."

Toby, for example, could not judge size. When he came to bat, he was not sure how big or small the softball was that the pitcher was sending his way. Most people learn from experience that a softball is always the same size no matter how close or far away it is. If the softball is close, its actual image on the retina is equivalent to that of a beach ball.

But an approaching ball is not judged to be growing, even though the retinal image is expanding; nor is a softball judged to be diminishing in size as it moves away, even though the image on the retina dwindles to a pin point. Objects maintain a constancy in spite of their changing appearance. An apple looks the same shade of red, no matter what the light conditions may be. A circle still looks round, even if it is tilted to the point where its image on the retina approaches that of an oval. A man looks his normal height from a block away, though the retinal image may be that of a nearby midget. These constancies are held to in spite of environmental changes that alter color, size, shape, location, movement.

Some children are confused in their awareness of direction: up and down, right and left, front and back. Danny could not catch a ball because he was unsure how fast it was coming, from what direction, how high or how low it was. When he had to throw a ball, he was a mass of confusion. Precisely where was the ball to go? How fast or slow should he throw it? Should he throw it high or low? He lacked that exquisite sense of timing that tells most children whether the ball will get to its destination—the first baseman—before the batter does.

If the school-age child with perceptual problems is perplexed in his sense of direction, he may be unable to carry out a school errand, because he is unsure which corridor to take to the principal's office. If he cannot tell up from down or right from left, he may persistently reverse his letters or copy numbers upside down. He may be unable to draw or write because he can't distinguish forms and shapes. He can't perceive that something is big or little, rectangular or square, pointed like the letter *A* or rounded like *O*.

Some perceptually handicapped children can't tie together the individual things they see into a unified whole. Ida, eleven years old, always has her workbooks and papers in total disarray. She sees only fragments, bits and pieces. If she looks at a picture in a book, she can see each individual element in the picture, but can't understand the relationship of one item to another. So she doesn't know what the total picture is about. If she tries to write in columns, she is able to write each individual word, but she can't visualize them in column form. So the words fall helter-skelter all over the paper. She can't put together puzzles or build with blocks. If she sees a tree stump, she's unable to tell that it is the part of the total tree that remained when the top was sawed off. Life is so confusing for this detail-oriented girl that she literally trips over a busy pattern in a carpet.

Still other youngsters cannot combine the information they get from one sense—vision, say—with another—hearing. In the normal child, the information coming in through both these senses is interwoven smoothly to form a unified impression. He watches a skit on *Sesame Street*. The music he hears is instantly integrated with the dance he sees. He can efficiently convert what he sees into what he hears and vice versa. Not Bernice. When she sees the printed word *table* on a page, she has no idea that it corresponds with the word *table* she has heard countless times. Each of her senses seems to operate separately. There is no crossover from one to the other. She is not able to "see" what she hears or "hear" what she sees. Because she can't integrate her auditory and visual senses, she will not be able to read until this problem is overcome through remedial exercises.

Some children cannot make their hands do what their eyes see. There is a lack of integration, or a mismatch, between vision and movement. This is called a visual-motor or perceptual-motor impairment. The normal child uses his eyes to guide where his hands are going. If he is trying to copy a triangle from the blackboard, his eyes tell him whether he has done it correctly. The perceptually handicapped youngster's eyes do not serve as an accurate guide to his finger movements. When Leon, a nine-year-old with this problem, tried to copy a square, it came out looking somewhere between a circle and a lopsided rectangle. Betty couldn't copy designs, either. She had no perceptual-motor impairment, but a co-ordination problem that made it difficult for her to control her muscles for drawing or writing.

Language and Thought Development

Language and thought are related processes. Although there can be limited thought without language and restricted language without thought, in the normal child the two abilities must develop together. The growth of language makes it possible for thought to occur, for concepts to form, for ideas to become richer. The attainment of skills encompassing language and thought is called cognitive development.

Cognition includes perception, because everything an individual knows is based on his taking in and organizing information delivered by the world to his sense organs; it also encompasses concept formation, the development of ideas, inferences, conclusions about information received by the senses. These ideas and concepts crystallize through and around words and word combinations. Each person then has a means of sharing his thoughts with others who use his language.

But in many learning-disabled children, sensory impressions do not jell into meaningful information. The result is disorders of language development and thinking processes. These difficulties are among the most widespread and serious problems of learning-disabled children.

What goes wrong? The variety of these disorders is staggering.

Just as some children have difficulty with visual perception, other learning-disabled children hear perfectly, but for a variety of reasons cannot understand what they hear. They have *auditory*-perceptual problems.

Some children with auditory handicaps cannot tell if sounds are alike or different. Words like *cat* and *cap* may sound identical. If a child can't discriminate between those two words and you tell him, "The cat is in the car," he may think you're saying, "The cap is in the car." If you say, "Don't spill the milk," he may hear, "Don't fill the milk."

This child misses the point of what is said to him. He becomes bewildered, frustrated. He is somewhat like a person listening to a foreign language he knows slightly. Despite close attention, he will hear a blur of sounds and be able to grasp only fragments. Under favorable circumstances, he may catch enough to make out the gist of what is being said. But it's an extraordinary strain.

He never *knows* he is interpreting incorrectly or whether he has heard enough to have the whole picture. Adverse circumstances intensify the problem. If words directed to him are spoken rapidly, or at a party where there is a great deal of background chatter, or if the child is tired and can't maintain a high level of attention, he will be lost. He will feel foolish and out of it. The child with this auditory-perceptual problem must learn not only to discriminate among sounds, but also to pick out the sounds he needs from background noises that occur at the same time.

Another child with auditory-perceptual impairment may be able to tell the difference between speech sounds and background noise well enough, but he can't link the sounds he hears with the objects the sounds refer to. He may hear, for example, words like apple, book, minibike, but be unable to associate these words with the things they refer to. If his problem is very mild and occurs under circumstances that affect his understanding of only a small number of words and sentences, his handicap is called an auditory-perceptual problem, central auditory imperception, or dysacusis. If the difficulty is severe, affects more of the youngster's language comprehension, and persists for years, it is called receptive aphasia or central deafness. Children who have this impairment in moderate to severe form frequently are wrongly diagnosed as deaf.

Other children may have difficulty remembering what they

hear. This can be a particularly perplexing problem to the child, as well as an insidious one to parents and teachers. Helen, obviously very bright, is unable to answer questions and follow instructions in class. Her problem: she can't remember the beginning of a sentence by the time her teacher gets to the end. She can recall—hold on to—only three or four words at a time, no matter how hard she concentrates. John can't remember the sequence of sounds within a word. He hears each sound correctly, but immediately forgets their order. So aluminum becomes *alunimum* and basket becomes *bakset*.

Sometimes an actual hearing loss, rather than a problem of auditory perception, causes or complicates a language disorder. A learning-disabled child might have a mild, fluctuating hearing impediment. The child who cannot fully hear sounds, particularly speech sounds, will have obvious problems learning to speak. This mild hearing loss itself is not a symptom of central-nervous-system impairment. Usually it reveals disease or damage to the ear.

When it occurs, however, it can combine with other handicaps to block language development; so it is important to know that such problems happen. Unless there is some outward manifestation of ear disease (draining ears, earaches, and the like), parents and examining professionals might not know the child is experiencing a mild hearing problem, and he will not get the help he needs.

Hearing problems are not an all-or-none occurrence. It is a fallacy that if a child hears at all he hears normally. A youngster can hear at some times and not at others. He can hear some sounds and not others. He can hear only bits and pieces, such as some parts of a word but not enough to tell exactly what it is. He can hear under some circumstances—when there is relatively little background noise—and not under others. He can hear everything but so faintly that he has a hard time grasping the meaning.

Language disorders can also occur when children attempt to speak. Some youngsters are delayed in speaking normally.

They can't bring their pronunciation, voice quality, inflections, or rhythm into line with the standards accepted as correct. Occasionally these difficulties are so marked that the child cannot be understood. This is termed delayed speech or articulatory disorder.

What causes problems of speech clarity? There are a number of reasons.

1. The way someone speaks is related to the way he hears and to his understanding of what is said to him. People pattern themselves after models. On the basis of their accurate comprehension of the speech of others, they can make their own speech sound right and, more important, understandable. The child with an auditory-perceptual handicap who has difficulty grasping spoken language will be uncertain in speaking. If he has not heard sounds clearly or is not certain of the meaning of those sounds, he is almost sure to reproduce them inaccurately. He himself may be unaware of the way he sounds. Because he is weak in monitoring his own speech, he can't contrast it critically with the speech of other people. He doesn't know that the sounds he makes are far afield of the sounds other people emit.

2. A child might hear and understand speech sounds perfectly, but be unable to reproduce those sounds, because he can't make the complex sequence of movements to tongue, lips, jaw, and palate. He cannot control the movement of those jaw, tongue, and oral structures necessary for speech. This is usually called dysarthria.

3. Another youngster can't remember the precise jaw and mouth movements necessary to talk. He does not seem to know what he must do to make lips, tongue, jaw move correctly to produce the words he wants. This problem is called dyspraxia.

4. In yet another kind of speech impairment, some youngsters can't think of the right word at the right time. This child has heard the word, probably repeatedly. But when he needs it he is unable to bring it out. Everyone has experienced this tip-of-the-tongue phenomenon, usually when overtired. But the child with word-finding difficulty gropes after words under

the best of circumstances. This problem can persist. If it is exceptionally severe, it shows up as a serious restriction in vocabulary. The child will have a limited number of words with which to express his thoughts. This impoverishment of vocabulary is most severe with abstract words, rather than words that refer to some immediate, observable thing in his environment. The youngster seems unable to learn or to use abstract words like obedience, justice, reality. He finds it hard to use the wide variety of words that make grammatical speech possible. He may be unable to use prepositions, adjectives, or adverbs. All of these limitations can make his language sound telegrammatic, because he omits or misuses all but the basic nouns and verbs. He may persist in confused pronoun use: "Me big boy," "Him want baby toy," "Where you, daddy?" This is called anomia; if exceptionally severe, expressive aphasia.

5. Some children have great difficulty with "inner speech," the use of words in thought and in concept development. This problem is called central aphasia or, if severe, global aphasia. When the child is unable to think in words, concepts are limited, thought patterns are disorganized, and ability for abstract reasoning is restricted. The child does not understand or use nuances of meaning. He finds it hard to classify what he sees and hears or to organize his thoughts about it.

The normally developing youngster forms concepts based upon what he sees and hears, then pulls together. He is able to generalize from information. To the child unable to generalize, each thing in the world is seen or experienced as a separate entity: big chair, little chair, rocking chair, high chair, skinny chair, fat chair, stuffed chair, wooden chair, green chair, red chair. All are seen as separate and distinct objects. Of course they are separate objects, but a child must also develop the concept of *chairness* as a classification that embraces all the differences. When he has the category *chair* firmly in mind, he has engaged in a learning operation that makes the world less disorderly and splintered. He now has a tool for understanding and talking about a category of experience. He has abstracted a meaning from concrete things presented to him—all those different chairs.

Children who are able to abstract build up a storehouse of words. This action is a building-block process, because as youngsters hear abstract words they develop new concepts associated with those words. For example, all children hear the word *animal* from an early age. But no child sees an animal. He may see something called a horse, a gerbil, a cow. The word *animal* is an invitation to the normal child to understand that all of these specific beings are alike in some way.

He has to learn a whole variety of discriminations and associations to master this concept of animal. His perceptual powers have to be good in order for him to see that some of these animals, at least, have a good bit in common. For example, each has four legs. He then has to be able to transcend the visual realities. He must classify these particular things together even though they have different sizes, shapes, colors.

He must develop subcategories within the animal classification: wild animals, farm animals, house pets. He has to include within the category some that in no way look like those he already knows or that do not possess the distinguishing characteristics he has considered essential, perhaps their four-leggedness. Thus he will include, in time, crocodiles along with kangaroos, snakes along with elephants.

The child with a thinking disorder finds it hard to go beyond the immediate thing he sees—the actual dog or cow or cat. In school, he will not grasp word meanings or develop a rich vocabulary. Even if he tries, he may be unable to take part in discussion or contribute his own ideas. This is often the basis for his so-called short attention span: he *can't* pay attention to language and concepts he doesn't fathom. It also explains his shaky memory: he cannot recall information he has been taught if the ideas are beyond his understanding.

Willy doesn't understand that New York, where he lives, is something called a city. Or that it is part of a state. He can't see, feel, smell anything called state or country. He is puzzled that New York is south of Boston but north of Philadelphia. How can New York be north and south at the same time?

Willy can't categorize, or classify, experiences and objects. He finds it hard to believe that things that do not look alike to him have a common name. For him, *man* refers to his father; so how can all those fat, thin, tall, blond, short, and dark creatures be called by the same word, *man?* He may use words too loosely, ignoring the conventional boundaries of words. For example, he knows his "daddy" and thereafter calls any tall, skinny man who smokes a pipe daddy. This is a developmental characteristic of a much younger child.

Words referring to time, speed, distance, size, height, and length absolutely floor this learning-disabled child. He can't range back in time to discuss the applicability of something he may have learned. A normal child might say, "Mommy, you told me Uncle Tim just retired. Maybe that's why we didn't find him when we drove by his office last week. He probably goes in only part time now." The learning-disabled youngster might not be able to combine these facts to reach the same conclusion.

This child can't talk about the over-all lesson he should have drawn from some specific experience. He can talk in a specific way about what he has experienced, but it's hard for him to weave specific facts into a total fabric that leads to a clear understanding of problems and issues. So, while he is aware that striking a match can cause a fire, that babies don't know what they're doing, that his baby brother likes to play with the matchbox, and that when a fire breaks out it can destroy everything, he cannot see why he should hide the matches from the baby. His decision-making ability and his judgment are, at best, uncertain.

Any kind or degree of distortion in language form can occur. Distortion can take place even when the child talks a lot. Some extremely fluent children use language inadequately. The child may talk in a great torrent. Yet if you listen carefully you note that he is not always using the appropriate words and that he cannot generalize or even tell a simple story. He is unable to relate ideas in a logical sequence. A ten-year-old, for example, might not be able to report what he did on his vacation last summer. He will not be able to give even the simplest account of an event in American history, or in yesterday's newspaper. His ideas are vague and confused, his explanations incomplete and superficial.

No one knows how these impairments occur. Diagnosis of language disorders requires great skill. The learning-disabled child's inability to acquire meaningful spoken language by about the age of three and a half to four years can't be explained on the basis of deafness, mental retardation, serious emotional disturbance, paralysis of the organs of speech, or environmental factors. Delay in speech may be the sole forerunner of a learning disability. Many children with reading and writing problems show an earlier history of late or impaired speech. All these problems can be treated by language therapists. Without this kind of help, these children will have a hard time making sense of the world. Their limitations will make it difficult for them to learn in or out of school.

There is also a special problem with reading, writing, and spelling, called specific developmental dyslexia or specific language disability (these are the most common names, although others are used). Dyslexia is a form of learning disability, but it differs from other forms in several vital respects.

Dyslexia can happen all by itself or in combination with other learning disabilities. Some dyslexic children show a number of the characteristics described in this chapter. Others have few or none of them. These boys and girls might have no problem with their behavior. They might be engaging and mannerly. They might be good learners as long as they don't have to read or write. They might have practical ability, common sense, even outstanding manual and athletic prowess.

Their problem? The inability to associate printed letters and words with spoken sounds. A good reader understands that words are just sounds written down. The dyslexic child is baffled. To varying degrees, he doesn't learn that print makes up a kind of code that represents spoken language in a predictable way.

Why? There are many reasons. But the child is not retarded, stubborn, culturally deprived, or emotionally disturbed. In the majority of dyslexic children, the problem is hereditary. It can skip generations. It is usually found in boys. No one knows why. Sometimes there is evidence of mild neurologic disturbance. In a few cases the cause is a complete mystery.

But all dyslexic children have difficulty reading, writing, and spelling. So do some normal children, but most of them get over it. Dyslexic boys and girls don't respond to the usual teaching methods, and they don't improve much with time or ordinary tutoring.

Some dyslexic children with impaired auditory perception cannot hear the sounds of their language correctly. They cannot remember how spoken words sound. So their speech is defective. And when they get to school they cannot associate printed letters and words with spoken words. Some can't tell the differences in the shapes of letters (and sometimes numbers). They can't remember what the printed word as a whole looks like. Since they don't remember how words look, they often rotate or reverse their letters when they write. Their spelling is usually very bad. And they don't form their letters well; spacing and slant are poor.

A good reader efficiently and quickly translates what he hears into what he sees (printed words) and back again. These children, intelligent and capable, cannot do so without painstaking and intensive help—usually over a long time. Most of these youngsters benefit from expert remedial teaching. But it is difficult to predict how much a specific child will improve.

The degree of dyslexia can range from mild to severe. It can occur in slow children or in brilliant ones. Many dyslexic children learn to read adequately, but they rarely become good spellers.

Emotional and Social Development

The child who cannot perform—achieve—is a child in the process of being emotionally destroyed. The destruction will begin with parents and teachers who expect in vain; it will continue with agemates who laugh, finally ignore. Ultimately it will end with the child himself, for no person is destroyed without his own aid.

Frustrated everywhere they turn—at home, in school, on

the playfield—many learning-disabled children develop emotional disorders. They are true disturbances, but they are secondary to the basic problems already outlined. The emotional problems are *result*, not cause, of the learning disabilities.

The varieties and combinations of emotional problems are virtually unlimited. Their severity and the particular form each disorder may take vary widely from child to child.

The reason for the emotional entanglement: low self-esteem and fear in the face of continuing stress as the learning-disabled child faces challenges that are beyond his abilities.

Through his preschool and school career, this child has been exposed to uncertainty and humiliation. He might not be able to run well, catch a ball, or even understand the point of a game. In school, where he's held up to distinct and inflexible standards, his inadequacies are openly exposed for all to see. Evaluating himself in relation to other youngsters—all children do so constantly—he can't fail to see that he falls short in terms everybody values highly: achievement.

For the average child, the early school years are a period of great psychological and cognitive strides. They can be a painful time for the learning-disabled boy or girl. While most children are gaining social prowess, he is an isolate. He can't put forth a constant level of performance. He is the perpetual member of the low reading group. He might be promoted because he is getting older and bigger, but he does not have a firm grasp on academic fundamentals. That terrible thing called social promotion is an antisocial promotion, because it puts the youngster even more at odds with his classmates. He clearly sees the hypocrisy. He knows the promotion is an empty gesture, that it is not based on any achievement on his part.

He can't build a sense of values, a feeling of what is right and wrong, a strengthening of conscience, as youngsters in the six-to-nine age range normally do. These can come only from believing himself an important and accepted part of a world whose values he accepts and will come to cherish.

Things go from bad to worse at school. Parents who may

have been tolerant, or at least uncertain about how to judge their child, are more and more confused. The child is rejected by the school. Quite reasonably, he rejects the school in turn. When he finds out that he has no chance of success, that he is beyond his depth, he might struggle helplessly for a time, but ultimately he will tune out. Educational attainment, instead of being the road to success that many parents hope it will be for their children, has for him dwindled into a meandering road leading off heaven knows where, beset by detours and dead ends.

The child might begin to believe his own resources are so weak, in anything he does, that he develops a sense of futility. He becomes an anxious, inhibited child. He is afraid in the face of very real pressures he cannot cope with. He suspects every new task he encounters, because he is concerned that once again he will meet criticism and defeat.

He might even worry about the prospect of failure in areas where he *can* succeed. For example, he does not have any difficulty with muscular co-ordination, yet he refuses to play a game in which he might do well. He could be articulate, yet has been so humiliated by the derision of children on the playground that he is inhibited from bringing toys to school for "show and tell."

He might begin to exploit his inadequacy as a rationale for inactivity: "If I cannot do anything right, why should I even try?" He is afraid to attempt anything new, because he sees it not as an opportunity but as just another stress-filled situation that will bring him disappointment. He may become immobile, paralyzed with fear.

If the child is hyperactive, he has been at the mercy of impulses he cannot control. He strikes out unthinkingly at the child who accidentally jostles him in the corridor; he can't resist going through the coat pockets of visitors to his home. This inadequate impulse control leads to massive conflict with family and school—with society. The school's discovery of this child usually occurs because of behavior that disturbs a classroom, rather than from the youngster's difficulty in learning. His learning problems may be far worse than his behavior. But society reacts quickest to those things that inconvenience it—as, for example, the way a teacher or a principal reacts to a disruptive boy or girl—rather than to things that "inconvenience" only the child, such as his inability to read.

This is the primary reason why so many learning-disabled children who are *not* behavior problems slip through everyone's fingers, often until it is too late to help them. The quiet, withdrawn child who "merely" cannot read or do sums is neatly recorded as a slow learner or an underachiever and, in most school systems, promoted up and out, untouched by human hands. These quiet learning-disabled children are "sleepers." Because of their good-natured temperament and their socially acceptable behavior, they cause no problem and often are not identified as learning-disabled children—if they ever are identified—until they are in severe academic trouble. Because they are not found early, they fall far behind—usually becoming passive and withdrawn—before anybody pays much attention to them. They just quit trying and ultimately become among the most difficult children to motivate.

Poor impulse control is called by many names, chiefly emotional lability, erraticism, variability, excitability, organic driveness, low frustration tolerance, distractibility, exaggerated response, lack of inhibition. Whatever the name, the child overreacts; he cannot regulate or modulate his responses to the things that go on about him. In everyday language, he is high-strung, nervous, demanding, hostile.

One result of the child's classroom impulsiveness is the charge that he is inattentive. He doesn't concentrate, because he's constantly bombarded by extraneous stimuli. His inattentiveness might actually be more like a forced attention—an attention to *other* things, the wrong things.

He is distracted not only by stimuli outside himself, but also by those welling up from within. Inner impulses may drive these youngsters to boundless, excessive, and unselective displays of puppy-dog affection. Just as this child can't keep from touching and handling objects, he sometimes can't keep from touching and handling people. Or he is so filled with anger that he reacts in a bitterly hostile way to a classmate trying to be friendly.

His attempts to deal with confusion on the outside and angry, upset feelings welling up from within are futile. He might become so loaded with distrust that he has misgivings toward those who honestly offer help. He could simply not know how to react to anyone who holds out a helping hand, because his total life experience has not led to an ability to trust others. So he resents his mother's offer to cut his meat for him, although he knows he can't handle a knife and fork well. Because he is confused by the everyday complexities of life, he might easily feel slighted or misinterpret the reactions of others. A trivial incident can easily precipitate him into a tantrum. He has become basically self-centered. He has pulled in his boundaries to form a protective cloak around himself. He doesn't have the insight or awareness to know much about or care much about the effects of his behavior on others.

The injustice, pressure, and threats that adults exert—in school, at home—can crush this child. When parents feel betrayed by their youngster's ineptness (disappointment eventually gives rise to a sense of betrayal), there is no way they can keep the signs of their bewilderment, letdown, anger from showing.

They may try to soften it, but the child senses dissatisfaction with his efforts and the intimation, however subtle, that he hasn't worked up to his potential. Whenever this hint starts to come across to the youngster, self-doubt moves in. Observing how his best efforts have met not only with failure and frustration, but also with criticism, he becomes plagued by doubts. He becomes riddled with a sense that he is inadequate. He gradually develops a seriously diminished self-concept. ("I'm just defective," one ten-year-old with an IQ of 140 told his teacher. "I'm stupid, stupid, stupid," an intellectually gifted thirteen-year-old said. "I know the answers to my problems. Put me in the toilet and flush me.")

This is self-destruction. Self-concept is the way everyone regards himself. How he feels about his adequacy, his worth, his basic ability to meet life's challenges.

This child's sense of unfitness mounts as school requirements pyramid. The demands made on the average developing child conflict with this youngster's picture of himself as helpless. He doesn't know how to get and keep warm, protective relationships. He is easily led. He believes what other children tell him—falsified game scores, inane stories. He can be exploited. He can be treated as a scapegoat by other children or shut out from their company because of his "dumb" behavior. He "quickly comes to know [his] place along the school-yard fence," as child psychiatrist Samuel Stein phrased it, in a research paper presented in 1969.

His basic ego is cracking wide open. By the age of nine or ten, the average child should have a feeling of industry. He should begin to think that there's something worthwhile to aim for and that he has the basic tools to work toward meaningful objectives. It is a sense of himself as somebody who can do, who can accomplish, who is, in fact, a person.

The ego of a child is essentially the core of his psychological make-up. It is the mechanism that controls the child's impulses and drives. It directs the expression of these impulses to conform with the requirements of his environment and his society. If a child has a strong ego, he is better able to cope with stress. The learning-disabled child is more vulnerable to stress. He finds the world less well organized for him, more confusing, more unsettling.

His ego must find ways to mediate effectively between his impulses and desires and the pressures exerted by his environment. To survive, he must find some way—some defense mechanism. He makes the best deal he can.

One deal might be withdrawal. Seeing that people do not accept him, do not find him lovable, he comes to feel that the best thing to do is to get away. If he's alone he doesn't have to prove anything. So he pulls into himself.

Other children become clowns—silly, loud, obstreperous. It is as though this child were saying, "If I'm going to lack control and inhibition, I might just as well make a big deal out of it. People might not like me, but they won't shove me out of the way or forget about me. Maybe then I'll be considered a person, after all. I'm even a hero to some of these kids. I make them laugh. I put the teacher down and make her uncomfortable." He gets perverse gratification from irritating, upsetting, enraging. Believing himself to be weak and powerless, he can at least show he is effective in manipulating, getting others to do what he wants or getting them so unnerved that they simply "don't know what to do with him." This negativism and power struggle emanate from a child's belief that he is basically incompetent.

No matter how loud and aggressive this youngster is, under it all he is still beset by his fears of inadequacy and of punishment and retaliation—for both what he does and what he wishes. Many of these children harbor unconscious fantasies; if they can't get back at the real world in action, they can be as hostile and angry as they like in their fantasy life. They might have daydreams in which, like Superman, they defy their oppressors with death-dealing devices.

Some youngsters are so terrified of failure that they will do anything in their power to avoid challenge. Occasionally they escape the threat of failure by running away from school or by refusing to go to school in the first place. In other cases, avoidance is more circuitous. Some will avoid grappling with a task by talking about it rather than doing it. They unleash an endless and inane verbal stream. Others are so fearful of failure in the classroom that they rip up instructional materials, throw paper around, destroy books and equipment, or attack children around them who are succeeding in their work. Some children play down their own failings by ignoring the task in front of them to help a nearby student with an easier job. There are all kinds of avoidance techniques. They depend upon how clever and ingenious a child is at covering up and masquerading.

Many children overcompensate to distract attention from their areas of inadequacy. They might develop a particular area of mastery, often to an extraordinary degree. Jim knows railroad schedules and train destinations for every major line in the United States. Linda sings memorized arias from most of the well-known French and Italian operas in the original language (without understanding a word). David knows the rosters and records of every major-league baseball team for the past fifteen years, including individual players' batting averages. Many of these virtuoso performances are truly remarkable.

Other children distract from recognition of their inadequacies by engaging in constant needling and arguments of the splitting-hairs variety. Their discussions are pointless and are meant not to resolve issues, but to exert influence, keep a teacher off stride, prove their superiority in arguing. The learning-disabled child enjoys the ego gratification that comes from exerting a bogus skill or mastering a monstrous array of irrelevant information. Ultimately, of course, this kind of overcompensation deprives him of the sense of worth he would get from true accomplishment.

The child who is unable to control himself might try in desperation to control the adults around him, particularly his parents. He is fighting for some kind of an edge, somewhere. He might play upon their sympathies or their guilt feelings, exploit their weaknesses. Parents who are weak, uncertain, or guilt-ridden tend to overindulge. This child will take advantage of any parental tendency to give in. He could assert control by being demanding or insistent or by simply yielding to the parents' tendency to protect him. This prolongs dependence. The resulting sense of power in the child takes the place of the satisfaction a normal child gains from a developing sense of independence and confidence.

Most of these children are socially immature. They often stop developing at a level of emotional behavior far below what is reasonably expected of children with their intelligence. They might gravitate toward younger children, who are less competent and not so much a threat to their faltering self-esteem. In the face of the buffeting he experiences, this kind of youngster might regress to childlike, even infantile, behavior. He might feel he will be safer, more protected, if he acts like a small child. No one will expect very much of him then. This youngster has been admonished, cajoled, coaxed, bribed, and threatened. All because he is not as adequate as people think he should be. He is a stranger in a world *he* did not make. He feels alone. Why not, then, try to carve out some island of safety and security? Many of these boys and girls seek all sorts of refuges—most often, though, as a tiny, helpless child. Genuine fears begin: fear of darkness, of animals, of anything strange and threatening.

This youngster is uncertain and inept in social situations. He doesn't learn well from the ordinary experiences to which everyone is exposed. It is amazing how often these children act in good faith on the basis of what they believe to be a correct interpretation of what has been said to them. But they don't know how to react to the welter of shifting, variable, objective cues most people, adults and children, are able to interpret. When the average person is visiting friends, he can tell from the subtle shift of their bodies that they are ready for him to leave, and so he rises to go. If he is talking with someone, he can tell by the slight tone of annoyance that creeps into that person's voice that he has touched upon a delicate area, and he quickly moves away from that topic. But this child lacks social perception. He doesn't seem to pick up these subtle clues.

Nor does he figure out other signals. If a thing is not direct or explicit, he doesn't know how to act. For example, he is not sure, literally, when to come in out of the rain, because he doesn't know how to interpret gathering clouds as an indication that there will soon be a downpour. He doesn't know how to interpret the gradual darkening of the sky to mean it's time to go home for dinner. This child seemingly lacks common sense. In spite of his intelligence, something has to be quite sharp and explicit for him to understand and to react in a customary way. Other children in the family know these things without having to be taught. The signals are all around them, and they absorb.

When parents are told that this child doesn't know something other boys and girls his age know well, almost invariably they reply, "We never talked about it in front of him. We never taught him that, so how can he know?" But other children do know a great deal about where their relatives live, what service club their father belongs to, what his profession is, that their mother studies yoga. This child is fuzzy about the world of work, uncertain about social institutions, uneasy about human relationships—all understandings expected in the preadolescent youngster.

Change in routine terrifies this child. Desperate for familiar things—the same seat at the breakfast table, the same daily schedule—a new event introduced without adequate preparation, even something pleasant like a birthday party or an outing, can lead to a tantrum, a violent reaction that continues until it plays itself out. Moods, changeable and unpredictable, offer no clear-cut indication as to what triggered them. This child can move in seconds from tears to roars of laughter. He is as puzzled and bewildered as anyone else by his unpredictable, disruptive behavior. He doesn't want to act that way.

Fear of the unfamiliar sometimes causes the learning-disabled youngster to become stuck on one thing—one activity, one sentence—and he will concentrate on it until those around him think they will lose their minds. This child, who usually flits from one thing to another, will suddenly become persistent and stick with something in a strange, repetitive way. He might say the same phrase, sing the same snatch of song, over and over without apparent sense. He might chatter incessantly about one subject for months, play interminably with a particular object until he pulverizes it, compulsively persist in some ritual—like washing out the tub to perfection before his bath. This is termed perseveration or compulsiveness. Why does it occur? It could be that the youngster has finally found some gratification and is reluctant to let it go.

This child cannot tolerate frustration. He can't delay his reaction to an impulse or his need for gratification. He wants what he wants when he wants it. He does what he wants when he wants to. It is frequently in the area of action—punching, pulling, kicking. In large part, his high-strung, oversensitive, irritable emotional reactions have to do with his need for immediate, right-now fulfillment of every need. His inability to be patient destroys relationships with other children. Overexcitable in play, he cannot learn to wait his turn, to follow basic game rules. Sensitive about failure and socially inept, he is a "poor sport." He seems dominating, overaggressive, because of his insistence on doing things his way *now*. Large play groups or relatively informal activity overstimulates him to the point where he is seemingly half a dozen children simultaneously shouting, running, jumping.

Not only is he not good at sports or any vigorous outside activity, but his delay in maturation may also cause fear of heights, an inability to climb, and thus give him insufficient outlet for any exploratory urge. Again he is frozen, immobilized. He has so many options closed to him, avenues other children have to learn, play, explore, release normal tensions. Life for this young child becomes a closed box.

The learning-disabled child with secondary emotional disturbances needs a very special map to chart his way. This help can be given only through painstaking attention, by his parents and by professionals, to his basic learning problems as well as to his psychological impairments.

4 / Where Can We Go
for Help?

A mother believes something is wrong with her child. Now what?

She is not likely to find help for him easily.

In spite of the growing awareness among physicians and educators concerning learning disabilities, virtually all parents still have considerable difficulty getting both diagnosis and treatment for their children. The help they do get can be beset by confusion and contradiction. It can lead to despair on their part.

"Thoreau said that most men live lives of quiet desperation," one mother told the authors. "Nowhere is that more applicable than to the parents of one of these children. The constant wondering, searching, seeking, and conflict are a source of great anxiety and frustration to the parent, adding to the problem of the child."

Another mother writes, "Diagnosis was very slow. Our family pediatrician did not recognize the problem through Billy's infancy and early years. (He said later that even if there were a problem, 'It wouldn't matter when you parents learned because there's nothing that can be done.')

"We ran with our son at age five to three other doctors and to a large hospital before one doctor expressed the opinion—after a five-minute examination—that he thought our son was 'retarded.' He recommended a clinic for a full evaluation. After *a year's* study, the clinic team told us Billy was not retarded; he had minimal brain dysfunction.

"The public schools in our large city had no special classes

55

for this kind of child, so we were sent to an expensive private school: $3,400 a year. Now began a humiliating experience. We were a middle-income family and had always considered ourselves comfortable. But suddenly we found we could no longer pay our way.

"Things at home changed. We stopped buying clothes, gifts, virtually everything. We could no longer entertain our friends. Our food costs were brought to the barest minimum; the cheapest ground meat in different forms became our nightly dinner. My husband and I had to plan our days to drive our son two hours daily just to reach the school bus. We didn't dare get sick.

"Today, five years later, our son still attends a special private school—his third, cost $3,600 a year. We have all come a long way together through years of no diagnosis and mis-diagnosis and incorrect treatment and fear. We have a yet longer road ahead—desperately hoping our boy can be helped to become a 'close to normal' man.

"There isn't much peace for families in our circumstances."

Another mother said, "We visited kindergarten to see how our child was progressing and saw him trying desperately to do the bunny hop with the other children. He was totally out of step and acting rather silly to cover up. His teacher could not understand why his pencils were always lost and why he would not stay seated at his desk. The school psychologist informed us that we had just as well admit he was an epi-leptic and that he was a little spoiled. She also suggested that he ought to be taught at home. My husband asked if she could recommend any schools; she said she wasn't allowed to make recommendations.

"Our doctors told us not to spend so much time worrying over one of our children but to think about the others, and that they had seen kids twice as 'wiggly' as ours. They also said he should not go into special education. One doctor was a consultant to the Board of Education and asked that the principal of the school call him. She refused. When the school nurse expressed an interest in our child, the principal of our school said nurses do not know anything about education so they can't take their recommendations. I must add that I am teacher-shy although I have been a teacher. They intimidate me, which is not as it should be, of course. Now that I understand my son's problems better, I will perhaps be better able to defend him. As it was, I could only ache for him."

You, his parents, are your child's major resource.

You will lay the groundwork for his life. You will exercise the largest share of responsibility. You will have to know your child and yourself better than anyone else can.

Several vital aspects must be faced from the outset. *You must acknowledge that there is a problem for which you need help.* You will meet a number of parents of children like yours who will deny vigorously that something is wrong with their child. You must be determined to face your problem, to seek every avenue of understanding and assistance.

The learning-disabled child *can* be helped, but his rearing inevitably is more time-consuming and arduous than that of the normal child. You will have to be prepared to give him a lot of attention. This youngster needs his family and his home more than he requires the services of the pediatrician and teacher. No professional intervention can serve to train or educate your child successfully unless you offer full cooperation. No therapeutic or educational technique can help, no medication will combat impulsiveness and hyperactivity successfully, unless there is a loving, disciplined family. You are the ones who will seek out help, who will critically determine which aspects of the assistance offered you are pertinent and can be used within your family living style.

You are looking for two kinds of help—evaluation and, following that, a plan of treatment. Diagnosis of the learning-disabled child is a continuing process. *Initial* diagnosis will confirm—or refute—the presence of learning disabilities in your child. If the diagnosis is positive, it will lead to a *beginning* course of treatment.

Periodic review—that is, repeated diagnosis—will be necessary to judge the success of the treatment program and to make the necessary changes in it.

Overlap exists on two counts: (1) the overlap of diagnostic review and treatment, as just noted; (2) the overlap of the professionals you will consult, some of whom will be involved both in the initial and continuing diagnosis *and* in the treatment.

Both diagnosis and treatment are covered in this chapter and in the three chapters that follow.

The time to begin to find help is just as soon as you become aware of the handicap. If there is severe damage to your youngster, signs will show at birth or soon after. But if your doctor gives the child a clean bill of health during his first nine months or so, relax. No advantage will be gained by scrutinizing the infant for signs of impairment when your pediatrician feels development and behavior are within normal limits.

But no parent helps his infant by looking away from unusual behavior or development signs. Look into general growth and development patterns.* If your child deviates markedly from the composite picture of normal behavior at a particular age level, start to raise questions with your pediatrician. Some of the signs your doctor may be interested in following up will be these: failure to sit by nine months; failure to walk without holding by 18 months to two years; failure to speak understandable single words by three years; any severe spasm or repeated blackouts; any sort of distant vacant look about the eyes or a lack of recognition and pleasure at familiar voices and faces; exceptional clumsiness with the hands; stumbling gait and much falling; prolonged drooling; unusual and marked emotional reactions; gusts of violent response to *trivial* occurrences; lack of laughter; failure to enjoy ritualized games such as peekaboo and pat-a-cake.

Some symptoms of learning disabilities, much more subtle, may not appear until the child is three or four years old.

---

* The authors recommend especially *Infant and Child in the Culture of Today,* by Arnold Gesell and Frances Ilg (New York, Harper & Row, 1943).

Others may not show until kindergarten or first grade. Both of these situations were illustrated in chapter 3.

Help should be found when the learning disability is uncovered, regardless of the child's age. Aid may be especially hard to find for the preschool-age boy or girl, because preschool classes virtually don't exist for this youngster. However, a professional may be able to recommend a local nursery school that is capable with learning-disabled children. And if your child needs a specific therapy—in speech or in physical co-ordination, for example—these can be obtained as long as the child is old enough to benefit.

Parents who suspect and then confirm a problem in their child go through well-defined levels of response. Initially there are doubt and uncertainty, a vague foreboding that something is amiss mingled with disbelief that such a thing could really be true. Any suggestion of handicap is a severe blow to parental pride. It dashes the hope that the child will fulfill the parents' own unmet needs, will attain heights denied them. Parents smart under the burden of the social pressures of middle-class American society to produce, on demand, a picture-book child. At this point, the father is likely to charge his wife with the accusation that she is hysterical and has allowed her imagination to run wild. Even if the "hysterical" mother can persuade her husband that they should seek professional help for their son or daughter, their doctor at this stage may be just as uncertain as the parents. This is particularly true in the case of a *mild* maturational lag, which is difficult to diagnose confidently at an early age.

Then: "It can't be true." The diagnosis has been made. The parents' worst fears have been realized. In their shock, their ability to think constructively might become paralyzed. Here, also, too many parents are prone to deny the undeniable. Overreaction and anger can take the form of abrupt repudiation of the physician who made the diagnosis. The parents might suddenly doubt his competence. A period of frantic doctor "shopping" could follow, of rushing from one physician, medical center, or child-development specialist to another for proof that will either repudiate the diagnosis of impairment or support it so firmly that there can no longer be doubt.

So the parents are in flight, running from reality. They gradually modulate from anger and panic to a sense of futility. They are not yet able to believe that there is hope for the youngster, even though he is unquestionably impaired.

Parental bewilderment and dread are understandable. These feelings are abnormal only if they are prolonged or if the parents dwell on them obsessively. The parents are sitting ducks for well-meaning but misguided armchair experts. Already hoping against hope for a miracle cure, the parents may eagerly heed friends or relatives who assure them that:

"I don't know what you're worried about—he looks fine to me."

"He'll outgrow it. My little Joey didn't talk until he was six years old."

"You know these doctors. They just like to get you excited and keep you coming back so they can collect their fees."

"You know all kids develop at their own speed. Just let nature take its course."

Loose talk can lull the credulous parent into a dangerous sense of security. Valuable months or years of the child's life may be lost. Admitting the problem and facing the truth are the only path to constructive action and peace of mind.

Don't waste time in this sort of mourning, self-lacerating guilt, or recrimination:

"Nothing like this ever happened in my family. Didn't you once tell me about your mentally retarded second cousin?"

"I don't think you ever knew how to take care of that baby. You didn't breast-feed him or do anything right with him from the beginning."

"What kind of father are you, anyway? Don't tell me how to discipline a child. You're never home till Susie's ready to go to sleep, and even then you can't wait to prop up your feet and watch TV with a can of beer."

Some parents find refuge in passivity and withdrawal. There may be no bitterness and recrimination, but a submissive acceptance of the impairment as a burden to be borne stoically. The family may close in around the learning-disabled child and try to protect him from contact with the outer world. The situation is accepted as inevitable and beyond help. Instead of finding aid for the youngster, these parents, in misguided love, may suffocate him through pity and foster his unhealthy dependence on them and on his brothers and sisters. They may swing from the extreme of rejecting the child, whom they resent and whose existence now hurts them, to a guilt-laden denial of the rejection. They purge their guilt feelings by pitying and overindulging him.

Ambivalence exists in every parent-child relationship. No matter how much a father or mother cares for a child, there are times when he or she doesn't want to see him, doesn't want him near, feels an impulse of distaste and rejection welling up within. This love-hate conflict is found in *all* family relationships.

You can love your learning-disabled youngster deeply and still acknowledge that you are disappointed and hurt. But your hatred of his affliction and your occasional dislike for the child himself do not shield you from your obligation to find the help he needs.

Through all this, tension is attacking. Nerves become frayed. Financial strains begin. Parents often come to feel virtually imprisoned by a child who can neither be taken anywhere comfortably nor be left at home with a sitter. Families have disintegrated under this kind of pressure. Mothers have abandoned their husbands and other children to cross the country seeking treatment for a learning-disabled child. Parents have had mental breakdowns. Some have attempted suicide. Separation and divorce, sadly, are common.

"Sometimes I feel so alone and lost, as though Ellen's dependency and needs will go on forever," one mother told the authors. (She and her husband were divorced, they said, because of the strain of caring for their daughter.) "I am always torn by the feeling that I should be home and available to her, and at the same time that I should be working at a job to make enough money to create more opportunities for her.

I sometimes resent what I feel to be her causing my chances for remarriage to be more limited. Then I feel guilty about that. The unreasonable fantasy that I should love her unlimitedly at all times combines with the resentment, fatigue, and aloneness. I so often wish someone would help a little so that *everything* wouldn't be on me all the time. If she could have just a weekend somewhere else. It has been over sixteen unrelenting years of no help, no letup, no out."

The strain can be more subtle. A husband might sense a gradual change in his wife. She might become distraught. She might withdraw, neglect her daily responsibilities, refuse to socialize. The husband might become aloof and detached, and show less and less interest in the child, as his wife devoted every waking hour to working with the youngster or participating in organizational activities on behalf of learning-disabled children.

Stop feeling guilty. There's no point in blaming anyone. No magical cure exists, but there is hope for your child. Learn about his problems. Discover what you can do now to make things better for him and for yourselves. Your child needs—all of you need—a stable home life. Value him as he is, and help him to feel wanted and appreciated within the family. You'll need courage, honesty (admit the limitations his handicapping condition imposes upon him), and persistence.

Your attitude must change from "Whose fault is it?" to "What can we do?" You must learn to see your child as a youngster *who is more healthy and well than not*. You must find ways to help him overcome his problems at the same time as he builds on the abilities he does have and those he will improve and develop. You will have to help him stand in the face of the well-meaning but misguided sympathies of uncomprehending strangers and friends. You will have to provide him with strength to stand the cruelty of other children. You will have to be his advocate when he is confronted with the bureaucratic deadheadedness that is too often displayed by the schools.

As you seek help for your child and yourselves, you will sometimes run into resistance from professionals who find you troublesome, overly demanding, and nit-picking. Far too large a number of professionals and institutions don't understand the learning-disabled child. A lot has been learned in the last five or ten years. Information about these advances has been widely disseminated. Yet there are still many physicians who don't have the faintest idea of the nature of this disability. Many psychologists don't know the appropriate ways to test for it. Most public schools ignore this child.

"We've had a life of twitch and trauma," a mother writes. "Chip is ten now and in fifth grade. His eye-hand co-ordination is almost nil. Only he can read his writing. He cannot tie his shoes. He cannot work the combination on his gym locker. He cannot find his way back to his theater seat if he goes alone for a drink of water. He cannot find his way—period. His life is one failure after another. Private parochial school? He was kicked out. His long string of failures piles up. You can take his mother's word, he is not dumb. But, boy, is he ever clopped up. Both he and his parents are near wit's end. Isn't there some help anywhere? Help before it is too late?"

Don't succumb to a feeling of helplessness in the face of apathy or opposition. Don't feel so hurt and embarrassed that you're frozen into inactivity and hand over all responsibility for your child's welfare to the so-called experts.

You will have to pursue help and understanding. "If we had not pushed and hollered, Timmy would be in a class for the retarded right now instead of doing honors work in high school," one father said. Unfortunately, society has not yet reached the point where hands are extended to those who need help. No one is likely to bring aid to you.

There are a number of reasons for professional lethargy and ignorance. *Normal* child development is not widely understood. Learning disability is a young field. There is an acute shortage of every professional the learning-disabled child needs. These men and women are so widely scattered that there is no predictable or uniform quality of service across the country.

The best professionals cluster in metropolitan centers or in the more affluent middle-class areas of cities and their suburbs. Away from the cities, it generally becomes more difficult to find sound professional advice. It would be hard, for example, to find a pediatric neurologist or a highly trained child psychologist in a rural area.

Even large cities may not have the needed specialists, because some of the professions serving the learning-disabled child are also so new—for example, clinical psychology, child psychiatry, and pediatric neurology. The latter, a key medical specialty for this youngster, has perhaps 200 practitioners nationwide. The term pediatric neurology was accepted by the American Medical Association only about five years ago.

Only 12,000 pediatricians work in the United States, roughly one for every 4,000 children under the age of fourteen. The qualified classroom teacher of the learning-disabled child is rare. There are too few speech and language specialists, occupational therapists, and remedial-reading teachers.

You'll get your best help in finding interested and qualified professionals from parents of other learning-disabled children. The most effective way to reach other parents is through the Association for Children with Learning Disabilities, whose activities are described in appendix B. The ACLD cannot endorse anyone, but it can report who nearest you has been helpful with learning-disabled children. Ask psychologists or guidance counselors in your school system. If a university is close, talk with members of its special-education or speech-and-hearing department. If the university has a medical school, ask the chief of the pediatric-neurology or pediatric unit for help.

Understand that personal recommendations are intensely subjective. Everyone chooses people to help him according to his feelings about them. Some parents will disregard a competent man because he is stiff and cold; they will choose another because of instant rapport. Nothing is wrong with this.

Your first encounter, when you become aware that *something* is wrong with your child, will probably be with your family physician or your child's pediatrician. You're most likely to express concern, assuming he is a preschool child, if he is notably delayed in some aspect of his development, if he is hard to control or discipline, if he is markedly hyperactive or emotionally unstable. Sometimes you will not worry until your youngster is in kindergarten or first grade—especially if he is quiet and well behaved—when learning problems begin.

Whenever you first express your concern to a physician, realize that he might not initially be interested in the problem you are presenting to him. He might know little about maturational lag or a learning disability. Possibly there was nothing, or very little, in his training that would help him identify the problem. Physicians are still trained primarily to look for disease. Since your child appears healthy, the doctor might tell you there is "nothing wrong." He could view your opinion with patient condescension or disdainful dismissal.

You are justifiably concerned with your child's development and his behavior. You're seeking understanding and advice, and you're looking to the physician to offer it. *You should be able* to expect him to help identify a child with a learning disability as early as possible.

But at least 90 per cent of the treatment of learning-disabled children consists of remedial education, psychological guidance, and parent counseling. The physician by himself is not able to say whether or not a child has a learning disability. The educator and the psychologist examine a child with techniques the physician doesn't use. Treatment of the learning disorder itself does not take place in the physician's office. It occurs in the classroom, in the office of the remedial-reading teacher, in the perceptual-training instructor's room, in the speech clinician's office.

Some physicians will resent being brought in to make a diagnosis of a condition for which there are only subtle physical symptoms, if there are any at all; or an ailment for which most of the treatment is educational rather than medical.

If your physician feels and acts this way, he is not the man to help you. Some physicians will be hampered or even paralyzed if they can't identify the cause of a behavior or learning disability. If they become enmeshed in the vagaries of whether or not the problem has organic roots, they are likely to lose sight of the *key* question: What is the matter with this youngster in terms of his daily functioning and how can he best be helped?

The physician you need should have a practical approach toward helping learning-disabled children—particularly toward any physiological factors he might uncover. He should be prepared to prescribe and follow through with treatment for them. The role of the physician will be discussed more fully in chapter 5.

Society asks a lot of parents. It asks—really tells—them to be patient, long-suffering, resourceful, and persistent if they want help for their children. Don't give up. People exist who can help you. Don't accept second best.

Look in your own community first. But if there is no local program of evaluation and treatment, if none of the individual professionals offers you a satisfactory treatment plan, widen your search.

Parents tend to stop shopping and settle in with a particular professional or team when the parents believe they have been provided with a concrete program of help and when they are not blamed. If the people you select take a constructive attitude toward your child and your family, give you an assessment of the child's strengths and limitations that makes sense to you, and offer workable and direct suggestions for home and school handling, stick with that individual or team.

Don't spend your energies fruitlessly in a frantic shopping expedition. Too many parents spend too much (in time, money, and emotions) searching for *that* professional who offers a cure, who eases their guilt. "Every parent of the handicapped child has a spark of hope hidden deeply within the recesses of his or her functioning," says Doreen Kronick, the mother of a learning-disabled child, in her book *They Too Can Succeed*. "Long after they have virtually come to terms with their child's limitations and adjusted their expectations accordingly, that spark lurks, ever ready to be set aflame."

When you know your youngster's needs are being met satisfactorily, don't subject yourself and your child to the doctor-hopping game in search of some golden message. It's damaging to your family and to your child if he is repeatedly forced to go through the same kind of probing, questioning analysis. The confidence of the learning-disabled youngster needs to be boosted. It isn't when his anxious parents rush him from doctor to doctor, leading him to think there is something fearfully "wrong with me" that nobody seems able to "cure."

What should you expect from any professional who deals with your child, whatever discipline he is in?

He must be willing to take the time to listen patiently to what you have to say. He must understand that the parents of this child undergo their own kind of private hell. You should be able to express to him, openly and fully, your torments, your fears for the future of your child, and your own weariness and frustration. Too many professionals are curt. Too many look at a youngster who seems healthy and immediately shut his parents off. Such men and women give parents the feeling that they have little time to discuss problems in full, that a lengthy discussion insults their professional dignity or encroaches on the time of another client.

Any professional you turn to should listen with awareness and sympathy to your particular problems. "The memories of numerous parents of handicapped children," one parent wrote, in an open letter to professionals, "recall at least one occasion when they strongly disagreed with the advice of a professional, only to be told that they were overconcerned, overanxious, had too much time to worry, or they needed a vacation. . . . Please do not automatically dismiss parents' views when they differ from your own." No one you choose for aid should casually wave away your concerns or talk down to you from a lofty perch of professional omnipotence.

You, too, must be a good listener. Parents often say, "No one told us anything." It is not always the other person's fault. A professional frequently is not able to get through, no matter how hard he tries, because some parents are unwilling or unable to listen. These parents don't hear or remember what they are told, because of guilt feelings or their need to deny that a problem exists. This doesn't mean you must accept everything uncritically. But you will learn little if you are unwilling or unable to listen.

A professional's effectiveness can be based more on his sensitivity than on his training. The sympathetic man or woman will not make parents feel guilty or inadequate. You've had enough of that already. To blame the home or to assume a carping, critical attitude toward parents merely intensifies the denial, guilt, and resistance they are already likely to feel. Don't take it if any professional tries to spank you verbally, belittle you, or intensify your feelings of inadequacy. Find someone else. No one can be effective when he depreciates what you say or insults your beliefs and values.

He should understand your child and your family. He must not be so lost in generalities that he begins to discuss learning disabilities as an abstract concept, rather than your child's specific impairments. He must be willing to help you solve day-to-day difficulties. He cannot do this unless he understands your strengths, your frustrations, and your problems.

He must communicate clearly. Anything he needs to say can be expressed in simple, direct language. Don't accept technical jargon. Too many professionals capitalize on an aura of mystique and leave parents confused and bewildered. Ask him to explain or clarify until you understand.

Is he seriously weighing all the facts? If he is, this means he has taken a considerable amount of time to find out, mostly from you, a great deal about your child. He wants to know the child's characteristics, his behavior, and his emotional responses. He is interested in how the youngster behaves within and outside the family. How does he respond to his brothers and sisters? How does he get along with children in the neighborhood? How does he play? In other words, how is he affected by others in his environment and how does he affect them? The professional who goes after all this information has made you part of his team; he has made it clear that your observations and your judgments are invaluable.

The professional should be the type of person with whom you can build a long-term relationship. The man who sees your child or counsels you on a one-shot basis may tend toward infallible pronouncement in his haste to satisfy all your requirements immediately. But you want the human being who will develop a feeling of closeness with you, with whom you can establish and maintain a continuing contact.

Some parents shop around. But so do some professionals. They "collect" certain kinds of patients, who sustain them in their professional roles. This is especially true in the case of physicians who work with learning-disabled children. Whether they are general practitioners or pediatricians whose patients include a high concentration of learning-disabled children, these doctors have an interest and a breadth of experience that make them more prepared to work with these youngsters than equally competent physicians who simply have not had much experience of this sort.

Parents need a realistic doctor. "We would much rather a doctor admit he does not know or is uncertain of an outcome," a parent writes, "than to float on an empty cloud that is likely to break at any moment and send us, along with our newest heartache, plunging to the ground." The competent professional does not predict an optimistic outcome just to allay parental anxiety. If there is no solid basis, that kind of prediction is cruel. The honest professional does not pat you on the head with a reassuring "He'll grow out of it." He knows he compounds the problem if he offers the false reassurance that the passage of time alone—without treatment, care, or education—will resolve all problems.

There is a great tendency to rank people in hierarchies, to put a physician ahead of a nonphysician, to put a man who has earned a doctorate ahead of one who has not. Extra competence is attributed to the physician, to the holder of the doctorate. The most important qualification of the person who is to help your child *is his ability to help your child,* regardless of his profession or number of diplomas. Frequently a young man or woman with a master's degree and a sincere commitment to working with learning-disabled children will be far better for your child than a better-established Ph.D. who has not kept up with the field.

Expect anyone you retain to recognize that collaboration

with other specialists will help in diagnosing the exact nature of a child's learning disability, in establishing a treatment plan, and, later, in judging its effectiveness.

The professional you want working with your youngster should see himself as part of a team, rather than as a single arbitrary authority. He must be eager to help you find competent consultants in other disciplines.

Be wary of the professional, often well-trained and competent, who has little patience with the opinions of others, even in his own specialty, if they don't agree with his. This man, usually charming and convincing, tends to work alone. He might use the same treatment method for all his patients and tell you it is the *only* effective one. No sound professional will say or imply that there is only one treatment for learning disabilities, or that it works all the time.

Educational and psychological services and medical evaluation and treatment must be brought together into a coordinated program. This will be extremely difficult except in those relatively few clinics that contain virtually every discipline a child requires. Ideally your physician should be the captain of the treatment team, but very few are. It's the rare physician, apart from a member of a team in a clinic, who assumes this obligation.

Most specialists work in isolation. It is hard to put the child together again after they have all had their time with him. Someone has correctly called the learning-disabled child a victim of "the fat-folder syndrome." Communication between specialists—between one physician and another, between physicians and educators, between educators and psychologists—is abysmal. Specialists don't even talk the same language. Diagnostic labels and symptom terminology can vary considerably among workers in different fields.

Parents need someone to reconcile the differences in emphasis among the experts. For example, each consultant might place stress on a particular aspect of the child's problem. If a specialist says he finds nothing wrong with your child, this does not necessarily mean there is nothing wrong. He is merely saying that the part of the child he is examining is fine. You can be thrown off the track if the co-ordinator, whether he is your child's physician or someone else, does not put all these views together. "We feel that the greatest good we do," one physician says, "is a detailed and leisurely discussion with the parents in an attempt to help them understand a confusing and terrifying problem."

The physician is best able to provide proper co-ordination if he is an active member of a clinic team that works together, meets to review all findings, and arrives at recommendations in an organized fashion. A clinic that has been designed for the evaluation and treatment of children with developmental problems can best provide everything a learning-disabled child needs. These clinics usually are associated with large medical centers or medical colleges. Your family physician should know if any exist in your area. A number of university-affiliated facilities are listed in appendix A.

If not at a clinic, there might be good services available close to you from individuals. Your family doctor or pediatrician should be able to refer you to the appropriate professional, just as he would if you had a physical problem requiring a specialist. If he does not have the time or patience to refer you and to co-ordinate the information, someone else can provide that effort. It might be a child psychologist or a key person within the public-school system, perhaps the school psychologist, the school social worker, or the person responsible for special education.

Too frequently parents find themselves providing the *inter* in the interdisciplinary effort required for this youngster. Parents must keep after the professionals they retain to discuss what has been recommended and learn how these findings fit into a cohesive treatment plan. The physician can still be the traffic cop, even if he is not the team leader. He should learn if the child is receiving the various kinds of help that have been recommended. It is his responsibility to know what's going on with the child under his care and to make sure that everyone, including the parents, is carrying out all the recommendations made. It is the parents' responsibility to keep him informed.

Working with professionals is a matter of putting together the right combination of talents to meet your child's requirements at any particular time. Even if you are fortunate and find a multidisciplinary team in a clinic, it might not include everyone you'll eventually need. Your child, for example, could require the help of a remedial-mathematics teacher. He or she would not be a part of the basic team. If the special help is not available from a regular team member, whoever is acting as the captain should be able to find an independent worker.

Any program will need periodic re-evaluation and updating. Its emphasis and the individual most intensively in contact with your youngster can shift over a period of time in accord with the child's needs. This does not mean that any other aspect of the program would be neglected. A young child with a severe perceptual-motor problem might have his most active contact with a perceptual-motor-training teacher, an occupational therapist, or a developmental optometrist at first. Later, when he had overcome that problem to a considerable degree, he might need regular support from a tutor. In some cases, the child will be so emotionally bound up that he can't respond properly to remedial education until he has had psychotherapy. Or remedial reading might have to take precedence over other treatments.

The professionals you consult will give you a diagnosis and a plan of treatment tailored to your child's unique set of learning disabilities. You must expect, and insist if necessary, that the diagnosis and treatment plan for your child explain as fully as possible *why* he behaves and learns as he does. It should be made clear what the plan will contribute toward improving the child's behavior and learning *and* toward reduction of stress and tension within the family. At the same time, the professionals you're consulting should give you some idea what the child's future might be and what response to treatment can reasonably be expected.

Expect the professionals to confess they are puzzled about learning disabilities. They will not be able to lay out a plan for your child with absolute confidence. Vast areas of uncertainty exist in the evaluation and treatment of any learning-disabled child. No psychologist can tell you precisely what your child's learning potential is, although his techniques permit him to make a fairly accurate estimate in most cases. The educator should admit that he can't predict with assurance whether, and to what extent, your son or daughter will overcome a reading block. The physician cannot predict to what extent or how soon any medication he prescribes will ease your child's distractibility and hyperactivity.

The view of anyone you retain should be provisional: "This is the way we interpret the facts we have about your child. As we observe his response to treatment, we may have to change our opinion. On the basis of this information, we believe he is likely to respond thus and so, achieve this much, acquire that amount of skill or self-control."

This uncertainty will trouble you. But there is uncertainty in everyone's life. The professional, knowledgeable though he may be, is a human being. He is all the wiser if he admits the possibility of error and looks for it as he evaluates and treats children. If he is authoritarian and arbitrary, denying that he could ever be in error, he might grievously misinterpret what he sees, to confirm his self-protective cloak of infallibility.

Parents tend to pressure the professionals for more complete predictions of exact outcomes. The honest man will tell you what he is *able* to tell you, in the light of his knowledge, and what he is *unable* to tell you. Don't think he is evading if he doesn't commit himself unalterably. He will deserve your confidence if he tells you what he is trying to attain for your child.

5 / Where Can We Go for Help: The Physician

To judge by the current attitude of eight out of ten physicians in private practice, medicine has not yet decided if it should help the child with learning disabilites.

Decades ago, some physicians began to suggest that injuries to the brain could result in disabilities of perception, language, and co-ordination. Dr. Samuel Orton, in the 1930's, was the first great American neurologist to show that problems in the way the brain functions affect the way a child perceives and remembers letters or is able to write them. He worked directly with an educator to develop a system of remedial teaching. In the forties, Dr. Alfred Strauss, a neurologist and child psychiatrist, described the following characteristics of learning-disabled children: perceptual and thinking disorders, perseveration, hyperactivity, and lack of inhibition. His studies revolutionized special education as well as pediatrics and neurology. From these researchers came the understanding that medicine, along with education and psychology, has a special contribution to make to children who have learning problems of organic origin.

Physicians today are called upon by a growing number of sophisticated schools and parents when a child is having trouble with his behavior or his academic achievement.

The doctor should take primary responsibility for: detection of disease, physical handicap, or any organic deviation that might affect a child's behavior or learning; co-ordination and interpretation of all evaluations to parents and to schools; medical treatment for the child; periodic re-evaluation; parent counseling.

This is what physicians should be doing. Perhaps two out of ten pediatricians and general practitioners take this kind of comprehensive approach.

The physician finds himself in an awkward spot in dealing with learning disabilities. His training has directed him to look for and treat disease. If he sees a youngster with fever, he looks for the cause of the symptom of fever. For years, when he saw a child who was not doing well in school he assumed it was an educational problem. Now that he is learning he must look for organic impairments in apparently normal children who are having difficulty in school, he finds himself working in a gray area, especially since the treatment for learning-disabled children is mainly educational.

"We're being overwhelmed by children who are not learning at the rate they should be," one physician stated, at a 1972 symposium on learning disability, and "this may continue until each physician has a problem-oriented functional approach and not a disease approach to learning problems in children."

The primary purpose of evaluation is to find appropriate treatment. The physician taking care of a particular child who is unable to read must be concerned not just with the fact that this child is having difficulty in school *now*, but with the child's entire history from before his birth to the time when he began to have difficulty. How did the child get to be the way he is?

Both parents should be interviewed before the child is examined. The physician needs some understanding of how both regard the problem; and he should know their attitude toward the child and toward each other. The joint interview also will help later in counseling the parents. Fathers don't always come to the initial examination. This might indicate that they don't recognize their importance to the youngster, don't understand the problem, or are denying it exists.

What specific things should the physician get in the first meeting? He should start with written reports of the child's school performance and of all prior testing. He must take a detailed family history that asks if either parent or any close relative has ever had any learning disability. For example, is the father a very slow reader and a terrible speller? Was this a common trait on his side of the family? Some youngsters with learning disabilities have specific developmental dyslexia, which is often hereditary. Genetic endowment in such things as eye color, body build, and facial features is an accepted fact. So is inheritance of temperament: "He's stubborn like his father"; "She has her mother's artistic talent with her father's disposition"; even "She's not very bright, but neither is the rest of the family."

Isn't it possible that a style of learning, even special disabilities, might be inherited? Jimmy's father, an engineer, is concrete in thinking, excellent in mathematics, and interested in spectator sports. He's an action-oriented kind of person, who rarely reads anything other than the newspaper unless it's related to his work.

Jimmy emulates his father. He, too, is concrete in his thinking, likes to work and build with his hands, and hates to read. His arithmetic is fine. Both Jimmy and his father are a little clumsy. Jimmy's father remembers that he never did very well in school in English and related subjects, but that didn't seem to matter so much when he was a boy. He thinks he might have had to repeat a grade, because of reading, and he's never been too good at spelling. He is, however, a successful engineer, and dammit, he wants his boy to shape up and do better in school.

In the prenatal and birth history, the physician is concerned about events that could be responsible for damage to the brain: bleeding during pregnancy, difficult or prolonged labor or delivery, overmedication of the mother, and precipitate delivery. What was the condition of the infant at birth? Did he breathe and cry immediately? (One of the leading known causes of learning disabilities is insufficient oxygen supplied to the brain at birth.) Was there jaundice, exchange blood transfusions, prematurity, or extreme infant irritability to the extent that sedation was required? Was there a severe feeding difficulty because the infant either had a very weak suck or was unable to suck and required assistance? Excessive spitting or vomiting?

What is the maternal reproductive history? Physicians frequently overlook the significance of a history of prolonged infertility or several abortions. This mother is much more likely to give birth to a neurologically damaged infant.

Is there a history of illness or injury of possible neurological significance, such as convulsions, measles with possible measles encephalitis, dehydration severe enough to warrant hospitalization, head injury—especially one that resulted in loss of consciousness or was followed by behavioral changes—any chronic illness?

What were the child's primary temperamental attributes, his personality, at birth and immediately afterward? Every mother knows she didn't deliver a lump of clay. Was this a very quiet child or a very active one, even when his mother was carrying him? If a particular child is described as hyperactive by his mother and his teachers, was this hyperactivity present from birth or did it develop later?

Hyperactivity is a good word to examine. It is a relative term. Hyperactive compared to whom? A passive, quiet woman who has an easy-to-live-with little girl might call any active little boy-explorer hyperactive and hard to handle; she will be a different mother with him than she is with her "good" little girl. Mrs. A. is a volatile, dynamic woman of Latin derivation, whose son, Peter, is considered a "holy terror" at school and in the neighborhood. Mrs. A. can't understand why his behavior is so "bad" away from home; she enjoys his company more than that of her quieter children, because "he and I are alike—we like to have a lot going on." Her Teutonic in-laws avoid visiting this group as much as possible, and Mr. A. works late at the office rather often. Peter is not hyperactive in the sense that a learning-disabled child is.

The physician should take a careful developmental history, especially of the child's first three years. How old was he as he went through his milestones? At what age did he sit, start to creep, walk, first ride a tricycle, a bicycle? Is there any history of poor co-ordination or clumsiness? A history of slight delay in the major motor milestones and a history of clumsiness or awkwardness are not uncommon. Was the youngster a little fearful of riding a tricycle? Did he have any trouble running around, or fall more often than his brothers and sisters? Was he generally clumsier? The classic picture is that of Charlie Brown, who's never going to catch the ball. This is the child who is never asked to empty the garbage, because he'll probably spill it en route. He manages to break a lot of things without knowing how he did so. Whenever something crashes in the house, nobody ever says, "Who did it?"; the entire family yells, "Oh, Charlie, not again!"

Charlie never did learn how to tie his shoes until he was in the first or second grade, and they still don't stay tied. He has difficulty buttoning and unbuttoning shirts and keeping his pants zipped up. He may seem to be a dawdler because he is clumsy in dressing and undressing himself. This can create monumental friction in the average home.

How did speech develop? It is often found that this child was a little slower than his brothers and sisters in starting to talk. When he did begin, he was difficult to understand. He spoke immaturely well into first grade.

How does he behave? Did he begin to wet his bed after he started school? This may be a signal of anxiety in the child, but it needs to be checked medically. His school history starts with nursery school if he attended one. Did he pay attention and work with a group? Was he hard to handle? Did he have difficulty with drawing, coloring, cutting and pasting, building with blocks? A report from the kindergarten teacher might include information to confirm difficulty in co-ordination, in paying attention, in speech or language or behavior.

Once a child starts first grade, a variety of symptoms can appear. Sometimes parents report that the child had no difficulties with his behavior; but he didn't learn to read, write, and spell. The teacher might confirm that this youngster just doesn't seem to be able to master graphic symbols. He can't grasp the fundamentals of reading, regardless of the method she uses to try to teach him.

When a physician looks at a child's history, he is trying to get a clear picture of everything that has happened to him from birth. He also needs to understand how this child fits into his family. What are the parents' expectations for their children, and for the learning-disabled child in particular? How does the family operate as a unit? How does this child get along with his brothers and sisters and with his parents?

The physician examines the child last. He knows a lot from the history. He will now try to get confirmation or denial. For example, the child might bear a teacher's or parent's label of hyperactive. But the office's receptionist might report that he has been quiet in the waiting room. The child might also behave well with the doctor. This could contradict the suggestion of hyperactivity, because a truly hyperactive child manages, no matter where he is, to leave his environment in a shambles. At this point, a physician alone cannot confirm a diagnosis of hyperactivity. Other professional opinions must be sought.

The major difference between the physical examination given to this child and the examination given an adult is the study of the youngster's sensory-motor functions. Much of the neurological portion of the examination is done by observation. The child dresses and undresses himself, without any assistance. It's important to watch how he unbuttons, unzips, takes his shirt off, takes off his shoes and socks, and then how he buttons and gets everything back on again. Does he put the right shoe on the right foot? Can he tie his shoelaces?

The most frequently encountered physical problem in children with learning disabilities is clumsiness. Can the child extend both arms and spread his fingers, eyes closed, without tremor, jerkiness, wandering kinds of movements, or odd posturing of the arms when they are extended? Can he extend his hands, close his eyes, and touch his nose (he may be unable to find it)? Can he rapidly and in alternating movements flap his hands over, palms up and then palms down, on his lap? This should be done simply and easily by a nine-year-old.

Can he touch each finger to the thumb on the same hand, and then do it with both hands at once? A child of nine should. Can he clench one fist while keeping the fingers of the other hand extended, and then switch hands rapidly? A nine-year-old with poor motor control might be unable to perform these movements smoothly. A school-age child should be able to stand on one foot with his eyes closed, and to hop on each foot. Most six-year-olds are able to skip, and to walk heel-to-toe along a straight line, forward and back. By the time the child is around four, he should be able to walk on his heels, as well as on his toes. (A word of caution: failure in any of these few simple items does not mean that the child has any kind of brain dysfunction. Many children with no learning disability do poorly in them. A lot of clumsy people are running around who are very good readers and never had any difficulty learning in school. Clumsiness *alone* is insufficient evidence for a diagnosis of learning disability.)

Testing the child's reflexes is a traditional part of the medical examination. Are reflexes normal, sluggish, exaggerated? The physician will determine if the child's muscle tone is firm, and especially if there is any difference in the quality of the child's muscle action between one side of his body and the other. These are the kinds of things that tell the perceptive physician whether neurologic development is up to par.

How do the youngster's eyes move? Poor eye co-ordination and crossed eyes are fairly common among children who have minimal neurologic problems. The inability to use both eyes together can affect the formation of three-dimensional concepts. A child's visual abilities at a distance of sixteen to eighteen inches are almost more important than his visual acuity at twenty feet. Most of his school day will be spent reading and shifting the focus of his eyes between the blackboard and his book.

The physician can roughly screen the child's hearing by altering the tone of his voice, by speaking to the child in a whisper when he isn't looking, by observing his reactions to sound and to voices in general, and by checking his hearing with tuning forks.

Does the child know his right from his left? He should by the time he is six. A child learning to read and write must be able to move his eyes smoothly from left to right. *All* children tend to reverse numbers or letters when they're first learning to write, because they do have some directional confusion. But the average child learns to go from left to right in reading and writing before the end of the first school year. The child with a learning disability may demonstrate continuing problems.

A physician experienced in evaluating children with learning disabilities might add to his physical examination a variety of tests, or his adaptations of some tests, that overlap other fields, such as psychology. He might use some tests of intelligence, perception, memory, and school achievement. All of these are for preliminary, or rough screening, purposes. For example, he will ask the child to copy forms and to draw. This gives the doctor information on the youngster's visual perception and visual-motor control. A three-year-old child should be able to make a circle, and a seven-year-old should be able to copy a diamond. Copying of forms or a drawing test should be used as part of *every* child's physical examination.

It is helpful to ask the child to repeat numbers, polysyllabic words, and short sentences. The purpose is to learn if he has difficulty remembering numbers, sounds, or words in sequence. A six-year-old child should be able to repeat five numbers in sequence and to remember his own telephone number.

The physician can screen for ability in auditory perception by administering a simple, short test. Paired words are offered, some of which are the same, such as *car–car* or *cat–cat*, and some of which are different, such as *cat–cap* or *pat–pet*. The child is asked whether the words are the same or different.

The physician needs to have a rough idea of the grade level at which the child is functioning. He can ask the child to read a commercially standardized series of paragraphs; each one of the paragraphs represents a different grade level in ability. It is important to have the child not only read each paragraph, but also answer questions about the content, to be sure he has understood what he read. The physician can also check the child's arithmetic grade level.

If a child does not do well in certain of these tests, the physician will often suggest that a comprehensive examination be done by a psychologist, a special educator, or any other professional whose specialty seems to be involved.

The doctor might order some combination of laboratory procedures, to look into the child's physical status. Children with learning disabilities might have conditions, related or not, that should be treated medically or surgically. For example, if the youngster has allergies, his ears might be so stuffed that he doesn't hear the teacher. Another child might have a heart condition that reduces his energy level. Such boys and girls are often out of school for long periods, losing touch with what is going on in the classroom. A child with a glandular disturbance might be slow-moving and lethargic. Any such physical condition must be fully diagnosed and treated. If the physician suspects a metabolic problem such as thyroid deficiency, for example, he will request X rays of the skull, long bones, and wrists to determine skeletal growth. Metabolism is the process by which the body feeds and regulates its parts. Usually the routine laboratory tests, including blood tests, serology, and urinalysis, are all that are necessary.

An electroencephalograph reading, or brain-wave test, may be ordered. Its findings alone, however, can't indicate a brain dysfunction. Research suggests that the electroencephalogram, or EEG, someday will be important in diagnosis and treatment of learning-disabled children, but in the present state of knowledge it is not extremely helpful. EEG tests of learning-disabled children often are normal. (Studies examining *groups* of learning-disabled children, however, show them to have a significantly higher percentage of abnormal EEG's and neurological signs than groups of normal children. This finding is of limited value in individual diagnosis; each child presents a unique picture.) Any EEG examination and reading should be done by an electroencephalographer who is familiar with the use of the EEG on children.

When a child is unable to control his behavior, medication *could* be useful. Anticonvulsants, tranquilizers, and stimulants are the drugs most commonly used by physicians to bring a child's behavior under better control or to reduce his tendency to convulsions. Stimulants often have a paradoxical effect on children; the same medication that stimulates an adult might calm a hyperactive child. No one understands this reverse action. A number of medications can be prescribed, singly or in combination. Different physicians will use different ones. Medication might be used in combination with psychotherapy.

When medication works, the effect is almost miraculous. It would be wrong to deprive a child of it in such a case. But parents must not feel that medication is the sole answer to controlling the behavior of a learning-disabled child. Many children will do better under medication, but there also has to be a change in the way they are dealt with at home. Management at home and in school is part of the treatment, with or without medication.

Physicians have to rely on the judgment of those around the child to evaluate the effectiveness of medication. Such opinions are often influenced by factors that have no relation to the usefulness of the prescription. A teacher, for example, believes that the learning-disabled child is showing improved behavior in the classroom, but the mother reports no change at home; stress within the family might be influencing that parent's judgment of the child's behavior. The physician can be confident of the effectiveness of medication only when reports about the child's behavior are similar from everyone who comes in daily contact with him.

The use of medication to alter a learning-disabled child's behavior is a trial-and-error process. Science has no way to predict how each child will react to a specific prescription. No one knows the exact amount that will work, so the physician must keep in close contact with the child's family to find out if the medication is successful, if he needs to change the dosage, or if he must alter the times of day the medication is given. Repeated changes in medication might be necessary before an effective one is found. This requires the co-operation of parents and teachers. Parent counseling is *always* necessary when drugs are prescribed.

Some parents resist the idea of medication or are afraid the child will become addicted. So they "forget" to give it to him on a regular basis. No medication among the many used for these children is known to cause addiction, no matter how long it is taken. Although the use of medication for hyperactive children has been criticized, no significant evidence has been offered to indicate that appropriate medication should not be used, provided the child is under proper medical supervision. Usually the need for medication ends when the child reaches puberty.

The prescription of medication for behavior disorders is relatively new. Its use is not accepted by many pediatricians, neurologists, and psychiatrists. More information is needed concerning the relationship of various kinds of medication with behavior response, neurological findings, and EEG results. Like aspirin, this kind of medication can ease symptoms. Neither provides a cure. However, when the medication is effective, the child's attention span increases and learning is easier. With thoughtful selection, careful regulation of dosage, and watchfulness for possible side effects, medication is a major medical tool for the learning-disabled child.

When the evaluation of the child is completed by the physician and any other professionals who have been consulted, it is essential that the parents get a full and correct interpretation of all findings and guidance concerning the recommendations. Both of these elements—interpretation and guidance—are just as important as the tests performed on the child. One person whom the parents respect should put the findings and recommendations together in such a way that the problems as well as the necessary steps involved in handling the child will be understood. Ideally this person should be the child's physician. His interpretation usually adds considerable weight to what has been said by others who were involved; his is often the opinion most readily accepted by parents. However, not every physician will undertake this role or can be a successful interpreter, especially of nonmedical results and advice. Then the psychologist, the special educator, or the social worker should join the physician during some of the counseling sessions.

An adequate examination of a child that includes all the steps mentioned here requires more time than most physicians give. It can take from ninety minutes to two hours on the first visit. However, if the physician will spend that much time with the child and his family *prior to his entering school,* it could forestall many subsequent hours of concern on the doctor's part, and of heartache and misery on the part of both parents and child, should the boy or girl turn out to be learning-disabled. Parents should expect to pay more for this kind of time involvement on the part of the physician.

If no doctors in your community perform this kind of examination, for lack of training, interest, or time, physicians exist elsewhere who do. Look for a diagnostic clinic where an interdisciplinary approach is available (see appendix A).

An increasing number of pediatricians *are* extending their usual physical examinations to look for children with possible learning problems at earlier ages—five and younger. They are not waiting until the children reach the ages of seven to ten and the school begins to refer them. Physicians especially are starting to identify "high-risk" children earlier. High-risk youngsters are boys and girls whose medical history or poor environment warns of possible neurologic problems. These children are discussed in chapters 10 and 11.

Some doctors are also going beyond "medicine" to recommend, for preschool-age children, specific nursery-school placements, some—such as Montessori—for boys and girls who have perceptual-motor problems, other kinds of schools for those who require a tightly structured program.

Other medical specialists might be called in to help with diagnosis of the learning-disabled child, and often with treatment as well.

The child psychiatrist. Until little more than five years ago, very few child psychiatrists in the United States played a significant role in the evaluation and treatment of learning-disabled children. "For years, child psychiatrists fell into two camps: Those who felt psychotherapy could cure all learning problems and those who felt the presence of organic factors completely precluded psychiatric intervention," psychiatrist Mary Giffin writes, in volume 1 of *Progress in Learning Disabilities.*

The myth that the psychiatrist—or anyone whose exclusive approach to this problem is psychotherapy—could alone significantly affect the achievements of learning-disabled children has pretty much been disproved. The tendency on the part of some child psychiatrists to back away from any problem that might originate in genetic or neurologic factors also is dwindling.

The child psychiatrist, often working in conjunction with a psychologist and a social worker, is especially qualified to assess a youngster's emotional responses, the "feeling" aspects of a child's life, and has a key role in the diagnostic process. He has to determine whether upsets in the child's feelings are causing learning disturbances or whether learning disabilities are a reason for the youngster's lack of trust in others and his poor self-esteem.

This specialist also helps determine if a child's environment —his family life and his school experiences—provides a setting that promotes his feelings of security and worth, helps him to mature, and allows him to handle the routine frustrations that inevitably occur.

The child psychiatrist is particularly able to understand the anxieties and uncertainties of both the youngster with learning disabilities and his parents. He can re-evaluate the child's emotional development as he meets new stresses. Some problems will diminish, but new conflicts might appear, especially during adolescence. The psychiatrist can best determine if a conflict can be resolved (in which case, he works with it), or if a realistic confrontation and acceptance of the handicapping condition must be attained by the learning-disabled child and his parents (in which case, he would work with both the child and the family). Because he is a physician, the psychiatrist can prescribe medication. If he does not do so himself, he should be aware of any medication that a pediatrician or pediatric neurologist has recommended, especially in its effect upon the child's emotional development and behavior.

The psychiatrist's principal job is psychotherapy. If psychotherapy is necessary, the psychiatrist will use that technique to help the child understand and adapt to reality better, meet challenge constructively, and use his abilities more effectively.

The pediatric neurologist. Until recently, neurologists who examined children used the same procedures with them that they administered to adults. Within the last decade, a great deal of doubt has been cast on the suitability of those methods for children. The medical specialty of pediatric neurology is the result. These physicians are beginning to use more relevant techniques in assessing the child's developing nervous system, methods that view the child *in the totality of his functioning*, rather than as an aggregate of simple sensations, movements, and reflexes.

Pediatric neurologists take an active interest in the neurological development of children who are inefficient learners. Some of their techniques are similar to those used by clinical psychologists.

The ophthalmologist. This eye specialist is not directly concerned with the visual-perceptual problems that learning-disabled children so often display. The ophthalmologist concentrates on diseases or refractive errors of the eye. Visual-perceptual impairment is rarely traceable to disease. This must be kept in mind in interpreting what the ophthalmologist says. He might say there is "nothing wrong" with your child's eyes. He is really saying there is no *disease* of the eye that he can diagnose and treat. This does *not* mean the child's *functional* vision is necessarily good. As was discussed in chapter 3, visual-perceptual disorders can occur when the eyes themselves are healthy.

Similarly, a child might have an auditory disorder, even one so severe that it interfered with his understanding of speech, without any evidence of active disease or hearing loss that the otolaryngologist, or ear specialist, can identify. Many parents are astounded to find that their child has problems with auditory perception, and will report with consternation, "I took Johnny to an ear specialist, and he said there was nothing wrong with my child's ears!" But the specialist did *not* say he had ruled out the possibility that there was something wrong with the child's *hearing*.

The otolaryngologist. This physician specializes in the ears, nose, and throat. He is most likely to be consulted if there is some suggestion that the learning-disabled child does not hear normally. He will be principally interested in determining if disease has reduced the efficiency with which the child hears sounds. If disease or injury has affected the nerve path-ways that transmit sounds to the child's consciousness, the otolaryngologist usually will not be able to treat him medically or surgically. If the disease has affected the mechanical ele-ments of the ear apparatus that pick up and transmit sounds before they arrive at the inner ear, where the nerve fibers are located, there is often the possibility of helping by surgery or other medical treatment.

The orthopedist. This physician diagnoses and treats dis-orders of neuromuscular development, especially when de-formities might result. He might perform surgery on the muscular-skeletal system, or prescribe physical and occupa-tional therapy or such devices as braces.

Learning disabilities are one of the most devastating prob-lems of infancy and childhood. The physician, because he is usually the first professional to see an impaired child, must learn to identify this condition as early as possible, and to work with other disciplines in a comprehensive treatment plan. Failing this, he is avoiding one of his basic patient responsibilities.

6 / Where Can We Go for Help: The Other Professionals We'll Need

In addition to the physician, the typical learning-disabled child usually requires the skills of a number of nonmedical consultants for diagnosis and treatment. The other professionals who are most often called on are the subject of this chapter.

The psychologist. At some point, preferably as early as possible after you sense your child is in trouble, arrange an evaluation by a psychologist. (Your son or daughter may then have to be examined at least once every two or three years until the mid-teens.)

A psychologist is trained to provide objective and detailed studies of several vital aspects of a child's functioning. He judges the youngster's intellectual ability, using one or several standardized intelligence tests. These tests sample a wide range of intellectual abilities by means of many carefully selected individual items. These test items break down into two general categories: verbal, in which basically the psychologist makes a statement or asks a question and the child responds; and nonverbal, in which the psychologist shows the child a problem and the child must try to find a solution.

For example, in the verbal portion of the test, the psychologist might ask the preschool child to explain what some everyday object is for and what it is made of. The five-year-old should be able to answer such questions as: What is a chair for? What do you wear on your feet? What do you do with a pen? Tell me what a table is made of. When he is old enough to start school the child is ready to define words. The psychologist will ask him to explain what a toy is, what a glass is, what a comb is. He will expect an older child, of about eight, to define words like telescope and artist. The child of eleven or twelve should be able to explain words like exaggerate, secede, and autocracy.

The verbal part of the test will also examine the amount and accuracy of the information a child has amassed at different ages. For example: How many glasses of water make a quart? How far is it from Philadelphia to Boston? What color is an emerald? Usually children will be able to answer questions like these by the age of eleven or twelve. In addition, the child is expected to use reasoning ability, to work out relationships of many kinds. He might be asked which number is more, eight or ten. An entering first-grader should know. And before long he also should know how many things make a half-dozen, and how much change he would get back if he gave a storekeeper a nickle for two cents' worth of candy.

The youngster is tested, too, for his ability to understand how things are similar or different and in what ways they can be grouped. The early-school-age child—five through seven or eight—should know, for example, how a train and an airplane are the same, or a grapefruit and a pear. A little later, by age ten or so, his understanding of logical categories should have grown sufficiently for him to tell that a snake, an elephant, and an eagle are all animals, or that a dollar bill, a check, and a money order are all means of payment.

The nonverbal part of the intelligence test helps the psychologist examine how the child's mind works in solving problems that do not directly involve the use of language. The preschool child might be given blocks to see if he can copy structures like bridges or towers that the psychologist makes with other blocks. The psychologist might give the child jigsawlike puzzles to assemble, ranging from a couple of pieces for preschool children to much more complex puzzles for school-age boys and girls. He might show the youngster pictures and ask him to indicate what small part is missing. Or he might show the child separate cartoon pictures and ask him to put them in the correct order to tell a good story. By nonverbal means, the psychologist is sampling the child's knowledge of the world, his logical processes, his ability to understand relationships, and his ability to solve problems.

The psychologist will compare the child's over-all performance on tests like these with the performance of other children his age, in order to determine his relation to the average. On the whole, is he on a par with other children? Is his thinking ability better than that of others his age—and how much better? Is his thinking generally at a lower level than boys and girls his age—how much lower? Conclusions like these can be stated by the psychologist in numerical terms, either as the child's mental age or as the relationship between his mental age and his chronological age, which is called his intelligence quotient, or IQ. Although far from perfect, the IQ score—when the test is given to an individual, not a group —is the best tool anyone has yet devised to indicate *roughly* the child's intellectual functioning at a given time.

In addition to evaluating intelligence, the psychologist determines the presence and nature of a child's emotional and social problems. In carrying out this function, he and the child psychiatrist do much the same kind of thing: they evaluate the child's family background; appraise the stresses he has been under throughout his life; determine how he feels about himself, how he reacts to other children, and how he fits into group activities in the neighborhood, on the playground, in school. The psychologist might learn about the child's fantasies —what he imagines about life, whether, for example, he believes it to be safe or full of threats—by showing him the commonly used Rorschach ink-blot pictures and asking him what they make him think of. Or he might show the child pictures of people in various relationships (a woman and a child, or a boy and girl playing together) and ask him to make up a story about them. He might ask the child to finish sentences in any way he sees fit: "The things I like to do best are . . ."; "My mother always . . ."; "In school, I . . ." The psychologist learns a lot about the way a child thinks and feels about people and situations from questions of this kind.

The psychologist also is interested in other vital aspects

of a youngster's development: his language skills, his perceptual abilities, his co-ordination. These are all related to his intelligence, and the intelligence tests yield information about them. But there are, as well, specific tests beyond the IQ measurement that go into each of these functions in detail. Some of these tests, which can also be administered by other specialists, were mentioned in the previous chapter—such as having the child repeat words and sentences in imitation of the adult giving the test, to judge auditory perception and memory, and the copying of designs, to determine visual perception and muscular co-ordination. But, to repeat, the physician does this only for screening purposes. The psychologist administers such tests in greater detail. He will come up with an over-all picture of the child's strengths and weaknesses that will lead to a sound program for the child.

The psychologist, in common with other specialists, determines a child's academic level of achievement, the way in which he learns, and any blind spots or points of breakdown in such basic skills as reading, arithmetic, and spelling.

The qualified psychologist must be sensitive enough to determine if the learning-disabled child is performing approximately at the level of his native ability or if there are particular inhibiting factors that keep him from testing as well as he might. This specialist must be alert to interferences posed by a handicapping condition, so that the child with a speech defect will not be penalized because he is unable to answer questions clearly, or the child with mild cerebral palsy will not be underrated because he cannot copy a design accurately.

Why is it important to estimate intellectual potential? A child who is not as bright as most other children his age will have difficulty keeping up in the classroom. He might not be learning-disabled. He could be working to his capacity, which just happens to be below that of most other children his age. This child might have fooled his parents, doctors, and teachers, who have not suspected low IQ. Children who are attractive, well brought up, and polite often appear much smarter than they really are, especially if they come from highly verbal backgrounds and have learned to speak and act nicely.

Such children might do satisfactory work in the early grades, because they could learn the basic academic skills on a memory basis. But later, when more reasoning and abstract thinking are required of them, they fail to reach expectations. Intelligence testing helps parents and teachers understand what they can reasonably expect of this child.

Parents and teachers often make the mistake of basing expectations on the child's size, not his age. The big boy is expected to do grade-level work, whereas the small boy of the same age might get away with poor achievement without incurring penalties. It is the child's performance in regard to children his own age that is important, not the accident of his size. It's hard to persuade parents and teachers of this except by an objective psychological evaluation that reveals how the child is performing in comparison with other youngsters his own age, without any regard for how big or how little, how fat or how skinny, he happens to be.

Without the benefit of psychological examination, both the child who is big for his age and the one whose physical attractiveness and good social graces obscure his inherently low normal ability can be victims of the chilling indictment "You could do better work," even though each is working as hard as he can.

Intelligence testing identifies children with specific learning disabilities and separates them from those who have limited intellectual ability. Confusion between the two is not uncommon.

The learning-disabled child who is of at least average intellectual ability will be found in the psychological examination. Parents and teachers can learn from the examination how far below reasonable expectancy he is falling because of his learning disability.

Psychologists, using their test and interview information, counsel parents concerning the child's education, home management, and discipline. They confer with teachers to help guide school instruction for the child. Some psychologists also offer psychotherapy to boys and girls whose emotional development is markedly disturbed.

Psychology encompasses many kinds of specialization. The

man or woman who examines your child might be called any one of the following: clinical psychologist, school psychologist, educational psychologist, child psychologist, pediatric psychologist. The child psychologist and the school psychologist usually are the most experienced with children who have learning disabilities.

The special educator. Diagnosis of the learning-disabled child is more than a one-time occurrence. It takes place when his handicap is first suspected. It then is done again periodically to assess his progress—or lack of it—and adjust his treatment plan accordingly.

This continuing evaluation is part of the job of the special educators who are learning-disability specialists. Some of them test the child to learn what he can do in school, particularly in reading, spelling, and arithmetic. The tests pinpoint the areas of weakness in the child's skill development that need special teaching attention. These same tests might also be given by a variety of other specialists, such as psychologists, remedial-reading teachers, and speech clinicians. There is no sharp line of demarcation between the educational tests given by special educators and those given by these other experts, although each looks at different aspects of the child's behavior.

The special educator—primarily the classroom teacher of learning-disabled children—plays a key role in the continuing evaluation, or diagnosis, that no one else fulfills. This is called diagnostic teaching, and it is described in detail in the next chapter.

The social worker. This professional helps you, as parents, to set limits, to be consistent, to exert discipline, and to provide security for your child. As a rule, he or she works in an agency or clinic, rather than in a school or independently. Although the social worker does not make the diagnosis of learning disability, he can help identify the problem. He then can aid the family in accepting the diagnosis and in handling the child. He probably will know more than any other professional about organizations designed to help parents of learning-disabled children.

The social worker often is assigned to work directly with

parents in individual or group counseling. Discussion groups involving parents of learning-disabled children try to provide the factual information they need regarding their children; these groups also assist parents in coping with their own feelings concerning their learning-disabled youngsters.

The social worker can aid parents to develop realistic attitudes toward their child's problems. He or she works with families to ease acute family strains. These might include relationships with brothers and sisters, how to communicate aspects of the child's problem to relatives, friends, and neighbors, how to deal with family feelings of shame, anger, and guilt. The social worker provides guidelines by which the family can help their child develop a sense of adequacy in meeting reasonable expectations. Ultimately the social worker may help plan the learning-disabled child's school program and career preparation.

The *school social worker*, or *guidance counselor*, does not do the same work. He is likely to be called in by a teacher who is concerned about the learning or behavior problems of a child. He then will often recommend examination by a school or private psychologist.

The audiologist. He is a hearing specialist, not an ear specialist. He is trained to examine, often with elaborate electronic devices, the ways in which children respond to a wide variety of sound stimuli. The audiologist determines how loud sounds must be before the child becomes aware of them. He determines if the child reacts to sounds within certain frequency ranges better than he responds to sounds with other frequency characteristics. He can determine, for example, whether a child's hearing is essentially normal for most of the speech range but suddenly exhibits gaps that cause certain words to be gibberish to him.

The audiologist will also be concerned with whether different kinds of sounds, particularly speech, are intelligible to the child. It is possible for a child to detect sounds but not be able to identify them. He might hear speech perfectly, for example, at the same level of loudness as the normal child does and yet not be able to recognize words. If he can't recognize words he can't understand what is said to him, and he experiences a curious perplexity and frustration that are hard for parents and teachers to understand. The audiologist can help recommend a treatment program, usually with a speech clinician or a speech and language clinician.

The speech and language clinician. This specialist may work in a hospital or clinic, in a school, sometimes in private practice. Some have been trained to concern themselves largely with the accuracy and fluency of the sounds children produce. Others have broader training; they are concerned, as well, with the child's vocabulary development, choice of words, and grammatical structure. Since many learning-disabled children do have problems in these areas, it is wise to see that the youngster who needs the help of a clinician is being treated by one with this broader background.

The optometrist. The optometrist is an independent professional who usually works out of his own office. Initially optometrists limited themselves to testing vision and prescribing glasses. While many optometrists in private practice still restrict themselves to this responsibility, a growing number have greatly expanded their area of professional activity.

This latter group now views the child's visual development in a broad manner. They are aware of the total vision process, including the child's interpretation of what he sees and the way the child moves. They are interested in the way these functions develop as the child grows and as he is faced with the challenges and responsibilities of school. They apply an array of training methods to the visual and visual-motor disturbances they find.

Developmental optometry, as a new field, has been criticized. One problem has been its sometimes vigorous description of visual-motor development as its exclusive domain. Other professionals believe that it is a legitimate concern of theirs as well.

For this new specialty within an old profession, a very wide range of training and ability exists among optometrists who deal with developmental vision. Many are respected professionals who are developmental experts. But some explore the wider field of visual training without sufficient technical preparation. Often they are limited in their understanding of child development and the learning process. They ignore or underrate the influence of limitations or distortions in the child's intellectual life, his social-emotional make-up, his language development.

Some optometrists treat visual disorders alone, rather than as part of the total treatment program, which must involve other significant, and sometimes major, aspects of the child's over-all ability to function. Because the optometrist most often works alone, he does not get the benefits that come through co-operation with other professionals. He might apply his techniques without regard to what anyone else is doing with the child, in and out of the classroom. The situation is better when, as in a growing number of cases, the optometrist does function as part of an evaluation and treatment team.

The field of optometry has played a significant role in calling attention to the perceptual-motor process and the effect of perceptual-motor impairments on the child. In some parts of the country, the optometrist is still one of the few professionals who express and act on these interests. In other areas, knowledge of perceptual-motor problems is widespread, and the optometrist is doing essentially what can also be accomplished by other skilled professionals: *occupational therapists, physical-education teachers,* and *special-education teachers* who are trained in perceptual-motor corrective work.

7 / Where Can We Go for Help: The School

The so-called average child is a statistical fiction. No youngster moves neatly along some foreordained developmental schedule. This is a mirage conjured up out of society's preoccupation with norms, standards, guidelines. Large-scale public institutions like the schools would prefer to stamp each boy and girl out with a cookie cutter. It would make things much more convenient for them.

Schools are not as child centered and respectful of individuality as people like to think. There isn't a great amount of latitude they permit the individual youngster. Virtually none forgive or excuse marked deviations in behavior or in skill development. The large-group setting demands that each child conform in behavior. The curriculum requires each youngster to learn certain tasks at an established rate of speed.

"Children are lined up and spray-gunned," one educator told the author. "If that does not take, the pupil is 'a problem.'"

Thus children in today's society who do not conform to group settings or to curriculum requirements become "problems."

Boys and girls are put into first grade when they are about six years old. This is done in the assumption that all children are ready for a first-grade program at six. This is a myth.

The Gesell Institute of Child Development, in New Haven, Connecticut, has shown how tragically inappropriate this mechanistic approach to school readiness is. Age cannot be the sole or even the major indicator of readiness. Learning disabilities and emotional problems often result from the sheer immaturity of youngsters who are forced into a first-grade setting before they are ready. Society ignores clear indications of individual differences. Normal boys, for example, are much less likely to be ready for first grade by the age of six than girls are. It's possible for a child to start school at seven years. But what if he's not ready until eight or nine? He's in trouble. There is usually no provision for him unless it is a special class (special-education classes are for children clearly out of the ordinary, whether handicapped or gifted). A few schools allow some flexibility by providing a transitional first grade; this is a kind of intermediate grade between kindergarten and first grade. But by the time that year is over a child has to be ready to go into a regular first grade whether he has caught up or not.

This placement of children in a first-grade academic program before they are ready to succeed is common practice. Sometimes it's done when there is no kindergarten in a community; the school system has had no experience with a particular child and doesn't know he isn't ready. In other communities, kindergarten teachers know a child is not ready and parents or schools ignore the information. The youngster is put into first grade because the teacher or parents hope his development will spurt and he will catch up academically and socially, or because he is "too big" to stay behind.

Part of the problem is an emphasis that pervades the American ethic—the idea that every child can be a "success," with success defined as financial achievement. The middle-class parent typically sees only one available path to material success—high scholastic standing and admission to college. He finds it hard to understand that not all children are born with the same mental capacity. Only 7 per cent of all children can do college-level work without excessive strain. But most parents of the other 93 per cent are pushing to squeeze *their* youngsters through the bottleneck. The fact that only half of all children who attend college graduate should tell them something. Yet parents and schools are in league in establishing values and requirements.

"Symptoms" of the learning-disabled child in school are largely produced by pressures he cannot handle. This child and his world—especially as represented by that most demanding institution, the school—are "out of sync." He simply is not matched to its requirements. His capacity and potential are out of line with the responsibilities demanded of him at that moment by contemporary society. He is in conflict with his environment.

Through the Industrial Revolution, the child was considered essentially an adult, a small one, perhaps, but one who could work side by side with those much older than he. Gradually childhood became a separate and distinct stage of life, one that prepared the child for adulthood; so modern society has taken most children out of the ranks of labor and put them in school.

School has become the major vehicle for conducting the child toward adult responsibilities. But the responsibilities education leads to depend upon the *needs* of a particular society. Learning requirements therefore differ from one society to another according to its needs; what is considered a learning disability differs as well.

A disability in one culture is not at all a disability in another. Physical strength, agility, and stamina are much more important in a predominantly agricultural society than in an urban, technologically advanced culture. A food-gathering society is essentially nonliterate. Since no one bothers to teach children to read or write there is no such thing as a reading disability. But someone with a disorder in co-ordination that interfered with his ability to break a horse or draw a bow would be considered disabled. The factory system that developed in the last century demanded that workers learn to read and write so they could follow printed instructions. Suddenly a whole population segment was disabled. (Through most of recorded history, the ability to read has been a social nicety limited to an elite class. Only by the time of World War II did the average American complete ninth grade.)

In every society, one's ultimate mission in life is competence and mastery in terms that are valued in that time and place. The society enforces its particular time schedule for the development of its children. Youngsters must master required developmental tasks to meet that schedule.

If school is the primary vehicle to adulthood, achievement in school is essential. As virtually all schools are now organized, that means achievement from Day One. Yet poor development of *basic* skills, including language development—those skills that are taught early—is probably the major reason for scholastic failure in many intellectually normal children, learning-disabled or not.

Somewhere between the ages of four and eight, every youngster in today's culture meets academic challenge. Teachers and parents expect children to measure up to requirements. Friends the same age exert pressure. The children themselves are anxious to perform more or less like others in their group.

These requirements are rigid. Many learning-disabled boys and girls begin to fail academically in kindergarten. The degree of failure a learning-disabled child faces will depend a lot on how much his school emphasizes conformity to group standards of behavior, social participation, and skill development.

Dr. Jean Piaget, known for his research into how children learn, once noted that while the gradual, systematic unfolding of intellectual abilities is now acknowledged throughout the Western world, "only in America" are people likely to see these stages in their utilitarian sense. Others marvel at the beauty of a child's development. They watch with respect the pace of attainments during the growth of a particular child. Americans, though, are much more likely to see these stages as a necessary prerequisite to *ultimate* productivity, material success, and status. It is for this reason, Piaget has said, that only in the United States is he asked how the child's intellectual growth can be speeded up.

Most learning-disabled children will benefit if the early grades are easy and slow-moving. There is enough time for youngsters to get into a pressure cooker that stresses the acquisition of a certain amount of skill or information in a specified period. Some schools are fairly relaxed toward formal learning in the first few years. They stress basic skills, but also social participation and a good deal of arts-and-crafts activity. Other primary schools are free and unstructured; students can select their own activities. A small but increasing number of schools are nongraded. This means no arbitrary levels exist according to age breakdown—all six-year olds in first grade, seven-year-olds in second grade, and so on; children, instead, progress at their own pace.

If a child has a severe learning disability, he probably will need special education full time. *That* class will be highly organized and will allow little freedom of choice to the child. This kind of class is discussed later in the chapter.

But if the learning disability is mild, the child might be able to work in a group with normal children. This kind of class ideally should allow him to move ahead at his own rate of development and interest; the classroom teacher or others in the school would provide any supportive services he needed, such as speech therapy or remedial reading.

(Children with a mild degree of learning disability overlap with normal youngsters starting school who themselves are not ready for formal learning requirements. Some normal children come to school with insufficient experience to allow learning to mean anything. Too many homes afford little stimulation. These are not only economically impoverished homes. Some children from middle-class families are culturally deprived. In their barren homes, however plush, they have heard little good music, seen no art, are not surrounded by worth-while literature. They go on few outings. They might never have been to a zoo or museum. But they are exposed to television for countless hours, in lonely isolation, with little chance to share activities with others. These children simply don't know how to learn.)

Most children with learning disabilities can be helped by slight modifications within regular school programs: transitional or nongraded early classes; special arrangements in the regular classrooms, such as grouping by ability level; team teaching; adaptations of the teaching techniques used in full-time special education; effective parent guidance; and the appropriate supportive services.

Too few schools do this. Some meet the problem of learning-disabled children, after their identification in kindergarten or first grade, with nongraded classes for a year or more. These groups, called extended-readiness classes, offer individualized teaching based on a diagnosis of each child's problems. The class is smaller. It reduces demands on its members. The teacher is a specialist in learning disabilities. Each child is led gradually toward formal, traditional schoolwork. The teacher looks for and helps fill the gaps in each child's learning background as the child moves along. If the youngster succeeds, he is ready to go into a regular primary class.

This kind of special class relieves both the child and his teacher of the intense pressure of the usual grade-achievement expectations. A boy or girl may be in this program for two or three years, or for as little time as he needs. Regular grade steps are suspended. Every child moves at his own rate. He is steadily encouraged by his teachers. He never learns to think of himself as a failure.

Good school systems provide a number of alternatives beyond the empty social promotion or grade repetition for children who are not learning. Social promotion means that a school promotes a child to the next grade solely to keep him with boys and girls his age; the fact that he is not succeeding is ignored. Merely having the child repeat grades without giving him special help is almost always a bad idea. It's never possible to have a student repeat more than once. That puts him completely outside his own age group.

Wherever tried, social promotion and grade repetition have proved shoddy and fruitless. They are confessions of failure on the part of a school district that has neither the resources nor the desire to help.

Among the most beneficial new approaches to the young child with a mild learning disability (along with the slow learner and the immature youngster) are the use of itinerant teachers and what have become known as resource rooms. Both of these are for boys and girls whose problems are mild enough to allow them to remain in regular classes.

The itinerant teacher is a specialist in learning disabilities who moves from school to school, class to class, to bring special education into the regular classroom. This specialist shows the classroom teacher how to adjust her approach to the child; helps her to understand more clearly why each child behaves and learns in the peculiar way he does.

While the itinerant teacher's major role is to interpret to the classroom teacher, she may also offer direct service to a youngster. She often will start a program of what is called diagnostic teaching for the child, so that she herself can understand his learning style. Diagnostic teaching rests on the premise that all intelligent children can learn, but in different ways. The itinerant teacher is trained to experiment with individual teaching methods for individual children.

The diagnostic, or clinical, teacher is thoroughly aware of a child's abilities and disabilities. She has his characteristics in mind at all times. She knows where his strengths are—his intelligence, his emotional organization. She knows what difficulties the child has and where his actual learning level is. If he falters at some point and can't proceed, she can determine—from her own observations as well as from tests that might have been given by other specialists—what weaknesses account for his inability to learn.

In setting up a prescription for help, she establishes a rapport with the youngster—a spirit of working together in an atmosphere of mutual trust divorced from any sense of blame or criticism. She is able to use this rapport to develop a better individual working relationship with the child than the classroom teacher can have. She teaches each child as a distinct person whom she knows well. The program is tailored specifically to the child. At this point, it is more important that he learn with satisfaction than that he receive a set body of information within a fixed period of time.

The diagnostic teacher steps back to a point before the child began to have difficulty, when the work was still easy for him. From there she builds slowly to the point of breakdown. She avoids any possibility of frustrating the child or overloading him with material he is not yet ready for. Then, step by step, proceeding cautiously, she leads him into work to overcome his weak areas while continuing to encourage him in things he understands well. There is little stress. The teacher moves slowly and watches to determine that the child succeeds at every stage.

An example: Eric, a second-grader, can't read. The diagnostic teacher learns that he is totally lost at second-grade level, in fact can barely read at the beginning first-grade level. She finds that Eric has little awareness of the sounds of the English language. If he can't recognize sounds when he hears them, he certainly can't associate the letters of printed words with them.

So she steps back to an earlier level and starts training Eric to listen. There are many games that promote listening skills. Eric is led, step by step, to listen carefully to loud and soft sounds, high- and low-frequency sounds, sibilant (*s* and *z*) and fricative (*f* and *v*) sounds, to tell them apart and repeat them after the teacher. When Eric understands the likenesses and differences in sounds, his teacher starts to move slowly in the direction of pointing out which letters represent which sounds. Gradually Eric begins to use these word-analysis skills to sound out words that are easy and phonetically regular—where the sounds and the letters conform, as in *ship* and *hot*.

All of a sudden another weakness shows up: Eric is confused by the order in which letters and words appear in print. As he gets into words that are a little more difficult, he confuses *saw* and *was*, *top* and *pot*. The diagnostic teacher then starts a series of exercises to improve Eric's directional awareness. Again there are games she can use or improvise to teach him the concepts of left and right, up and down, near and far.

She has Eric go through a lot of physical exercises relating body movements to letter forms. He is asked to point to the left when the loop goes in that direction, as for *d*, and point to the right when the loop faces right, as for *b*. She has Eric trace over letters until he has securely built into his memory an awareness of the direction of the strokes for written letters. Gradually Eric learns letter forms thoroughly and relates them to the sounds they make. The diagnostic teacher then takes him step by step through more complex words, enhancing his ability to associate letters and sounds, until his reading level approximates the level of other children his age.

Through such diagnostic teaching, the itinerant teacher demonstrates how this child can be helped by the regular classroom teacher to control his behavior and to pay more consistent attention. The itinerant teacher will usually be able to draw out the child who is passive or withdrawn. She will be able to demonstrate techniques and materials from special education that are unfamiliar to most classroom teachers. While some of these are specialized, a classroom teacher can usually step in and work with them once she has been shown how.

The itinerant teacher demonstrates that the learning-disabled are not exotic, far-out children. The fact that a youngster has a mild but identifiable learning problem is no reason why he should necessarily leave his regular public-school class or be labeled an exceptional child and placed in a segregated special-education program.

The itinerant teacher might bring in other services to back her up. These could include the full range of specialized supportive help provided to both special and regular classes within a school system. The psychiatric consultant, for example, can observe a child's behavior in the classroom, his social adjustment, his response to challenge, and his approach to classroom requirements. The psychiatrist might also help the itinerant and classroom teachers gain insight into the child's emotional development and group behavior. The perceptual-motor specialist will determine to what extent a child's learning is affected by such things as problems in visual-motor organization and visual perception. The language specialist might conduct a detailed language evaluation.

Some school systems go a step beyond the itinerant teacher. They provide a separate classroom—a resource room—for the learning-disabled child. If Billy can't handle regular classroom requirements for the whole school day, he can be sent for part of the day to the resource room, where he is given individual or small-group instruction in his particular problem area. The resource room is another kind of intermediate step between regular education and an intensive full-time program in a special-education class. It helps children who have more serious learning problems than do those who can remain in the schoolroom full time with normal children.

The resource room has two other benefits:

1. It can serve as a cooling-off or quiet room when the learning-disabled child starts acting up in his regular class. Judy's irritations often reached crisis proportions. At that point, she was sent to the quieter, more controlled, and smaller resource room until she calmed down.

2. The resource room also is a way back into the educational mainstream for children who have been in full-time special-education programs. Julius spent three years in a special-education class. Now he reads at grade level and is back in the regular classroom; but he goes to the resource room three periods a week just for help in sounding out unfamiliar words.

Sometimes the child with a mild learning disability can remain in a regular class even when itinerant teachers, resource rooms, and other supportive services are not available. But then the burden is thrust squarely on the parents to find an after-school tutor for the child. Caution: Parents should try to get somebody who is a trained special-education teacher, a speech clinician, or a remedial-reading specialist. Incompetent tutoring, no matter how well-meaning, is useless. Parents often retain any classroom teacher to help their child get over his reading and writing hurdles. They assume that no diagnosis of his reading disability is necessary, that reading is such a simple matter that any classroom teacher, or the parents themselves, can do the job. But most elementary-school teachers in the United States know very little about how to teach reading. They have had no training, or limited training, in teaching these skills. They might be fairly effective in getting the skills across to the average child, who just about teaches himself to read. But these teachers fail when they are faced with unusual problems or have to improvise special techniques for a youngster who is not learning by the method his teacher was trained in college to use.

If none of these school services are available, or they don't provide adequate help, the child might have to go into a full-time special-education class. Parents should not face this with foreboding. Don't chastise your child and blame him because you think he is stupid or not trying hard enough.

Jane started talking late. By the age of five, in kindergarten, she still could not make herself understood. She had a year in a transitional first grade and then moved into a regular first grade with an itinerant teacher. A language specialist tutored her regularly. Her parents worked hard with her at home. By the end of the first grade, it was clear that she still had limited speech. As a result, she could not learn to read.

It would have been cruel to advance Jane to a regular second grade, even though she was then eight. The school psychologist convinced Jane's parents that she was a learning-disabled child who needed an intensive remedial program. They agreed to a special class. Two years there, with all-day diagnostic teaching and language instruction planned solely for her, were enough. Jane reached her normal grade level in achievement and returned to the regular class.

No stigma should be attached to a special class, no feeling on the child's part that he is being punished because he is bad or stupid or isn't trying. At this point, the child probably *isn't* trying any more. Neither would anyone else who had to put up with the obstacles that face him.

"How would you feel if, day after day, a boss determined how much work you had to complete, and each day gave you much more to do than you could possibly finish?" one parent asked. "Then he graded you and sent the marks to all your relatives." "Pretty awful," most people would answer.

That's how children react when adults create unbearable tensions within them. As has been pointed out, many learning-disabled children can succeed in a regular class with some sensible modification of requirements. But others cannot. It then becomes folly to oppose the child's assignment to a specialized program. Parents are lucky if their school district has one.

The parents of a learning-disabled child (or any handicapped boy or girl) live in understandable confusion: Should you buck segregated class placement or try to get it for your child? If this book is successful in its purpose, it will lead you to fight for segregated class placement *if* careful evaluation and your own common sense tell you that your child is failing, feels ostracized, and is lacking in any sense of achievement and self-esteem. If he is transferred to a special class, he has a much better chance for survival and ultimate school success. Be grateful such a class is available.

Full-time special-education classes are effective for a number of reasons. Classes are small, so the teacher can give individual attention, help each child organize his work, and help him keep his impulses in check. The teacher *knows* each child intimately, what he is ready for and how much he can handle. A child can progress one step at a time, move ahead at his own pace. There is no universal, sure-fire teaching method. The teacher must discover each youngster's weak areas and then find the best available techniques and materials to combat them. She also searches for each child's best areas and uses his skills to overcome his learning deficits.

Your child might not like the special class at first. Don't panic if he regresses. Sometimes a child temporarily reverts to bed-wetting, to screeching, to hitting. He might hate and resist the special class, especially if it strengthens his belief that he is a disappointment to you. He might sense your unspoken feelings of shame, guilt, or embarrassment. Discipline yourself to be open about the class with your child and with relatives and friends. Make the point that your youngster needs special help. He's not going to learn without it.

It's amazing how much of the problem can be handled simply by being forthright, to the child himself and to others. If John asks why he has to go to special class, you could say, "Because you need it. They know how to teach you better there. You *know* the work was too hard for you in your regular grade."

If the special program is what Trudy needs, she will be infinitely reassured at seeing that you are not swayed from your resolve by her tears, by transitory whining, by wretched behavior. Some parents turn to jelly when eyes ooze and lips quiver, let alone when the child emits shrieks of protest and stamps his feet. Assert your authority. If you know it's right for your child, insist that he go.

The situation will be more difficult if the child has a younger brother or sister who is in a regular class and may even have passed the learning-disabled youngster academically. It's hard for a learning-disabled child to take the hot breath of an achieving younger brother or sister on his neck—especially if the younger child teases him and chips away at an already weakened self-esteem.

Sit on the younger child hard. Don't tolerate an attitude of smug superiority. But the learning-disabled child's resentment at being in a special class when a younger child is in a regular grade must also be talked about directly. You could say, "You and I know that your brother is better than you in reading. I'm sure that makes you angry. We know he doesn't let you forget it. There are some things you can do better than he, and some things—especially reading—he's much better at than you. But that's right now. Many children who are slow in learning to read catch up later. We want to be sure you have every chance for this to happen." Often the learning-disabled child's anger and resistance clear up when he realizes he is beginning to succeed in areas that in the past brought only shattering failure.

Once your child is in a special program, work closely with the school. You should know and understand what he is being taught and how he is being taught. Participate in any parent groups the school offers. Stimulate formation of these groups if they don't exist. Find out what's going on. If you're not satisfied, speak up (see chapter 11).

Don't be embarrassed to ask for frequent conferences with your child's teacher or with supportive personnel. You need to know as much as possible about the child's learning problem, about the *specific* factors that are identified as causing his failure to learn. You need to know what kinds of special help he *needs* and what kinds of special help he is *receiving*. Get as much detail as possible about the way the program is being tailored to the specific disabilities of your child. The special-class teacher will be pleased to talk with you. However, remember that your job is to understand, not try to teach.

Every parent hopes the special-education program will eventually allow the youngster to return to his regular classroom. The aim of special education for all handicapped children, including those with learning disabilities, is to prepare them, wherever possible, to get back to regular classes. Many learning-disabled youngsters do return, *if* they have average or better intelligence and *if* they start the special-education program early enough, say by the age of eight or nine. Children who have reached age nine or ten and haven't learned to read yet, or still display severe perceptual-motor or language problems, might have more difficulty.

The learning-disabilities program in the Bucks County, Pennsylvania, public schools is one of the most successful and ambitious programs in the nation. A suburban and semi-rural area, Bucks County has thirteen school districts, with a total school enrollment of some 100,000 children.

The county has been operating programs for learning-disabled children since 1963. The work continues to be refined. The basic aim: to provide a learning-disabled child with all the specialized services he needs; to adapt the school program to the child, rather than try to shoehorn the youngster into a set, conventional school setting. Bucks County provides diagnostic and prescriptive services that use every available specialty—medical, psychiatric, psychological, and educational—to evaluate a child and determine his needs.

School personnel screen children entering kindergarten with a battery of tests to examine intelligence, perception, language development, and co-ordination. About half the children who are judged to need help are left in the regular classroom, but receive the kinds of supportive aid discussed in this chapter. The other half need full-time special education.

All the elements previously noted are included in the Bucks

County program: a full array of specialists, full-time and part-time special classes, resource rooms, itinerant teachers, and outside consultants, such as the psychologist and psychiatrist.

The Bucks County public schools recently examined the effectiveness of their special-education efforts. Eighty per cent of the learning-disabled children with at least average intelligence who entered special classes there by the age of eight returned to the regular classroom before they were twelve. Of these, 20 per cent were placed in their proper grades; 40 per cent were one year behind; 40 per cent were two years behind.

For children who entered the Bucks County special-education program before they were eight, the average stay in a special-education class was about two and a half years. The average stay was three and a half years for children who entered at the age of eight or older.

It took at least one full school year of special education for the typical learning-disabled child to gain confidence and self-respect, to change his basic attitude toward himself. It then took another year before his learning gaps were overcome enough that the child could *begin* to move ahead. The child with a learning disability *and* a behavioral disturbance had to have his behavior improved before formal learning could begin. Factors other than the age of the entering child seemed to have a bearing on how successful these learning-disabled youngsters were. Above-average intelligence, a sound and co-operative family, and lack of secondary emotional problems helped them return to normal classes faster. Children with borderline or low-average intelligence progressed more slowly; some were not able to go back to regular academic classes.

Bucks County found that children with auditory-perception and language problems required special education for a longer time than did youngsters whose primary difficulties were related to visual-perception disorders.

Sometimes experts wind up with egg on their faces. "In 8 per cent of the cases," the survey reported, "the program was not successful. Indications are that in spite of every effort, for certain pupils the key to development is difficult to find even under directed effort." The professionals who deal with learning disabilities just don't know it all yet. No matter how competent the psychological examination and the educational evaluation, they miss at times. Some learning-disabled children are very promising; they initially show every evidence that they will need only a brief period of special education before moving on to glowing success. With some of these youngsters, a snag is hit; the child cannot be moved off dead center. The reasons are a mystery.

In other instances, professionals come upon evidence of untapped resources in children who did not seem promising. Sometimes these untapped resources are not in the form of higher intelligence or over-all learning ability, but, rather, appear as an unsuspected talent. No one knows how to account for it, but Cornelia suddenly takes to the flute and plays like a concert artist. David finds himself as a soccer player. Agatha comes through with startling artistic talent. The vagaries of the human mind.

The most essential characteristic of special education for the learning-disabled child is the attitude of the teacher. If she is a good teacher, she will be an acutely sensitive person, one who can look at this child in a fresh, open way. She can "read" these children with accuracy.

She knows what each child needs. She teaches to his requirements, rather than to the label of learning disability, which is meaningless when it comes down to one child with his very special set of problems. She is aware that learning-disabled children do not make up a homogeneous group. These children, she knows, present a complex set of difficulties that require constantly changing instruction. She is the master of infinite variations in method and approach.

She is gentle yet tough. The elements of toughness include stamina and durability, because teaching these children is a hard job. It can drain one's energy. It is hard to be consistently patient while expecting a great deal of children; to be affectionate and understanding of youngsters and at the same time cool and objective; to control one's natural reaction of irritation, even anger, at a child who is disruptive, demanding, or defiant. Yet, within the classroom she must establish a climate of emotional understanding, warmth, and support that will foster the best development of each pupil.

All children must have the opportunity for success. Learning-disabled children who are placed in adjusted programs or special classes especially need this kind of opportunity. The program should be adjusted so that every day a youngster gets approval, the acknowledgment from the teacher that he is learning something, is doing a good job.

Teachers can be thoughtless and cruel to children and their parents:

"Is Karen really your older sister? She was a delight. I'll expect great things of you."

"Even if you can't do the work, I should think you could *copy* correctly."

"Spelling counts on your grades in social studies, language, and math. Even in art and music. No matter how good you are in these subjects, you'll get a low mark if you can't do the spelling right."

"Everyone *else* has learned to print properly. Why can't you?"

"I'm sure he *could* do the work, Mrs. Smith, if he would only *try*."

"Only babies sound out their words. You're too big for that kind of thing."

"But you just had that word on the last page. I can't believe you've forgotten what it is already."

"I just don't think you *want to learn.*"

"I'm pretty annoyed. You'll learn to read and write if I have to keep you after school every day for a year."

"Anyone can learn to read. If he can't read, he must be retarded."

"You've obviously given in to this child constantly, Mrs. Jones. How can we expect him to sit still and do his work when he can get away with *anything* at home?"

Teachers everywhere say this kind of thing every day. Not only are these comments unjustified; they accomplish nothing that is good.

"Teachers, for the love of humanity, remember that the child is never to blame," says Dr. Alice Thompson, a California special educator, in "How to Do It—A Baker's Dozen of Suggestions to Teachers." "Circumstances may be to blame; planning may be to blame; prior management and teaching may be to blame. But never the child. He does whatever he can within the program you provide. Improve the teaching and you will improve the behavior and the learning.

"Try success—try courtesy—try recognition—try independence and adequacy—try fitting the difficulty level to the child —try almost anything *except* derogation and reproach."

What do each of these challenges signify?

"Try success." *Effective* teaching of the learning-disabled child has one principle: the child must succeed. He has experienced the devastating effects of frustration and defeat so keenly that he no longer believes he can do anything well. The child must find *proof* that he can make it in school, that the school will reward him with the satisfaction that comes only from being able to do something right for once. No one, child or adult, can function properly without knowing the thrill of achievement. The teacher must select tasks she knows a child is ready to undertake and from which he can get an immediate reward. She must know when he has the skill to move to the next-higher step. Success-oriented instruction is fun. The child finds it exciting. Success-oriented teaching is active. It recognizes that learning-disabled children—all children—learn best by doing, rather than by passively accepting what is shown or told. Most youngsters stop being troublesome when they succeed at tasks that interest and gratify them. No amount of pressure to produce, no exhortation, will be as effective as the child's *discovering for himself* that he can cope.

"Try courtesy." The teacher must try to help the child toward dignity and fulfillment, basic human rights. The teacher must *respect* each child as essentially good in spite of behavior that may be distasteful—repulsive, nasty, stubborn, even profane. The teacher must be aware that the child's turbulent emotions perhaps have no other outlet for expression than through anger in class or aggression directed against her. This is not easy.

"Try recognition." One of the toughest things any child must overcome is the devastating effect upon him of the attitude that he can do it if only he will try. That is asking a child to do what might be hardest for him: sit still, pay attention, plug away at a job he can't do. The attitude must change to: he can do it if someone makes it possible for him to. The burden is now *on the teacher* to recognize the child's individuality, pace, and learning style. The onus is on the teacher, not the child.

"Try independence and adequacy." The only way to promote independence and adequacy is to make certain the child can succeed. In most classes, teachers try to cover a required quantity of material during the school year. The emphasis is always on moving ahead. A *better* approach is to lay down a broad foundation of basic skills first. Take reading as an example. Once a child is ready for reading instruction, he enters a first-grade program. If he shows good recognition of words and comprehension of content, he goes on. But first he must have the skills essential to reading. He may not have grasped the relationship between the sounds he hears and the symbols—the words—he sees on the page. If he has this problem, he'll need help in learning how to listen properly, retain what he hears, and match sounds to letters.

"Try fitting the difficulty level to the child." Learning is hierarchical. A child's ability to engage in a higher mental process, in a more difficult activity, depends upon his mastery of a lower or earlier skill. Instruction must be flexible enough to accommodate the wide range of development in learning-disabled children. Diagnostic teaching may even have to go back to ground zero. The child knows *something*, has *some* skills. But nothing can be taken for granted. The teacher has to find the stage at which the learning-disabled child can operate, move him forward step by step, and help him capitalize on his strengths while she provides remedial help for his weaknesses. She selects appropriate materials and techniques from among the many that are available. She must stress process rather than content. In the latter, the teacher essentially funnels facts, information, and details into the student's head. The teacher who stresses process is concerned more with *how* a child learns than with *what* he learns. This teacher looks at the mistakes children make as information that will allow her to improve her teaching. She is continually asking, on the basis of each youngster's errors, what *she* needs to do to make it possible for the child to eliminate those errors.

"Try almost anything *except* derogation and reproach." No learning-disabled child should be teased, chided, shamed. The teacher—or the parent—who does so may rationalize that it's for the child's good, but this is merely her way of releasing her own anger and frustration. The child becomes a safety valve for the adult's irritation. Chiding or shaming the child will *never* motivate him or increase his attention and effort. It will only increase the already heavy burden of shame and guilt a learning-disabled child carries.

If schools are going to handle children who are a little outside the norm, they must pay attention to individual differences. If a child has a quirk—any kind of difference—that does not allow him to fit into the system, the system has to change to help him. "Children would rather co-operate than resist, would rather succeed than fail, would rather get along with others than engage in strife, would rather enjoy themselves than be miserable," Dr. Thompson writes. Schools that share this understanding will have children, normal as well as learning-disabled, who co-operate, enjoy learning, and ultimately succeed.

Learning-disability specialists know what kinds of school programs these children need and how important good ones are. Nonetheless, there are still too few public-school classes for learning-disabled children.

Most communities make no provision for learning-disabled boys and girls. Others provide partial service, much of that too little and too late for substantial good.

Private schools have been established to fill the vacuum, and there now are a number of good ones across the country. They can take over the child's schooling when nothing suitable exists in the local public schools. The Association for Children with Learning Disabilities (see appendix B) will provide parents with information about private schools; these might be nearby day schools or, if there is nothing within commuting distance, boarding schools. The federally sponsored program called Closer Look (appendix C) also will send lists of schools in specified areas. Knowledgeable professionals—psychologists, pediatric neurologists—sometimes are able to direct parents to sound private schools.

These schools are expensive. They provide small classes, well-trained teachers, and the necessary supporting services, such as speech therapy and perceptual-motor training. Tuition usually starts at $3,000 per school year for a full-time day school. Boarding schools are about $6,500 per year—more for children who need additional aid such as psychiatric treatment.

More and more local school boards and state departments of education are contributing toward the cost of sending a learning-disabled child to a private school (day or boarding) or to another public-school district when the child cannot be provided for locally. According to the Council for Exceptional Children, a private organization concerned with both handicapped and gifted children (see appendix C), this financial aid might range from $720 to $4,200 per year, depending on the state.

If no adequate program for learning-disabled children exists within a local system and a child is eligible for admission to a good private school or to a nearby public-school system that has classes for the learning-disabled, his parents should find out whether their community or state provides this kind of financial help. They can ask their local school superintendent, the state superintendent of schools, (by phoning the statehouse in the state capital and asking to be connected to his office), or the ACLD.

8 / The Child at Home

Dear Mr. and Mrs. Brown:

We left too many things unsaid when you were in the office the other day. Let's discuss them.

We've examined Billy and believe he will do well in the new program his school has designed for him. Unfortunately, it's impossible to be explicit concerning the why and how of his learning disability. None of us know enough yet about children like Billy to tell you exactly what's happening and what to do about it. We wish we could say, "Oh, yes, it's blankitis, and a few shots of blankillin ought to clear it up."

We'd like to ease your anxiety. You are loving, caring parents. You have done a fine job raising your two older children. Then along came Billy, and all hell broke loose.

You know that Billy, like all other children, has certain basic needs. You are doing your best to satisfy them. You provide comfort within a close, tightly knit home. You see that Billy is kept safe from danger, well nourished, healthy. Because you want to provide the best care you can, you've had expert professionals analyze his behavior and his learning characteristics. They helped you make decisions concerning his education and medical treatment. But they told you little about handling the painful, upsetting problems that haunt you daily. Just where you need help the most—in your home life—you feel lost.

The methods you used with your other children don't work with Billy. Maybe your first two children had nap schedules that gave you, Mrs. Brown, time to yourself while they recovered a bit from their fussiness. But Billy was always wound up and jumpy when he should have been sleepy. You couldn't get him down to rest, and you couldn't get away from him to find a moment's peace. Your other two children quickly learned to hang up their clothes neatly. Billy scatters his pell-mell around his room. You have the devil's own time getting him to breakfast, while his brother and sister appear promptly and clean. You wonder if you are to blame. It occurs to you that if somehow you were only a little bit smarter you could handle Billy better. Your distress increases when grandparents or family friends, who mean well, suggest you are spoiling the boy, that you don't know how to handle him properly. Society's judgment in these matters is usually criticism of the parents—what could be easier? This is galling, because you know that Billy was different from birth.

Both of you will have to tread a fine line with Billy. He will absorb more than his share of your energy. Yet try as much as possible to give time and love to the rest of the family. Your other children can take an amazing amount of "benign neglect" if they understand *why* you have to devote so much of yourself to Billy and if they are offered assurance that their time will come as well. Plan activities with them alone. Handled right, Billy's brother and sister could be of great help. But not if they resent the child who seems to get most of the love and attention. Most youngsters behave with remarkable awareness and compassion if the emotional climate within their family is good and if their parents have a wholesome attitude toward themselves and their children, including the child with the problem.

Don't get so caught up in Billy's care that you lose outside interests. Keep up an active social life. Involve yourselves in recreation and community affairs. Try to relinquish his care periodically to a competent babysitter. It might be extremely hard to find a sitter who can handle and be trusted with a learning-disabled child. But attempt to find one who will learn, with encouragement and help, to stay with your child. You might trade time with the parents of other learning-disabled children. Both of you need the independence and the morale boost that will come from taking some time off, especially if you can go on vacation—even a long weekend— without any of your children. In sharing Billy's care, you'll free yourselves from the feeling of confinement and the ill effects of the tension and resentment that will inevitably build up if you alone are responsible for him.

Interpret his needs not only to people like babysitters or friends who come in briefly to pinch-hit for you, but also to your neighbors and relatives. Take the time and patience to try to help them understand Billy's problems. Most will gradually lose their apprehension about him and treat him as they do any child his age.

Keep channels of communication open within the family. Fathers sometimes play down problems and think their wives are unduly nervous. They come home from the office and are incredulous to be faced by an exhausted and now angelic child who, they are told, was raising hell earlier. A man may turn against his wife and berate her, because he believes he can control the child and his wife can't. Arguments can rise to bitter proportions.

SHE: You're not alone with him all day. It's fine for you in your air-conditioned office. I have to struggle with the laundry and the cleaning with this nagging brat hanging on me.

HE: If you think I'm going to put up with this after a busy day, you're crazy. What is this nonsense you're giving me about the kid's yelling and screaming in the supermarket? You let him get away with it. If you give in to him, he'll get a lot of satisfaction out of screaming his head off.

SHE: Just once I'd like to see you try to stop him when he takes it into his mind to go amok. He'd soon have you running back to your office.

So it goes. Parents must talk with each other, try to see each other's point of view, and respect each other's efforts to help the child. Instead of pulling in different directions, you must try to work together in your joint responsibility.

Our tests show us that Billy is bright and healthy, but his physical co-ordination makes him clumsier and his rate of language development has been slower than those of most children his age. He couldn't handle play tools in kindergarten and was lost with written symbols in first grade. But there were many other things Billy could do—until he decided to quit trying anything, because he had become convinced he was dumb.

Both of you are crushed by his school problems. You appear to take his difficulties personally, as affronts against you and your family. You believe that whatever he does reflects on you. You consider Billy—probably all your children —to be an extension of yourselves; by this reasoning, Billy's failures are your failures. So many parents feel this way. What a mistake and what a waste this is.

Our children are not extensions of ourselves. Unfortunately, in our society the achieving child is the ultimate status symbol. Perhaps it's because he is the only thing left we can't buy on time. When we think of our child as an extension—reflection— of ourselves, we put him in relentless competition for *our* rewards, the achievement of *our* victories, and we call the plays, whether or not he's ready or able.

Why did you both reject the kindergarten teacher's advice to hold Billy out of first grade for one year? For his sake, or because it might have reflected poorly on you or been awkward to explain to your family and friends? Mr. Brown, how could this possibly have been such a blow to your pride? You're a success in your business; you weren't going to be held back. Mrs. Brown, were you worried about Billy's feelings or your own? Children are innately honest little realists. Billy knew he couldn't do the work. He didn't need or want sympathy or excuses. All he wanted was someone to help him in a way that was right for him.

So often we try to rush nature, to push our children into activities for which they're not ready. We try to make them fit into a mold of our design, not theirs. This leaves them with little recourse. They can try halfheartedly to please us, really to get us off their backs; they can rebel, actively or by passive resistance; or they can just quit—withdraw into a world of daydreams. Children can develop many deviant behavior patterns as a reaction to pressures at home or in school, but in so doing their valuable constructive energies are dissipated. Learning becomes no longer a source of joyful discovery and mastery, but a painful striving to meet arbitrary, often inappropriate standards imposed by the adult world. Many children under stress begin to hate school, and they dawdle—sometimes actually get sick—in the morning so they can avoid it. At home, their inability to cope leads to excessive dependency, fearfulness, disobedience, and painful feelings of inferiority. Billy has tried many of these reactions.

They are the wrong reactions, but the best he can do under the circumstances. School and home are inseparable. Problems in one spill over into the other. If a child can't handle his classroom work, he's likely to be nasty and irritable when he is with his family. Unless he feels secure and believed in at home, he's likely to blow up when he gets to the classroom. All children are learning something every waking minute. Billy has learned, with conviction, "I can't." His life (school and home) has taught him: You don't just *feel* inferior; you *are* inferior. You're a failure, a disappointment to everyone around you.

All children have abilities. These must be found; each youngster must be made aware of them. "Every child," says psychologist Gardner Murphy, in his book *Personality,* "is in some ways like all other children. In some ways he is like some other children. And in some ways, he is like no other child." Parents must look objectively at their children, see them as they truly are. In what ways is Billy like all children—with the same qualities and needs? What characteristics does he share with other learning-disabled children? And what are his unique personal strengths and weaknesses, the things you need to understand and work with?

The two of you must approach these questions together. You share the responsibility for helping Billy to solve his special learning and behavior problems. Your son will be far better off if he can't exploit rifts between his parents. You must create a favorable atmosphere within your home for seeking and finding ways to handle the tantrums and sulking that will occur. You will have to find ways to weave Billy into your family life; his management cannot be farmed out to a school or doctor.

His problems and behavior can't be viewed apart from your reactions—and those of relatives and friends—to him. He can't bear alone the burden of "causing all the trouble" in the household. For every action of his, there is a reaction. The reaction can aggravate the problem. Or it can reduce and correct it. "A barometer of human emotion, [this] child is unusually sensitive to parental feelings," a mother writes, in the newsletter of the California Association for Neurologically Handicapped Children. "If you cannot remain calm when he is disrupting the household, he will sense your feelings immediately and his own disruptive behavior will get worse. Strive for some objectivity, for [this child] needs your stability when he can't control himself. A good question to ask yourself is when does his behavior stop and your reaction begin?"

If you're truly objective, you won't let yourselves be beguiled by the notion that Billy's behavior is merely a phase he's going through. If you think—as some people will assure you—that it's merely a stage he'll grow out of, you will be inclined to procrastinate. You will not think of taking action to resolve his problems. Uncorrected, Billy could continue to pile bad behavior on bad behavior; this poor behavior might then harden into habits that will become more and more difficult to uproot.

Being objective means being realistic. Both of you must examine carefully the areas in which Billy does need help. Like many learning-disabled children, Billy in effect has to be taught how to live. You can't assume that he will pick up the basic rules of life by himself. You might have to spell things out for him. For example, you should see to it that he gets off to school well fed and appropriately dressed—comfortable with himself. You might have to ask him daily quite specifically— and as kindly as possible—whether he has brushed his teeth, washed his face and hands. You might have to remind him that the seasons have changed and it's now a wintry rather than an autumn day, so he ought to wear warmer clothing.

If you get to know his uniqueness as an individual, you'll

also be aware of many tasks in which he is competent. Insist that Billy do the things you know he can do. You have seen him cut his meat at dinner, so don't do it for him. He can sweep with a push broom; assign him the job of keeping the garage and sidewalks clean. Gradually withdraw help as his need for it decreases, so he can assume greater initiative and self-reliance. Parents become so emotionally lopsided in the way they think about their learning-disabled children that they forget they must continually re-evaluate and try to take a fresh look at their youngsters. Parents frequently remain pessimistic, because all they think about is what's wrong with their child—never what's right. Billy is not helpless. Don't anticipate helpless behavior. Expecting his continued ineptness or difficult behavior will not make it more pleasant to tolerate—and he will act the way you expect him to act. Your other children will be quick to point out that you're applying different standards to Billy than you are to them. This can lead to resentment and quarreling.

Be alert to any hint that Billy is good at *something*, even at this early age. The discovery of areas of unimpaired ability, often of considerable native talent, allows the parents of learning-disabled children to give their youngsters new and venturesome chances for success. They need these opportunities. Don't impose your value standards. Don't be too quick to label genuine talents trivial or foolish. If Billy begins to show a talent for fly casting, for example, encourage it. Be enthusiastic if he decides he likes to cook. Whatever it is, be proud and support it. If you expose him to a wide variety of experiences, something *will* capture his interest.

Listen to what he says. Have an open mind. Don't step in and help him unless you're sure he can't do something alone. If he is always helped, if your impatient, quick, more able hands deny him the chance to try, he won't ever learn to master things for himself. This seems obvious, yet parents of learning-disabled children often are stunned when they are told they have overlooked abilities their youngsters have.

Don't worry about immediate usefulness. One learning-disabled twelve-year-old who had such poor co-ordination that he couldn't write very well started practicing magic. Inexplicably, he became a master at sleight of hand. His parents frowned on the pursuit, considering it an intrusion on his "more important" schoolwork. But magic was what this boy wanted to do. He also needed it to gain a feeling of importance and to fulfill a latent talent for showmanship. When he performed tricks that mystified his classmates, he gained a sense of satisfaction he could get no other way. His parents were persuaded by an understanding psychologist to buy him equipment and to take him to magicians' conventions. He began to earn money giving magic shows at parties and school assemblies. In time his co-ordination, which hadn't developed even after years of training in a special school, began to sharpen to an incredible degree, and the improvement carried over into writing, typing, and woodworking. Magic had become a worth-while pursuit in its own right, as an ego-building outlet; and ultimately it brought the boy an important return in the academic area.

Encouraged to do things in which he can succeed, no matter what they are, the learning-disabled child will discover self-respect. Find every conceivable way to help Billy learn that he can be successful. "The real remedial work for a child with a learning disability goes on at home," writes Mrs. Margaret Golick, a psychologist at Montreal Children's Hospital, in *A Parents' Guide to Learning Problems*. Parents are the most important guide this or any child can have. Not in academic instruction. But you can work side by side with Billy in areas that intrigue him: the care of animals, model building, appliance repair. You can go fishing or camping with him. You can help him learn to swim, to dance. Many parents of learning-disabled children have become masters at finding ways to provide rewarding and productive day-to-day learning experiences for their children.

"Only the home can provide the variety, the repetition, the relevance that [this child] needs," Mrs. Golick says. "Parents can make mealtime, bedtime, a drive in the car, a trip to the supermarket and ordinary household activities into meaningful teaching situations. . . . If mother or father takes the trouble to teach systematically some of the skills involved in cleaning, cooking, shopping, gardening, there is an ideal opportunity to develop finger dexterity, visual and auditory perception; to teach order, logic, arithmetic; to sharpen a child's ability to use language. . . . Involvement in the life of the household gives a feeling of competence that can help to counteract the sense of failure instilled by low marks."

(Parenthetically, there is rarely a parent, even one who is a good teacher of academic subjects for other children, who can be effective tutoring his or her own youngster. Parents are too emotionally involved with their children to be objective. When the mother-child relationship, or the father-child, is converted to that of teacher-child, the child in effect no longer has a mother, or a father, but only one more mediocre teacher. Yet so fixed is present-day society's lunatic demand for academic excellence that the minute a child starts to experience failure in first grade, his parents sweep in to tutor him. This usually is the beginning of misery for both parents and child.)

Parents help most when they know what a child can and cannot do. Encourage Billy to work only on tasks he can accomplish. There are a number of assignments suitable for him around the house, if you'll only think. They can be as simple a part of family living as folding napkins, setting the table, or helping with a minor kitchen chore like shelling peas. These give the child a feeling of success, and they are also helpful exercises for eye-hand co-ordination. If Billy makes a mistake, he need not incur anyone's wrath. Learning to hang laundry on a line could be a helpful activity for him if you don't insist that the clothespins be placed exactly at the seams or if you can bear to see things rumpled while he figures out a way to get them across the line.

If Billy fails at a job you've given him, it might be because you have expected too much. Find challenges that are within his abilities. If you match tasks to his level of functioning, Billy will succeed. And if you've paved the way with easy-to-wipe-clean surfaces and break-proof containers, for example, spills will fade in importance compared to the newly learned co-ordinative skill involved in concocting a salad. Montessori books, available in your local library, describe in detail a number of jobs for children that you can easily adapt to your home. (These are Dr. Maria Montessori's "exercises in practical life.")

No child should feel he's being pressured to learn something every minute of the day. But, comfortably and consistently in his daily life, Billy should get a happy feeling that he is helping at home, handling things well, and having fun. All children, but especially learning-disabled boys and girls, learn best by practice in real situations. No lecture will be as effective as a demonstration of the activity itself—and then letting him do it lots of times.

Parents differ in their standards for doing a job right, so you should decide beforehand how strongly you feel about results. Reward any honest effort that is in the direction of the desired result. Children who are clumsy learn much more when they are free of pressure and criticism.

Too many parents get irritated by children who do their best and still get things wrong. Why should Billy try to hang up his trousers if, after he does so, you criticize him because he's done a sloppy job? He's trying, and he's getting there little by little. That deserves praise. Mothers get too impatient with fumbles in household routines, or when a child puts his shoes on the wrong feet and cannot tie his laces. Fathers become disappointed and impatient if their children are not good at sports or working with tools.

Think about *his* problems. Can you figure out something that will help Billy put his shoes on correctly? Perhaps you could draw outlines of his shoes on the closet floor and indicate which is left and which is right. Or could you mark the inside of the shoes with pictures to show where the big toe goes?

Mrs. Brown, you're concerned because Billy doesn't listen, can't remember his lessons, forgets his lunch money, dawdles over dressing and eating. We discussed this dependency— for that's exactly what it is—because it irritates your husband to see you "baby the boy." Billy is overly dependent on you. You're much more protective of him than of your older children. Because of his handicap, his slowness and clumsiness in learning how to take care of himself physically, you bathed, fed, and dressed him long after you needed to. Your concern leads you to respond to Billy's whims instead of to his needs. Parents who do this, who give in at every turn, add to their children's problems. They cause their youngsters to regress, to become more, rather than less, infantile.

Billy can't stand up for himself. You feel sorry for him and fight his battles. He has learned to rely on you, to exploit you to get everything he wants without effort on his part. So he stands in his own way in developing independence. And you, like so many loving mothers, have become enslaved by the chains of dependency you helped forge. Listen to your husband when he says, "Let him do it himself." Try to develop some of his detachment. Fathers seem to understand the laws of cause and effect better than mothers do. Mr. Brown is legitimately concerned every time you allow Billy to miss school or get out of doing his homework because he has complained of a headache or that his stomach hurts. Mr. Brown lives in a real world; nobody in his office cares whether he's got a headache, as long as he produces his work. He feels, rightfully, that Billy has to learn this way of the world. He expects Billy to grow up to be a productive citizen and knows the boy must start learning to produce now. But Billy thinks his mother has given him a free ride.

Learning-disabled youngsters need firmness, consistency, and clarity more than other children do. "Routine is to a child what walls are to a house," psychiatrist Rudolf Dreikurs and Vicki Soltz write, in *Children: The Challenge*. "It gives boundaries and dimensions to his life." This is true for all children, but especially for youngsters like Billy. You have described the quarrel you had because Mrs. Brown let Billy miss school one day so he could sleep late. Mr. Brown had come in from a trip the night before, and Billy had been allowed to stay up past his bedtime to greet his father. He slept late the next morning. Mrs. Brown, you even wrote a note to Billy's teacher saying he hadn't been well. You were hurt and angry because Mr. Brown criticized you for letting

Billy skip school and for writing that note. By allowing Billy to stay up late, you denied him his right to attend to his own business the next day, and you interfered with his right to proper rest. It also ruined the next day for all of you, because Billy was even more active and disorderly than usual. The false excuse you wrote to the school told Billy that lies could be used to avoid unpleasant consequences.

Like all children, Billy will test limits. He'll try to see how far he can go. If he finds no boundaries, he'll become confused and will demand more and more license to do as he pleases. When someone finally clamps down on him, he won't know what hit him, and he might erupt like Vesuvius. Be sure Billy knows what you expect, the rules of the house. Tell him what the consequences will be if he does not obey the rules. Always follow through. Don't let yourself be swayed by his wiles. If a child senses his parents are wavering, he could provoke them to criticize each other in front of him. Try not to let this happen. Help Billy realize that he is responsible to both parents equally. But be sure he understands the rules and the penalties for infractions.

Not long ago one of the authors was stopped by a policeman, for speeding. The policeman politely handed out a ticket. With equal grace the judge accepted payment of the fine. Neither the policeman nor anyone in the traffic court yelled or nagged. The law was understood; there had been signs along the road to remind drivers of the speed limit. The author knew he was violating the law. The penalty was also known, and it was administered quietly, without scorn, without anger. Thus does everyone learn effectively that he has to pay for his actions. The penalty for speeding was paid in the same way that Billy must calmly and emotionlessly be brought to account for poor behavior. Calmly and deliberately, without rancor, without humiliating criticism, without derision.

Many adults who pride themselves on being loving parents somehow don't see anything wrong in mocking or teasing their children. They are surprised when told that their teasing is a harsher punishment than any honest beating they might administer. Somehow people believe scorn and derision don't hurt children. "But it was just a joke," some will say. Derision is not funny. The fact that you are criticizing with laughter makes the criticism more scathing to youngsters, who would rather you told them straight out that you are angry—and why.

This doesn't mean you should not get angry. Try to deal with Billy as calmly as possible. But everyone is driven to angry outbursts at times. Express your anger honestly and directly: "I'm *damn* mad. You know I won't stand for your using my tools without asking. I looked all over for the wrench when the toilet wouldn't flush. And now I find it, two days later, lying in the grass and rusting. I'm furious, and you might as well know it."

Kindness and sympathy are essential, but they cannot take the place of firm, fair discipline for the learning-disabled child. When you punish, try to do it fairly and calmly—as the policeman did. "Punishment should be prompt," says pediatrician George W. Brown, in an article in the *Journal of Learning Disabilities*. "Delay causes the child to be confused about what he did wrong [and] gives the child a long period of worry and resentment that may be out of proportion to the situation. Let the punishment fit the crime. Do not impose a major punishment for a minor transgression. Don't punish the same behavior with widely different penalties at different times. Avoid long sermons, talk, logical reasoning. Make the handling of the problem direct and simple. Don't demand verbal assurances that he will never do such a thing again. . . . Try to avoid punishments that are violent or lead to great excitement. Don't let your own feelings of anger and frustration distort the situation into something it isn't. . . . Use punishments that involve withholding of privileges or putting the child in quiet isolation. Make clear to the child that you dislike his action, not him. . . . The child usually needs an improved self-image, not degradation. Avoid self-defeating threats, bribes, promises, and sermons. Politeness cannot be taught by . . . harangues; bickering and harsh criticism are sometimes more inflammatory than instructive. . . . It is a mistake to be too strict and then too forgiving. Avoid cold anger at one time, then loving embraces soon after. Hold your temper if you want [your] child to learn that temper can be held."

A family must set up a structure, or routine, within which all members can live comfortably. Billy should have a regular time to get up every morning. Get him an alarm clock. Make out a timetable *with him* and pin it up in his room. Include time for play, homework, reading, television, going to bed, waking up, and meals.

He needs a list of chores, too. It doesn't matter whether you have a maid or Mrs. Brown is the maid. He can make his bed, clean his room, put away his own laundry, empty the trash, and run errands. He might not do these things as well as you would, but accept his efforts and express pleasure when he handles something particularly well. Don't rob him of his dignity by doing anything over again. Don't remake his bed. Never mind how it looks to others. Be pleased he got it together at all. You might even show him how to get it a little smoother next time.

Children need and love order. When rules and routines are established, they will live within them with a strong sense of security. And so will parents. There are times that rules or routines will have to be changed for good reason. But it must be made clear that those are exceptions, and are not just to satisfy parental or child whim.

Since you two are the authorities, the rules in your home will depend on your values and the kind of home you want. They should be based on the principles you have taught your children, the principles *you* live by and that your youngsters can understand and respect. Children who are taught to obey principles, rather than parental whim, are less often confused, rebellious, or misled by temptation. Be sure every member of your family understands the rules and the punishments for infractions.

Once you have set the rules, see that they are enforced evenhandedly. Don't let Billy badger one of you for an extension of bedtime when you both have already agreed what that time should be. Don't let him appeal to anyone else. Refuse to be drawn into a popularity contest with grandparents, for example. Be direct with them. Be sure they know they aren't doing Billy any good when they vie with you for his favor by being permissive toward him. You should also be able to check if your other children are complying with the rules. Rules are meaningless unless you can enforce them.

Physical punishment is rarely good. Physical restraint, presented to Billy as your way of helping him to control himself so that he won't hurt himself, is a better idea. One of the authors learned a valuable lesson some years ago from his work with a number of learning-disabled boys who were "wall climbers." Some of these boys had withstood every effort of their parents and professionals to calm them. They were defiant, aggressive, accustomed to having their own way. Their tantrums were ferocious. These youngsters had learned to control any situation they were in. The adults around them, fearful of setting off small riots, had refused to exert their authority. One day, in desperation, the author firmly and unemotionally placed one child face down on the floor and sat on him—astraddle on his buttocks. The boy screamed and thrashed wildly, but soon realized he was helpless in that position. The dead weight on his buttocks, unyielding to any entreaties, persuaded him that freedom would come only if his antics stopped. The technique worked. He, and others on whom this method was subsequently tried, could have their freedom—could rejoin the human race—only by quieting down. It was amazing how quickly they did.

It is hard for parents and teachers to handle this kind of youngster. Usually a method can be found, but parents often let up too soon, before a technique has had time to work. Professionals usually have to prevail upon parents to try a method long enough to allow it to take effect. So it's often wise to begin a program of behavior control under guidance. Professionals can be objective concerning goals, the extent to which the child's behavior is being improved, and how long a specific method of behavior control might be needed before it could reasonably be expected to help. You might need professional help to teach you to observe Billy, to define your goals for him, to identify what is acceptable behavior and what is not. More and more psychologists and special-education teachers are prepared to offer instruction in handling the behavior problems of learning-disabled children.

Whether their behavior is seriously out of control or not, most children, normal or learning-disabled, become more manageable when their parents are consistent with discipline. It is hard to be consistent, and virtually impossible to be so all the time. But few parents realize how uneven they are. Parents who talk with counselors about their disciplining efforts are often amazed to learn how many times what they *do* actually contradicts what they intend.

Children are keenly observant. They readily mimic what others do. The learning-disabled child is even more inclined to copy. Parents who contradict their discipline by their own actions will have major problems with a learning-disabled child. This boy or girl is most uncertain how to behave, and sometimes he is confused about the principles that are supposed to govern his behavior. However, he understands what he observes, and that is what he's going to use as a model for his actions. If you value a certain type of behavior, don't just talk it up; do it yourself. That's what Billy will learn. If you behave inconsistently, he will too.

The point applies to anything you tell him. There is no value in stressing the benefits of industriousness, for example, if Billy doesn't see you engaged in serious work. If you talk about learning as good for its own sake and he sees no evidence that you read books or discuss issues seriously, he will have no impulse toward valuing knowledge. If you decry material-ism at the same time that you boast of each glittering new possession, Billy will sense that hard work is not necessarily its own reward and will expect to be paid off, as he thinks you are, for every effort he makes, for everything he learns. Set consistent, dependable models. Be sure there is no distance between what you practice and what you preach.

Keep your word. In the throes of a screaming tantrum at

the shopping center, Billy once got you to placate him with "If you stop crying, I'll take you to the zoo Saturday." Billy stopped, Saturday came, and you did not take him to the zoo. He had been rotten all week long and didn't deserve to go. But you had made an explicit promise. You should not have said it unless you meant to carry it out.

When Billy behaves well, try giving him simple immediate rewards or use tokens—things like poker chips—that can be translated later into things that appeal to him. If his good behavior always earns him an instant reward, even if it is a piece of candy, he will see a direct benefit, one that will be forthcoming consistently. Promises are empty to children with learning disabilities. They refer to a far-off time. Both you and Billy are likely to forget. Billy can't learn to control himself in public that way. He *can* learn if he is given a poker chip— later to be traded for something he really values, perhaps an ice cream cone—each time he keeps himself quiet and under control on a trip to the supermarket. All parents properly reward their children for good behavior by recognition, praise, often a treat. Learning-disabled children need a reward that is as immediate and concrete as possible. You're not bribing the child; you're helping him to control his behavior and to understand that he will benefit directly from this self-control. In time he'll learn to control his behavior without immediate, concrete rewards.

Be wary of making threats. So many parents usher their children through stores—and childhood—with virtual nonstop commentary on the order of "If you touch the counter one more time, I'll smack you!" The youngster keeps grabbing everything on the counter, and nothing happens—just another empty threat that the child comes to dismiss scornfully. Often the clever youngster understands that his mother will carry out the threat only after six to eight warnings, so he's fairly safe the first five times. Or he can detect a rising intensity in his mother's voice with each repetition and knows at about what decibel level she'll carry out her threat. What Billy will learn is not respect for his parent's wishes, but that his parents may or may not mean what they say, and he will learn how to manipulate them. Don't threaten until you mean it. If you do threaten, fulfill the threat just as soon as Billy does the thing you have been warning him about.

Be direct in talking with your son. Don't be inveigled into tortuous explanations. Explain simply why his poor manners upset you. It doesn't make any sense to him when you say, "I just can't stand the way you act at dinnertime. I want you to be better behaved." It's much more understandable to spell it out: "The last time we had mashed potatoes I noticed that you tried to eat them with your knife. Tonight we're going to put just the mashed potatoes on your plate. I want to see you eat them with your fork."

Be brief; be clear. If you give an order be sure it's understood. Give the child time to follow through. Show your satisfaction. Then give the next instruction. Spell out what you expect in simple, easy terms. Try to be positive. Support and direct, rather than criticize. Avoid saying, "Billy acts like a baby, so we're treating him like one." Instead say, "Billy is learning to sit still at the table and eat his meal without a fuss." Give your instructions in a pleasant and encouraging tone of voice. Remember that Billy is not deliberately malicious. While his annoying behavior might be beyond his present control, you can eventually lead him, through your understanding, to learn to control himself better. A behavior pattern like Billy's is not immutable. He will mature and change.

Like many learning-disabled children, Billy frequently has difficulty following instructions. You won't always know if this is defiance or if he simply does not understand. Be as concrete as possible when you ask him to do something. One helpful technique is to phrase your directions simply, in short, terse sentences. Tell him, "Look at me while I speak." If you are not sure he understood, ask him to repeat what you said. If, in spite of his repetition, you still believe he doesn't know what you meant, ask him to demonstrate what you asked for.

Most of the behavior problems learning-disabled children have at home can be prevented by removing excessive stimulation and by making their activities as predictable as possible. Learn to anticipate what situations will be overstimulating to Billy. Keep those within simple, clear-cut limits. Over-reaction to things that other children take in stride—a party, a picnic—need not be a fixed, unchangeable part of your young-ster. A learning-disabled child's reaction can sometimes be altered if you clearly understand what causes it. Then you can modify the aspect of the family environment that triggers Billy's outbursts. For example, does having guests for dinner set him off? First, let him know in advance that company is coming. Then encourage him to stay in his room until the guests are assembled, because you understand that he becomes unnerved and overexcited by each new arrival.

Keep Billy's room simple and, if possible, in the quietest part of your home. It should be a retreat, a place in which he can relax. If he cannot have a room to himself, give him the part of a room that is farthest from the door and hallway, perhaps behind a folding screen. Keep as many of his possessions as you can on shelves in a closet. Few toys should be strewn about. As one mother suggests, modern laundry appliances enable most of these youngsters to get along with fewer sets of clothing, and therefore to benefit from less confusion over what to wear and from less of a visual jumble of clothing thrown about the room.

If you're not sure what activities overstimulate Billy, ob-serve him carefully. It may be that activities do not bother him as much as his brother does, by picking on him inces-santly. The two of them may have to be kept apart as much as possible. If you're not sure about cause, alter just one thing at a time and observe the effects carefully. Be sure you allow enough time for any behavior change to show.

Simplify family routine. Many children with learning dis-abilities are especially fussy and irritable at mealtime. Most people don't regard mealtime as anything out of the ordinary. But think how complex a situation it can be. Everyone in the family is talking. The table is laden with food; aromas assail the nostrils. The room is bustling with activity. There prob-ably is teasing and banter. You think nothing of this, might even find it pleasant. Then everybody's serenity is shattered when Billy—unable to cope with all the sights, sounds, and smells—yells, kicks his brother, and throws his fork across the table.

If this happens, don't let the situation get overheated to the point that everyone becomes upset. Step in immediately and take charge. Give Billy an escape route. You might let him leave the table and sit at a small table off to one side of the room. He might have to sit by himself, with a pared-down table setting, for a while. When he can take that much stimulation, you might ask him to rejoin the family group for dessert. Give him some extra space at your table. Move him bit by bit into more difficult situations. At first he might still become overexcited by the talk at the dinner table, and all of you would have to control yourselves. If the dessert experiment is successful, let him rejoin you for a full meal. Perhaps by then he'll be able to juggle his food and a bit of conversation, too. Later he can share the experience of eating at a friend's home, and later still in a restaurant. Start with the simplest situations, and gradually introduce complexities as you believe Billy can take them. The goal is *to help him* join the family in as much of its routine as possible, as long as he can keep himself under control, enjoy a family experience, and not shatter the rest of the family.

If Billy gets seriously out of control and simplification of family activities doesn't do enough, you will have to consider other techniques. Try a "time-out" room. Tell Billy what kind of behavior you expect of him. Define what you will accept as good behavior and what you will punish with isolation. If he doesn't comply, calmly and unemotionally place him alone in any quiet room. You might have to restrain him to get him into this time-out room. In this case, pick him up firmly, without hysterics, and *move* him.

Billy is there to regain his composure, to settle down. Tell him he can rejoin the family as soon as he has himself under control. Combine use of the time-out room with rewards, praise, and support for his good behavior.

Billy doesn't play well with other children. He hasn't had much chance to learn. First, he can't keep up with them.

Second, your excessive concern leads you to behave differently with him than with your other youngsters. You don't interfere with their squabbles; you don't try to protect them from getting hurt. Unlike Billy, they are learning to give as well as take, to know that other children have the same rights as they do.

Billy has to understand that he must live with other children in a world that doesn't revolve around him. Yet he still requires organized routine and help. Consider sending him to camp next summer. He will be nine—that's old enough. Don't worry about his wandering off or losing his shoes. He'll learn to keep track when no one is there to take care of things for him. Camp also will give him good training in physical coordination.

In the meantime, Mr. Brown, work with Billy on game skills. He can learn to succeed at some games, at first simple ones broken down into small component parts that will be easy for him to handle. Try to adapt some of these games to your home. Start with ones that don't demand the abilities he lacks. Gradually introduce others that require more and different kinds of skills. Card and board games come in all levels of difficulty, and with judicious selection you can gradually introduce concepts at higher and higher levels. Elements of popular games like baseball can be taught separately. There may be no hope for Billy's batting, but he can be helped to play an easy position in the field. First teach him to catch large, slow objects—yarn balls or balloons.

Build his confidence and interest so he will welcome being with other children, playing with them. He must feel he has something to contribute. This is extremely important. The most miserable child in school is not the one who can't learn to read, but the one who always loses the race, who can't handle a ball, who is never chosen to be on anybody's team—clumsy Billy, who needs him? He's miserable on the playground, because other children don't want him. You might be upset because Billy can't carry a glass of water, even one only half full, without spilling it. But your concern doesn't come near the agony that Billy must feel every day. (It's ironic that after a boy grows up nobody cares if he's clumsy. How many times have you asked your chairman of the board to play tetherball?) Parents often find that their learning-disabled children get involved in their worst quarrels during games they cannot play well. It's little wonder that many develop into poor losers. Be alert to help Billy *avoid* frustrating games in which he has no chance of success.

The child who learns to live comfortably within his family unit as a rule-abiding young citizen will learn self-respect and the initiative to take responsibility for his own actions. Parents can encourage self-starting tendencies, or they can squelch them without even knowing it. In the office, Mrs. Brown, you were constantly trying to help Billy by undressing and dressing him, answering questions for him, interpreting for him, admonishing him, even trying to help him draw. He wasn't able to carry one action through to completion. It was a superb illustration of the way most parents interrupt their children's activities or do things for them unnecessarily: "Put that away now, honey, so we can go to the store"; "Hurry up; mother's late. I'll do it for you." Just as a youngster is about to put the last block on a tower of twenty, a feat he looks upon as a triumph, some adult will either finish it for him or knock it over with "Okay, that's enough time wasted. Put the blocks away and go up for your nap."

Children surely must come to consider themselves insignificant creatures, always at the mercy of some powerful intervening being who looks upon their actions as having little or no value. Most parents treat strangers with more respect than they do their own children. When a visitor comes to their home for dinner, they never tell him, "Close your mouth when you chew" or "Shut up and pass the salt."

Every child needs to learn that he is significant. He will realize it only when he is treated with respect and allowed to do his own work—even if it's building a tower of blocks. His mother could say, "That's a great tower. Daddy will be home soon, and we'll save it to show him. As soon as you finish, it's time for your nap, dear." The child will learn to respect himself and his property, and this will, in turn, allow him to respect others and their property. Your Joe and Lisa have been gaining self-respect all along, but Billy hasn't, because others have usually completed his work for him or made excuses for him, instead of helping him to do things *in his way,* however slower and more awkward that is. He has not been allowed to learn that he can be master of his own actions. He can be, you know, but it will take more time and patience on the part of everyone in the family.

By now, perhaps you've begun to realize that much of your anger with each other has grown out of disagreements over Billy. Your son might not have caught on to reading, but he has learned to tyrannize the two of you. Remember when you canceled the trip to New York because of a fight over him? He had staged a tantrum and torn up some of the other children's toys. Mr. Brown, you punished him severely, and Mrs. Brown fell apart. Billy came downstairs calm and serene after his explosion to fix himself a glass of chocolate milk, but you two canceled a vacation and spent that time storing up more resentment against each other.

Support, encourage, and appreciate each other, so that Billy will be able to reflect this strengthening kind of love. Help him move gradually to independence, so he can maintain the dignity of childhood and the self-respect that comes with doing as much as possible for himself. Accept his contributions to the family, no matter how small, with appreciation and a genuine pleasure that he can recognize. Accept his individuality. It will be harder for Billy to learn to cope with many things, but with the patience and kindness that accompany your respect for him, you can find a way to teach him.

Be optimistic, be positive, but most of all help your child to help himself. Don't hinder him. He needs you. Your job is far more important than that of the teacher, the pediatrician, or the psychologist. Don't get discouraged; don't let up. Ultimately you will see the success of your efforts, as Billy develops talents and becomes independent and his own master. The greatest gift you can give Billy is to provide him with a home life that teaches him he is a valuable and responsible part of it, a contributing member of the family, loving and very lovable. He can learn these lessons *only* at home. And they are far more important than spelling, the multiplication tables, and learning how to print neatly.

9 / Adolescence: You're Not Out of the Woods Yet

What is it like to be a teen-ager?

Psychiatrist Theodore Lidz, in *The Person: His Development Throughout the Life Cycle*, says that these are years in which a youngster "blossoms into an adult, beset by conflicting emotions, struggling to maintain self-control and to achieve self-expression under the impact of sensations and impulses that are scarcely understood but insistently demand attention.

"It is a time of physical and emotional metamorphosis. It is a time of seeking: a seeking inward to find who one is; searching outward to locate one's place in life; a longing for another with whom to satisfy cravings for intimacy and fulfillment. It is a time of turbulent awakening to love and beauty but also of days darkened by loneliness and despair . . . the transition from childhood to the attainment of adult prerogatives, responsibilities and self-sufficiency."

Adolescence is the critical years from thirteen to nineteen in which a teen-ager becomes responsible for himself while continuing under the family mantle of guidance and protection. Though still dependent, he is forging a new identity for himself. While his parents are still available, he is learning to know himself better and is exploring his world. He is finding opportunities to test his abilities by assuming new roles, donning and shedding new characteristics, to see which help him best to relate to others and to be comfortable with his limitations. It is the youngster's apprenticeship in living, his tryout period in adapting to the ways of the world.

Along with biological alterations, new inner yearnings and pressures arise. These create strange feelings and longings in teen-aged boys and girls. They therefore have a great deal of uncertainty and confusion in coping with the impulses and irrational forces they find welling up from within.

The same pressures attack the learning-disabled teen-ager. But he has greater difficulty dealing with them.

Ever since you knew your child had a learning disability, you have been agonizing: Can he learn to cope with life? What will his ultimate destination be?

You've taken him to professionals and listened intently to each diagnosis, each new recommendation. But as he becomes a teen-ager, you want to know how his pattern of behavior and learning will affect his future.

Will your learning-disabled child graduate from high school? Can he go on to higher education? Is he going to be able to get along with people, earn a living, raise a family? Will potential employers think him odd? Will he be able to work with others and handle constructive criticism?

Parents typically wonder:

"No one can tell us what his future holds. What will become of him? Is it possible that in time he can manage his own affairs?"

"He's so different. When will he get a feeling of belonging, of fitting in someplace?"

"Will he be unwise? Join bad company, give in to temptations like drugs and alcohol?"

Ultimately, although this very real question is rarely expressed (because it is so frightening):

"Can he or she be self-sustaining when all the props are removed, when we're no longer here to offer guidance and direction?"

"If only I could have more faith in Sue and her future," a mother writes to the authors. "She has many wonderful qualities. What do you do to prepare a child like this for the realities of a very cold, mechanized society? How do you prepare her for a world in which only the superperfect are accepted? How do you make her feel strong and confident when you yourself are shaky and hanging on? What happens to this kind of kid when she leaves a protective environment? How do you help her to look one day, one week, one month, one year ahead and try to plan something besides just drifting along? Tough questions; tough answers."

Your teen-ager worries right along with you. No matter how concerned you are in anticipating what his later life might hold in store, your son is just as painfully aware of the uncertainties that face him as he moves out of school into real life, whether he says so or not.

Let's assume your son is one of the relatively few lucky ones. He has had every break. You recognized his problem early. You had the good fortune to live in an area where excellent education and knowledgeable professionals in nonschool fields were available. He made progress. He came through the crucial early years and has made a reasonably good adjustment within the family and the neighborhood, as well as in school. You have nothing more to worry about, right?

We're sorry. You're not out of the woods yet. There will be more to think about in the coming years. In some ways, they could be the most difficult period your son will experience.

The problems that surface or are intensified by adolescence are little understood. You probably have not been prepared for them by the professionals who have worked with you. The kind of help you need now is not readily available.

In the first naïve gush of enthusiasm that greeted the initial research into learning disabilities, in the late 1940's, it was easy to believe the glib assurance that all learning-disabled children could be "cured." It was believed that if the learning-disabled child was properly diagnosed by the age of eight or nine and offered a sound educational program, he would not require further help as he moved into adolescence.

The experts have learned better.

Many learning-disabled adolescents still need some special attention. They don't get it in their junior and senior high schools.

Special education as it has developed in the United States is basically for young children. In most communities a sharp split exists between special educators and secondary-school personnel. Special educators have little influence on the junior and senior high schools, and virtually no communication with them. Special services are rarely provided in high schools, almost never in vocational schools. Even the few communities that offer good special-education programs for young children provide little as those youngsters move into junior high school.

Most special-education teachers are trained primarily to work with elementary- and intermediate-age children. They simply don't know what to do with the learning-disabled teen-ager. They, too, are conditioned by the belief that their materials and techniques are exclusively for boys and girls under twelve or thirteen years of age.

They're uncomfortable when confronted with teen-agers. They make the error of thinking that the adolescent who is unable to adjust to secondary-school requirements is so badly off that the prospects of his benefiting from further training are discouraging.

This attitude is dead wrong. There is considerable hope for improvement in the teen-ager. But his disability might not have vanished. He could have left some problems behind as he matured, but he might grow into still others.

As he develops, he might encounter social and educational problems that were not anticipated and for which his early school program has not prepared him.

Some children with learning disabilities might need only an understanding environment in high school, a slight flexibility in curriculum and teaching approach, and perhaps some outside tutoring. They can then work in regular classes. This kind of help is available in few school districts.

Vocational programs are useful, but they present problems of their own. Administrators of vocational or technical schools often require that a youngster be at a ninth- or tenth-grade achievement level before he can be considered for enrollment. This is unfair to the learning-disabled child who has, say, a great deal of mechanical aptitude but a specific reading disability that interferes with his over-all academic attainment.

He might be well able to master the skills of a vocational program if he were given a chance.

Whether the learning-disabled youngster stays in a regulation junior or senior high school or goes to a vocational school, lack of teacher understanding of his remaining problems is likely to interfere with his success. He might fail to follow directions, for example, because of a nagging and persistent problem with auditory perception; or, no matter how responsible the student is, some irregularities in his behavioral control might make him not quite as dependable as he would otherwise be.

The child with a mild-to-moderate disability is the one who is penalized the most by the ignorance of educators in the junior and senior high schools. (The child with a serious handicap is more readily noticed and might get some help.) As the authors have pointed out, some mildly affected youngsters are able to cope with a regular school schedule through the elementary grades, often with the support of individual remedial work outside of school, along with parent counseling or, sometimes, psychotherapy. In the case of other boys and girls with mild learning disabilities, an incorrect diagnosis or no diagnosis during the elementary years might have obscured the problem. These youngsters lagged in school, but not quite badly enough to fail.

As these children with mild-to-moderate learning disabilities get to the seventh or eighth grade, their gaps widen. These youngsters are simply unable to contend with the new and stiffer requirements. Whether a child has an undetected learning disability or has been properly diagnosed and educated, serious achievement holes are likely to persist into the teen years. If a lot of a child's elementary-school time was given to aid for specific disabilities, then that much less time was devoted to formal academic subjects. This teen-ager comes into his junior- and senior-high-school years with the likelihood of serious academic discrepancies. He might lag considerably in subject areas the school requires; for example, he may just not know enough mathematics to understand algebra.

Or he might still be plagued by baffling, apparently petty

learning disabilities even though his understanding of subject areas was very good. Bill knows as much about his high-school subjects as anyone else, but his poor small-muscle control doesn't allow him to write fast enough to keep up. It's hard for him to take notes in class. He has to depend on his mind to retain what it can. Then come quizzes and exams. Bill is required to write at top speed for fifteen to thirty minutes. He can get down on paper only about one-third as much as his classmates can.

Henry has the intelligence to do high-school-level work, but he is hampered by a continuing language problem. He knows what he wants to say, but he falters, slips, slides, and grinds to a halt when he tries to get it out.

Society, in the guise of the public schools, makes little provision for youngsters like Bill and Henry. It steps up its demands on the teen-ager as he tries to make the transition to a junior- and senior-high-school program. A youngster who felt protected in self-contained classes at the elementary level suddenly confronts a departmental format. Without preparation, the learning-disabled adolescent has to adapt to the varying personalities, requirements, and methods of as many as five different teachers during the course of a day. He has to face a much more complex situation in the noisier, faster-paced school units. He has to contend with assembly hall and cafeteria, crowded corridors and limited time in which to find his way to his next class.

Learning-disabled adolescents typically are less mature and appear on the average a bit smaller and younger than most boys and girls the same age. The growth spurt and changes in appearance will come, but many of them are not ready for adult independence and responsibility until their early or middle twenties.

In time the learning-disabled boy is likely to gravitate, as most boys do, toward competitive activity and athletic endeavor. In both boys and girls, sexual urges will become intense, and will gain expression first in sexual fantasy and then in masturbation. Virtually all parents are uniformly distressed by this change: "My little boy get excited by *Playboy* center-folds?"; "My daughter shopping for a low-cut dress?"

The thoughts welling up in your youngster will initially cause him embarrassment and shame. Be as tolerant as possible. Don't do anything to compound the guilt feelings he may experience about these perfectly natural phenomena.

You can be absolutely sure that there will be an increase in masturbation, especially in boys, soon after puberty. This is natural and harmless. It is not wrong. He will not be damaged in any way. Nocturnal emissions and paradoxic sudden erections occur with learning-disabled adolescent boys as with all others. Discipline yourselves as parents to be casual toward such things or simply to ignore them. Certainly don't look for them.

Only when the shocked horror of adults suggests that it is shameful or harmful is masturbation likely to become a problem. Even those parents who are able to handle their feelings about their child's masturbation may become overwrought at other evidence of sexual preoccupation on the part of their teen-age son or daughter, such as using four-letter words or hiding sex literature and contraceptives. Don't rage even if your youngster gets hold of hard-core pornography. Trash of this type, distasteful as it may be, does not harm teen-agers. All studies show that satisfying their curiosity tends to inhibit, rather than intensify, overt sexual behavior. If you get all worked up and indignant, you will not quash your youngster's excitement. You will more likely heighten it, by causing him or her to keep it hidden. Simply overlook it, and be assured that your youngster will lose interest in pornography.

The learning-disabled adolescent has a special need to be helped in a matter as vital as sex. These boys and girls have a tendency to be out of touch in many ways. This is particularly damaging in the area of sexual awakening. They live in a sexually saturated culture. The adolescent who can't make sense out of the deluge of erotic stimulation is bewildered. He or she wants to know what other young people know—the four-letter words and all the acts the words refer to. No teen-ager can afford to be ignorant about sex. Learning-disabled adolescents must know more than most, to make up for their tendency to be naïve and for their inability to pick up incidental information the way most boys and girls do. It can do no harm—and, in fact, could prove helpful—to give them detailed, accurate information as soon as they ask for it.

One of the major jobs of every adolescent is to develop a feeling for what is right and appropriate in various situations and to learn how to behave acceptably with others his age. The learning-disabled teen-ager is worried about his role in adolescent society. He has a weak sense of identity. His lack of easy companionship makes it difficult for him to learn accepted teen-age behavior—how to act, talk, and dress. He can suffer from feelings of inferiority because he is uncertain about these things.

Parents complicate matters immeasurably by criticizing or prohibiting overt efforts on the youngster's part to establish himself with his age group. Every generation wages a battle about teen-age insistence on certain external *tokens* of apparel or appearance. The teen-age girl is adamant in her desire to wear hot pants, bell-bottoms, jeans, or whatever happens to be the style of the moment. The boy also wants to wear the sanctioned adolescent uniform. He may fight for his right to wear his hair long.

Every family has its own standards. But parents should be as relaxed as possible and accept as wide a range of behavior and dress as they can without losing sight of their own values. All teen-agers need friends desperately. Companions allow a teen-ager to develop a sense of who he is in the world beyond his immediate family. Within the security of the group, he gains a wide variety of experiences that allow him to define himself. He learns the guiding principles of behavior. He judges his capacities, his aptitudes, his weaknesses. He tries out various forms of adult activity and measures himself against other adolescents, some of whom he admires, some of whom he despises and rejects.

The learning-disabled adolescent often does not get this kind of opportunity. He might have little companionship with the opposite sex. He might fail to develop essential social skills. He might continue to act gawky and strange, to be unaware of the effect of his persistent odd mannerisms on others, and thus fail to manage the adult roles toward which he, like every other teen-ager, is striving.

While many learning-disabled adolescents are relatively comfortable in the presence of adults, they still have a lot of difficulty with other teen-agers. Although some will deny that they are troubled by their lack of friends or their inability to attract members of the opposite sex, many acknowledge feelings of loneliness, anxiety, inferiority.

In late adolescence the average teen-ager begins to see that he can love and be loved as an individual. His identity gets tied up with the warm feelings that come from being wanted and loved by someone his own age. This enhances his feelings of assurance and independence.

Too many learning-disabled adolescents lag behind others their age, male or female, in this respect. They are too tied up with their own uncertainties to feel confident about exploring the mysteries of sex. While they are eager to be part of teen society, they often look and act "different." Other adolescents tend to shut them out. A learning-disabled teen-ager might gravitate toward youngsters two, three, or even four years younger, because he feels more comfortable with them.

Many learning-disabled boys and girls need a great deal of help with social and emotional difficulties. They might require counseling or psychotherapy, preferably from someone who has experience with and an interest in learning disabilities.

The intense concern of parents and teachers with learning problems often causes them to overlook the significance of social relationships, which become more important as the youngster grows older. Adults sometimes have to help the learning-disabled adolescent move away from his isolated, self-centered perspective. These young people might have such a hard time attracting or keeping friends that parents or other adults would have to organize social experiences for them. The learning-disabled teen-ager should associate with normal children if he feels at ease with them and has the ability to make friends. If not, he should have the chance to become friends with other young people with similar problems, with whom he can be comfortable "rehearsing" his social skills.

Such a group could be established as a school program, offered by an independent agency, or sponsored by parents. The activities should include, for example, organized events to prepare these youngsters for everyday living, such as field trips and projects that would enhance their feeling of social adequacy; and regular group meetings during which general behavior was discussed by the teen-agers and their adult leaders.

The learning-disabled adolescent who is rejected by other teen-agers is likely to back away from further social challenge. If he can be helped to enjoy the company of others, he gradually will learn to feel more comfortable on dates, in theaters, on trips. He will learn to dress appropriately, organize his leisure activity, make proper use of conveniences like the telephone, manage such practical affairs as ordering a meal in a restaurant and having enough money with him to cover the bill. He can also benefit from tactful help in controlling his behavior; typically, learning-disabled teen-agers talk out of turn and much too loudly.

The learning-disabled adolescent, like his younger counterpart, has difficulty coping with new experiences. Anything unknown can paralyze him. He must be taught patiently how to handle himself in each new situation. Parents can demonstrate appropriate behavior. Many learning-disabled adolescents continue to have a great deal of difficulty in drawing on past lessons to guide their present behavior. Parents can show how everyone applies what he learns in one experience to a new one.

Even when the adolescent has overcome much of his learning problem, he may still have trouble getting along with people. One study, which followed a group of learning-disabled children from their preschool years into adolescence, found that many continued to exhibit "socially inappropriate behavior," which not only prevented them from making friends, but also limited their ability to function in public places. Problems arose through conversational idiosyncrasies like talking to strangers, telling pointless stories, asking personal questions. These boys and girls were also restricted in their understanding of the feelings of others, according to the study.

The tone quality of this teen-ager's voice might still be monotonous and harsh. The boy or girl whose voice sounds funny or babyish to other adolescents will provoke a negative reaction, even rejection. When he cannot express his own feelings in words, his sheer frustration will sometimes compel him to act in a hostile way.

Immersed in concern about the specific learning disabilities of their children, parents tend to forget that these boys and girls share the same problems and need the same guidance that normal adolescents do. The learning-disabled teen-ager, like his nonhandicapped agemate, is struggling to emancipate himself from his family and direct his own life. He wants recognition, and he hopes for prestige, wealth, and power. He goes through a period of keen uncertainty and vacillation, unsure who he is and what he wants to be. But in time he settles into a stable role, finds a direction.

Until he does find his way, you can expect that he will for a time be rebellious, nasty. Your teen-ager is likely to reject your cherished values and question traditional ways of behaving. He has a need to prove he is a person who can think for himself. He finds fault with adults, sees flaws in their thinking. If he can prove his parents wrong, he has a basis for relying on his own superior wisdom. He is feeling his oats, but you may find this period a severe blow to your authority and self-esteem. You feel betrayed. Is this the respect due you who have lived through so many troubles and made so many sacrifices?

But wait. Have patience, and show some forbearance, even if your teen-age son or daughter no longer looks up to you as a paragon, to be admired and emulated. Understand that he is subject to turbulent, contradictory emotions. No matter how much he sneers and takes potshots at your values, he *really* does not mean to destroy you. Challenge you, yes. Reject, no.

He *needs* you more than ever. He needs to test himself against you. In turning away from you he is seeking a path for himself, free and clear. Underneath his nonconformity, he is still intimately tied to his family. He is caught in a poignant conflict; he rejects his parents at the same time as he retains a grudging, hidden respect for them. He wishes to free himself from their way of life, yet he also experiences nostalgia for the security and affection of his home.

Your child loves you, but he wants to be a person in his own right, not *just* your son or daughter. If you respect his right to disagree with you, you will be surprised to see him later embracing many of the standards and values he seemed to be discarding.

The teen-ager's criticism and rejection of his parents wane as his confidence that he can act and think independently grows. He will make peace with you once he has proved to his own satisfaction that he doesn't need to rely on your judgment and advice.

How can you help? First, by a little honest self-awareness. Why do you feel so hurt by your teen-ager's rebelliousness? Maybe because you have let yourself be drawn into competitiveness with him, and you have a nagging sense that you'll come off the loser. You are, after all, middle-aged. You may no longer feel so confident about your sexual powers, your attractiveness, your earning capacity. Yet at the very moment when your feelings of worth are shaky, "that crummy kid" is trying to prove himself stronger, smarter, better looking than you. That is hard for anyone to take. But if you're going to fight him, fight fair; don't tease him, mock his pimples. Don't disparage in a sly or sneaky way.

Does this mean you should abdicate your parental authority, take a lot of guff from an impudent child? Absolutely not. Fight him honestly, openly. You can assert your authority and still win your teen-ager's respect. There's no need to be a limp spaghetti of a parent. Do not be overly permissive; you will lose his respect, and he will feel unloved. Do give direction, do set limits, do protect your youngster until you are confident of his judgment. But don't do so merely to assert your parental vanity and gratify your flagging ego. Do it because it is right, is for his good. The youngster will feel unwanted if his parents fail to place limits on his behavior that are reasonable and fair.

What is reasonable and fair? This requires a delicate balancing act on the part of parents. Be sure to say outright that the limitations you are imposing are for your son's or daughter's protection and well-being. Prove it, and be firm about it. For example, you may hate your boy's choice of rock music, but don't impose your own taste on him. This is not for his well-being, and he knows it. But you can say, in all fairness, "Look, you're not ready to drive. We don't think you're ready yet for tricky city traffic."

You are providing safeguards against his venturing into dangerous waters. Remain moderately strict in all matters in which his safety and well-being are concerned, but fairly tolerant and permissive in matters of taste and appearance, in which he is forging his independent identity. Be prepared gradually to relax your authority as he shows he can take on responsibility. Listen to reason; your child will appreciate it and grow from it. Be flexible; move slowly from imposing your will in a rigid, authoritarian way to offering advice, help, and support gracefully when you are asked for it.

Parents worry whether their learning-disabled children are likely to become delinquents, a subject that is discussed at greater length in the next chapter. The well-cared-for child rarely turns toward significant delinquency. This would be likely to happen only if the child were prone to delinquency, learning disability or not, or under circumstances of deprivation, severe academic frustration, or adverse family conditions. The learning-disabled youngster, typically less mature and less confident than other children, does not usually exhibit the independence, the strength of character—in a negative sense

—and the angry bitterness toward society that characterize the hard-core delinquent.

The immature, gullible learning-disabled child or teen-ager can be easily exploited, however. He might be drawn into petty delinquency through the influence of others. To be accepted as one of the crowd, the learning-disabled adolescent might use drugs or be pushed toward some form of gang participation or small thefts. Parents must watch the teen-ager's development closely. They must exert firm authority, so that the youngster who does engage in any minor delinquencies will incur strict penalties for it. If episodes of delinquency continue, the parents should seek professional help from a child psychologist or child psychiatrist *experienced* with learning-disabled teen-agers.

During adolescence the normal teen-ager makes a considerable spurt in cognitive development. His intellect takes new forms to help deal more effectively with his tumultuous feelings and urgent drives. He is developing the capacity to reason out a course of action on a logical basis. He is learning to restrain impulses and substitute logical thought for immediate action, to consider the effects of what he does on his own welfare and on others. He is beginning to be able to say to himself, "*If* I do it this way, what will happen to me? *If* I take this course of action, rather than the other, what will it do to my family, to my friends, to the greater social group?" His expanding horizons and enlarged cognitive abilities allow him to start considering issues beyond his immediate experience: war and peace, the state of the world, political ideologies.

He can think about consequences beyond the immediate present, because his views of his world are expanding rapidly and because the flexibility of his thinking and his capacity for making logical deductions are growing. Along with this expansion—and making it all the more possible—comes a growth in language skills, which become richer and more varied. The teen-ager is better able to express himself verbally, get his ideas into the open, invite the reactions of others, and appropriately modify his thinking on the basis of the language he hears and reads. The youngster can talk to himself in a more sophisticated way (inner language is essentially the same as thinking).

The logical-reasoning and abstract-thinking abilities of the learning-disabled adolescent often do not develop as early as those of his peers. His greatest continuing problem might be an inability to generalize from experience, to arrive at judgments that allow him to modulate his behavior, choose among alternative kinds of action, anticipate the effects of his behavior on other people, and select the guiding principles and ideals he wants to govern his life.

He might have a tendency to make snap judgments, reach unwarranted conclusions, or fail to consider more than one way of looking at a problem. He might have difficulty exercising practical judgment. When confronted with a problem, he wouldn't have the depth of understanding that allowed him to weigh the various factors involved. He would be prone, therefore, to yield to immediate pressure or to arrive at a decision dictated by the heat of the moment.

Charlie, seventeen years old, knows he has to take the train back to the station near his home so he can pick up his younger brother after the track meet at school. But all of a sudden his best friend urges him to stop for a soda. Because of the immediate enticement, Charlie fails to do what he knows, in his best judgment, he should do. Because he doesn't generalize readily from previous experience, he forgets that countless times before he has been late for appointments and has inconvenienced others who were depending on him. Because he has difficulty in thinking through and anticipating the effects of his behavior on other people, it doesn't occur to him that his brother will be stranded and, not knowing what has happened to Charlie, anxious as well.

Such practical problems frequently arise with the learning-disabled adolescent and make his social behavior chancy. He is much more likely to act on impulse than on careful thought; the balance between the weight of impetuousness and that of deliberation is tilted toward the former.

The learning-disabled adolescent who still cannot easily express his thoughts and feelings or who remains unable to understand language well is a more serious problem. In the average child, adolescence is a time when humor flourishes. The adolescent with a residual language problem might have difficulty in following the jokes, puns, wordplay, and slang other teen-agers toss around so casually. When excessive concreteness predominates over the capacity for abstract thinking, the learning-disabled teen-ager misses the point of teasing banter. He does not get subtle shades of meaning. He is out in left field when metaphoric language is used. Susan, at the age of seventeen, doesn't understand a joke, and she is not even sure what her friends mean when they say she is not "hip." She just doesn't know the current language. Her awkward efforts to communicate with other teen-agers intensify her feelings of inferiority and loneliness.

Language difficulty obviously affects academic work. The ideas dealt with in a college-preparatory high-school program become complex. The learning-disabled teen-ager might not be able to see subtle relationships, organize his thinking in a logical sequence, understand similes, get the meaning out of proverbs or allegories. He might have a hard time pulling a story together or organizing his thoughts well enough to present a good theme or book report. He might have a hard time understanding the difference between literal and figurative use of words. He might be completely out of his depth in getting to the heart of a Shakespeare soliloquy or in understanding an explanation of, say, the difference between a democracy and a republic, an oligarchy and a dictatorship.

Jack was sent, at the age of eight, to one of the best special-education schools in the country. In spite of significant gains in many areas, after five years of fine remedial education he still had obvious immaturities in his emotional and social development. Serious achievement lags also remained. His handwriting was virtually illegible; he read at about a fourth-grade level; his spoken language was inadequate. He had difficulty forming ideas, telling a story. It was hard for him to understand figures of speech or poetic language. He was advanced for his age in math and science, but his preparation for formal secondary work was too spotty to consider sending him to a regular junior high school. He still needed the custom-designed curriculum of his special school.

The pressure for achievement and the high status value assigned to college preparation put an added burden on the shoulders of the learning-disabled adolescent. This youngster is acutely conscious of time lags and achievement discrepancies. He knows it if he is academically a year or two behind other boys and girls his age. Adolescents are very much aware of their status in relation to other teen-agers. To a thirteen- or fourteen-year-old boy, an achievement lag of a year or two represents a big piece of his life. He has to feel pretty bad about himself.

Modified programs for these youngsters should be developed in junior and senior high schools. They should have many of the same features a good elementary school has for learning-disabled children: smaller class size, a higher teacher-student ratio, a maximum of individual help, learning tasks offered in graduated steps.

The secondary school, while continuing to try to correct these students' academic weak spots, must help each teen-ager feel better about himself, by developing the talents and skills he has. Most learning-disabled teen-agers turn out to be quite good in one or more areas of work, even without encouragement from parents or teachers. They can demonstrate remarkable and surprising skills. They might show unusual ingenuity in mechanical or electronic operations. Some boys can make anything work, although they might not be able to express the operating principles behind it. Some girls are much better at sewing or cooking than their mothers are. It is intriguing that a virtual nonreader can figure out the parts manual of a car he is trying to fix, that a spatially disoriented boy is able to follow complex graphs and working plans, that a girl with a form-perception problem can follow an intricate pattern to cut out a dress. Tasks like these could tap a high area of interest.

Why keep reminding a teen-ager that he is deficient in

English or math? Why not quietly help him to improve the academic skills he has, at the same time doing everything possible to enhance his image of himself as a competent person by encouraging and valuing the talents he shows? Many of these talents can lead in a career direction.

Jim was awful at most academic pursuits. He used to spend his time in class whittling on a block of wood. Some of his teachers tried to pressure him to pay attention. One teacher, though, saw his whittling as an opportunity. She thought the boy might have talent in art. She believed it might be worth while to let the academic subjects go for the time being and give Jim an individualized program, with a lot of woodworking and art courses. Jim became happy for the first time in his school career. His carving skills ultimately led him to a career in a dental laboratory.

The secret of a successful academic program is to gear studies to each student's *functioning level*, rather than to the conventional expectations based on his age, previous grade placement, and intelligence. Most secondary schools, like elementary schools, require each student to do almost everything at the same level. A young person might be at the fourth-grade level in reading, eighth-grade in social sciences, and perhaps tenth-grade in math. He is all over the lot. This makes him a nuisance to the school administrator, if he is among those who think it is a law that every student must be working at the same stage in every subject.

Schools should be able to teach the individual whose attention is limited and concentration uncertain. Perhaps a youngster like this should have only one or two academic subjects and spend the rest of his time in areas where he has skills and in exploring other areas where he might develop them. The adolescent who senses himself an academic failure has a lot of doubt whether reading and math will be of value to him in his pursuit of what he considers worth while. He wants to know if and where he's competent. If he can be successful fixing cars, why not encourage him and build his academic learning around that? Schools should arrange these students' curriculums to minimize frustration and discouragement and to offer practical values whenever possible.

Every adolescent wants the assurance that he can earn money, can look forward to having a car of his own, can eventually get a job and live independently. He must see school as something that contributes to these goals, or he will tune out or quit. If he is encouraged to work on a practical plane, he will begin to get the feeling that he can develop a marketable skill, and therefore he will learn better. He will begin to gain a foothold in the world of work and to see himself, in a pragmatic way, as part of a larger society.

Given the opportunity, many learning-disabled youngsters can meet the requirements of a great variety of worth-while professions that do not require a college education: office work, skilled arts and crafts, service and retail sales occupations, traffic management, practical nursing. The list goes on. Correspondence courses or individual tutoring can help the teen-ager succeed in subjects he failed in high school.

Residential school might have to be considered for a learning-disabled teen-ager if: you cannot obtain a flexible-enough education for him in your community; he is seriously disrupting the family; counseling with a competent therapist has not helped; the teen-ager has multiple problems, such as emotional disturbance along with the learning disability, for which a full-time residential program has been recommended; he has been ejected from the public schools; or he just feels so thwarted and defeated by his schooling that a drastic change is necessary. Few good residential schools exist. The most reliable information about them is available from professionals who work with learning-disabled children, especially psychologists and guidance counselors associated with private day schools. The Association for Children with Learning Disabilities, the Closer Look program, and several special-interest publications also offer information about schools (see appendixes B and C, and the "Recommended Reading" section).

Don't consider a residential school if it will cause great financial hardship or deprive other youngsters in the family of educational opportunities. There are other alternatives to a conventional school. Perhaps your youngster should be in the armed services. The learning-disabled sometimes thrive on military discipline and order, develop social awareness, and learn skills they can carry back to civilian life. The armed services offer training in a wide variety of jobs.

Or use your ingenuity to plan your teen's career education. One parent found eighteen-year-old Jack a job as a kind of apprentice in a bicycle-repair shop. He became an outstanding employee. Ginny loves animals, has a sixth sense about horses. She has been "apprenticed" to a race-horse trainer. There are many kinds of unique but valuable jobs any youngster can prepare for. The *Dictionary of Occupational Titles*, a government publication available in most public libraries, is full of suggestions. All of a sudden, something will pop into place. Blacksmith, zookeeper, customs inspector? All—and countless more—are jobs learning-disabled adolescents have held.

Why should there not be a nationwide clearinghouse of apprentice opportunities, a publication that would bring skilled older people into contact with aspiring young craftsmen? Say a weaver in North Carolina wants to share his skills with some talented young man, whether he can read or not, in exchange for chores. A master potter needs someone to cook and clean, and in exchange is willing to teach the mysteries of glazing. A teen-age girl is needed to take charge of two small children; in return, she can learn at the elbow of a gourmet cook.

"All education is career education or should be and all our efforts as educators must be bent on preparing students either to become properly, usefully employed immediately upon graduation from high school or go on to further formal education," Dr. Sidney P. Marland, U.S. Assistant Secretary for Education, said, in a speech in 1972. "Anything else is dangerous nonsense."

The education you get for your learning-disabled youngster should offer him job skills. Nothing is more relevant for these students than helping them prepare for careers selected on the basis of their interests and their aptitudes.

Vocational schools are slowly becoming aware of learning-disabled youngsters. Some are making provisions to allow them entrance in spite of their academic deficiencies. But little is yet available in prevocational or vocational training.

(Prevocational training is preparatory. It is concerned with such basics as punctuality, neatness, getting along on the job, holding to production schedules, learning how to communicate with supervisors. Vocational training teaches specific marketable skills.)

The best assurance of your youngster's ultimate self-fulfillment is to see that he has the fullest educational opportunity. With the necessary social skills, which you can help him acquire at home, with vocational preparation, and with emotional stability, your learning-disabled son or daughter can reasonably expect to meet the challenges and find the rewards of a satisfying career, a healthy inner life, and warm and intimate personal relationships. Given the chance, most young people with learning disabilities manage well and become happy, fulfilled adults: good family members, sound parents, and stable citizens.

10 / Learning Disabilities and Juvenile Delinquency: Cause and Effect?

Is there a link between learning disabilities and juvenile delinquency? If it exists, how significant is it?

The authors believe there is a relationship. Research has been limited. But signs do exist. Society should try to read them.*

Tim was fourteen when one of the authors first saw him, but he looked twelve. He was in solitary confinement, a five-by-ten-foot cell, in a maximum-security prison for juveniles. It was a penitentiary for children.

His major "crime": an inability to control himself.

Tim had been a problem "since he was nine months old," his mother later said. He destroyed "every toy he owned" in fits of temper. Rarely still for a moment, he had a low frustration level and would explode "without warning" when he didn't succeed immediately at whatever he wanted to do. Even before he started to talk, he would grab a household weapon—a vase, a broom—when provoked by one of his brothers or sisters.

Although obviously intelligent, Tim could not learn and could not be managed. In school, he was not able to read with comprehension, and he raged when called on to recite. He tore apart his classes with his fighting, cursing, and clown-

---

* The fact that some learning-disabled children have become delinquents does not mean it will happen to your child. Neglected or abused learning-disabled children typically are the ones who get into serious trouble. For the most part, firm, loving families adequately forestall anything more than minor incidents.

ing, and he virtually destroyed his home. Short, puny, he was in constant motion, usually starting fights. He was unable to pay attention to anything for more than a fleeting moment. He was out of his seat in a flash to investigate any noise outside the classroom door.

He was never out of trouble. At the age of eight or nine, he would walk down the street throwing rocks at cars and pedestrians. He started fires or turned in false alarms. Once he walked up to a parked motorist, shot him in the face with a bean shooter, and ran. Two electroencephalograms ordered by his family doctor were abnormal. Medication was tried briefly. It had no effect and was stopped.

Desperate for appreciation (he once told his mother that everyone hated him), Tim would spend all his allowance on candy, bring it home, and throw it into the air for his younger brothers and sisters to dive at. He stole some money from a classmate's locker when he was eleven, and two months later he gave another boy a beating in the schoolyard. Tim whipped the much larger boy in what a teacher described as a "cold fury." Five months later he walked into a store and took several cartons of cigarettes. He didn't smoke them himself, and he didn't try to sell them. Apparently he just wanted to boast. That same day, when a friend was set upon by two boys, Tim jumped in and became so angered that he pulled out a pocketknife and stabbed one of the boys in the shoulder. (When the author later asked him why, he replied, "I just got mad.")

For the last two incidents the juvenile court ordered him to a training school. Paroled fifteen months later, he was wilder than ever. He lasted three months at home.

A boy in school called him retarded. Tim became hysterical, pulled out a penknife, and waved it menacingly. It was forty-five minutes before the principal could calm him. Tim was suspended.

His parole was revoked. (His mother told the probation officer, "I love him, but I can't handle him.") He went back to the training school, but was so incorrigible that he was transferred to the maximum-security reformatory.

Unable to keep from lashing out at virtually everyone

around him, Tim spends most of his time, at this writing, in the isolation cell where the author met him. He is very much aware of his extreme misbehavior. One New Year's Day he mailed his mother three resolutions: "I will try not to swear. I will try not to steal. I will try to be good." Yet of the ninety days prior to the author's visit, he spent seventy-one locked up alone. When he was particularly troublesome, the cagemen—that's what the attendants are called—injected him, forcibly if necessary, with massive doses of a powerful tranquilizer commonly used in the treatment of psychotics. No physician has ever termed Tim psychotic. The drug served no useful purpose for him. The cagemen used it to make him groggy and quiet. "One shot in the buttocks keeps him out for six to eight hours," the superintendent said.

Tim was examined by a psychiatrist, who reported, "This is an infantile . . . helpless, underdeveloped little boy confused and overwhelmed by his impulses and his environment. The next few years could be crucial as to whether he goes into an irreversible personality disorder." The psychiatrist asked that Tim be given a medical evaluation, and treatment based on the findings. The medical evaluation was not scheduled. Four months later the same psychiatrist saw Tim again, and again recommended the examination. He noted, "His behavior has deteriorated. His prognosis is poorer." The psychiatrist asked for an endocrine study, a medical examination of how the body chemistry is functioning. Tim received no examination.

He sits in jail today, the victim of impulses he neither understands nor can control. After five years in and out of the state correctional system, he will probably remain there until he is eighteen, when he will be released, to carry his ungovernable impulses into society with him.

Two questions must be asked:

Could inability to learn to read be a major cause of juvenile crime?

Is it reasonable to believe that the behavior traits that mark many learning-disabled children—immaturity, hyperactivity, poor judgment, failure to cope with stress, inability to handle impulses—if not diagnosed and treated, might make these children as incorrigible in society as they are in school?

"Delinquency begins with truancy," Sergeant Joseph Phelan, a veteran in the St. Louis police department's juvenile division, told one of the authors. Truancy begins when a child determines that he is better off out of school than in it. *Almost all delinquents are failures in school.* Most of them, perhaps three out of four in some areas, are dropouts. Virtually all are dropouts in spirit if not in fact.

The delinquent child is often an underachiever who can't read. Dr. MacDonald Critchley, a British authority in reading and language disorders, found 75 per cent of the delinquents he studied to be functional illiterates. A functional illiterate cannot read well enough to understand street or bus signs and cannot write a coherent paragraph. In effect, he is in a foreign land.

Ninety per cent of 110 girls tested in a Tennessee state reformatory were from two to seven years below their grade level in reading. In California, 80 per cent of forty-nine "severely delinquent" children tested in one survey read below grade level, in some cases seven years below. In a second California study, 28 per cent of a group of delinquents aged eighteen through twenty-two could not pass a fourth-grade reading-comprehension test; an additional 30 per cent could read no better than sixth-grade level. Dr. Clifford H. Cole, chief of the Neurological and Sensory Disease Control Program of the U.S. Public Health Service, reported, in 1967, that "75 per cent of the delinquents" in New York are "illiterate."

"It is significant . . . that in at least 80 per cent of all cases taken to [juvenile] court, one can find that a school problem was an important factor," writes Howard James in *Children in Trouble,* a book about the juvenile-justice system.

Millions of schoolchildren are not learning to read. Virtually all of them are students who need extra, specialized help. "Public schools have been slow to recognize the [handicapped] youngster," said Sherwood Norman, of the National Council on Crime and Delinquency, a nationwide privately supported anticrime organization, in a speech in 1969. "They seem unable to let go of a grading system which exalts the easy achiever and punishes the struggling slow learner. As failure spirals downward, the child ceases to care, his behavior becomes worse, punishments increase, he is more drawn to other kids with problems. Soon, school pushes him out altogether. Characteristically, the school calls him 'dropout.'"

School failures pour out, about 900,000 each year, into streets clogged with the millions of dropouts who have preceded them. They can't read, so they can't work. ("Eighty-seven per cent of the hard-core unemployable adult men in one group we tested are not able to read their names," an unemployment task force reported to the mayor of Indianapolis in April, 1969. Ninety per cent of the inmates of federal prisons have reading problems, according to a Bureau of Prisons report.)

These boys and girls sixteen and under walk the streets: 60,000 in Philadelphia, 50,000 in Chicago, 36,000 in Detroit, 60,000 in Los Angeles. They are victims of their immaturities.

The crime rate goes up, 124 per cent from 1960 to 1971 for boys and girls under eighteen years old. The age of the average thief drops. "We are now getting nine-year-old muggers," the police chief of Washington, D.C., told a reporter in 1969. As the age level falls, the number of youth-committed violent crimes leaps—65 per cent in 1971. Almost half of all arrests for major crimes in 1971 were of juveniles.

Children don't learn for a variety of reasons. Schools don't expect certain categories of youngsters to succeed (poor children, minority-group children, boys and girls who have various labels attached to them like slow-learning, underachieving, emotionally impaired, mildly retarded). In classes of forty or fifty students, learning can be difficult for the best of them. The pressures of poverty—ill-health, inadequate clothing, hunger—are a fierce deterrent, which makes attention to school lessons a luxury. An inadequate family life forces a child's attention to his own survival. In slum areas, the call of the street for youngsters past the age of nine easily outdraws a dull classroom.

But, in addition, many children don't learn because of learning disabilities.

William Mulligan, a California probation officer, writing in the spring, 1969, issue of *Academic Therapy*, describes the school-failure-to-delinquency path taken by many learning-disabled children: "Their school problems begin when they reach the level where they are supposed to learn to read. As they progress in school, they recognize they are dropping further and further behind most of the students in their class. They are usually placed in a slow group and, although it is not indicated as a slow group, the children recognize it.

"No matter how hard they try, they are faced with failure each day in the school setting. They are frequently subjected to pressures by parents, who feel the teachers aren't qualified or that their child is lazy and doesn't want to do his homework. Many of these parents feel their child has average or superior ability but simply refuses to apply himself. As the child progresses through school and faces successive failures, he may very well begin to have some fears about himself and feel that he is dull or even mentally retarded, yet he is afraid to express these fears to his parents or to the school authorities.

"With these fears and daily frustrations, the child has only one or two recourses. He may withdraw and not participate in class work. He may also attempt to gain recognition by [misbehaving] in the classroom *or in society* [emphasis added]."

In the 1950's, the National Institute of Mental Health began to wonder if poor reading had anything to do with misbehavior. Its researchers followed 45,000 schoolchildren in one community for several years. First they identified all the poor readers in the fifth and sixth grades. A follow-up study two years later revealed that "nearly all" who had been bad readers in the fifth and sixth grades exhibited serious social problems in the seventh and eighth grades as well. "If academic difficulties were due to lack of intelligence," noted child psychologist Bruno Bettelheim said of this study, in an article in *The School Review*, "they would not be followed so uniformly by severe emotional difficulties."

What of the learning-disabled child who is the victim of

uncontrollable impulses, the youngster who—for reasons science has yet to understand fully—cannot restrain himself from shouting and screaming in class, from starting fights in the schoolyard? What happens to him if he is ignored?

"A hyperactive child, say at eight years old, is doing more than his share of lying or impulsive acts, such as taking change from his mother's purse," reported Dr. Mark Stewart, a psychiatrist with St. Louis University. "The child simply acts impulsively, never stopping to think about what he's doing. Things become serious if he is inadequately supervised at home. Each time he gets away with these acts, his tendency for this behavior is reinforced. When he reaches twelve, the physiological problem behind his restlessness may have disappeared; but by then he may be a budding delinquent. This child is vulnerable in a chaotic home situation."

A study of eighty-nine delinquents in California revealed that 38 per cent had learning disabilities. An additional 20 per cent were on the borderline.

Sixty-eight per cent of those 110 girls studied in the Tennessee reformatory had "a learning disability or a behavior disorder related to a learning disability."

"Sixty to 70 per cent of our population have serious learning problems," Mrs. Patricia Holliday, director of education at the New Jersey Training School for Girls, told the authors. "With such deficiencies, they needed special [help] to learn. The special attention was not received and school became a meaningless waste to them, a place to avoid." Sixty-two delinquent girls aged twelve through eighteen were examined at the New Jersey institution. Intelligence tests revealed that more than half had average or better intelligence. Only 10 per cent were below average in intelligence. Yet four out of five of these sixty-two girls could do no better than elementary-grade work in reading, spelling, and arithmetic.

Dr. Eric Denhoff, a Rhode Island pediatrician, examined 109 boys, from fourteen through nineteen years of age, who were school dropouts and delinquents. According to a report of the results published in 1969, 53 per cent of them had "cerebral dysfunction"—learning disabilities.

"We give little or no attention to any possible . . . neurologic factor which may [contribute] to . . . delinquent behavior," writes Dr. Camilla Anderson, former chief psychiatrist at the California Institution for Women, in a paper presented at a meeting of the American Psychiatric Association in 1967. "The well-established fact that there is a high incidence of abnormal [EEG tracings] among delinquents has been largely disregarded.

"Psychiatry seemingly [has] learned to think only in 'either-or' terms: If there [are psychological] factors present, we proceed under the assumption that the problem therefore is not related to organic factors." More attention to neurological impairment, Dr. Anderson's paper suggests, "would help us to understand that wherever one finds marginal people—people who are not making the grade, people who seem perpetually out of step or people who are stress . . . prone—one finds a high incidence of cerebral dysfunction due to organic factors."

"A high proportion of the women in prison [have] minimal brain damage or minimal cerebral dysfunction," she reported in an article in the *American Journal of Correction.* "In this group, we find many who have committed crimes of violence. We also find many of the most persistent and repetitive troublemakers."

As chief psychiatrist at the California institution, Dr. Anderson ordered EEG examinations of a group of 700 inmates, chiefly those who were problem cases or who had long records of juvenile delinquency or crimes of violence. Sixty-one per cent of this group had abnormal brain-wave patterns.

"Those who . . . are responsible for the management of delinquent and criminal populations are severely handicapped . . . ," she told the authors, "if they do not have a clear perception of . . . cerebral dysfunction."

Dr. Ben J. Sheppard is a Miami pediatrician specializing in neurological disorders, and until recent years he was a juvenile-court judge as well. In both capacities he has worked with delinquents. His belief: disruptive behavior, everything from truancy on, often results from medical difficulties of which both parents and authorities are unaware. "At least 25 per cent of our delinquency can be blamed on organic reasons," he says, in an article in *Today's Health*.

"If the youngster becomes a dropout," writes criminologist Robert E. Kelgord, in *Academic Therapy*, "the road is clearly marked to the police station . . . to the juvenile hall, and finally to some sort of correctional institution. While the criminological literature may be deficient in the . . . relationship between brain damage and delinquency, it abounds in descriptions of dropouts and delinquency.

"Generally speaking, the . . . literature shows a correlation of up to 90 per cent between these two factors. . . . Our juvenile institutions today confine many youngsters who should not be . . . detained, but who . . . have been processed through the assembly line of juvenile jurisprudence *without ever being seen by the competent person who could diagnose or even suggest evidence of brain damage* [emphasis added]."

Nothing like a consensus exists concerning the causes of violent behavior. Until the past few years, research on the subject probed solely into the influence of environment and family life. This probing was done by psychologists and sociologists. But medical researchers in growing numbers now are looking for possible biological causes of violence. Their primary focus: brain illness and injury, irregularities in body chemistry, a poorly developed central nervous system, the role of genetics. The federal agency sponsoring much of this new research is the Center for Studies of Crime and Delinquency, of the National Institute of Mental Health. "The work has established that biological causes of violence are as important as the psychological or sociological ones—that no single discipline has a monopoly on the subject," Dr. Saleem Shah, chief of the center, told a *Wall Street Journal* reporter in 1970.

"When I look at people with the most deprived sorts of backgrounds, I am always impressed at how few of them become criminally violent," said Dr. Frank Ervin, a prominent researcher into causes of violence, as quoted by the same reporter. Dr. Ervin, who is affiliated with Massachusetts General Hospital, in Boston, added, "It would be silly to deny that environment is important, but when I see people who have a long history of violence . . . many of them have medical histories that indicate organic brain damage."

Research into body chemistry has revealed links between hormones, brain function, and violence. "What we've found is that particular hormone balances make the human system 'touchy' or sensitive to the type of situation that might evoke attack," according to Kenneth Meyer, a psychologist at Carnegie-Mellon University, in Pittsburgh, who was also interviewed by the *Wall Street Journal*. "What we don't know yet is the way these balances act on the brain and thus modify behavior."

The researchers at Massachusetts General have learned that violent or loss-of-control episodes often can be traced back to childhood. In such cases, they note that an abrupt change of personality has frequently occurred after a head injury, a case of measles, or a prolonged and high fever during a child's early years. Some cases of brain damage can be traced back further, they have observed, to problems in infancy or in the fetal state.

The most dangerous period for brain damage is the years between conception and the age of three, when a child is most susceptible to the effects of any injury, illness, or high fever that might reduce the supply of oxygen to the brain. "The majority of what we call brain damage may result from poor prenatal care, a difficult delivery, inadequate postnatal care, and infant malnutrition," Dr. Ervin told *Today's Health*. "The brain is a very sensitive little computer, especially early in life. Factors such as lack of oxygen, low blood sugar, or [injury] may mean that the baby's brain doesn't have a chance to get well organized, doesn't develop properly.

"If there were good nutritional and medical care for all pregnant women and for all babies up to twelve months of age, what's considered brain disease could be knocked down to perhaps one-tenth of what it is today [emphasis added]."

Dr. Ervin and his colleagues emphasize the existence of early signs of violence. "We find that violence-prone [adults] have a childhood history of hyperactive behavior, multiple fire-setting, prolonged [bed-wetting], cruelty to animals," he adds in the same article. Many childhood signs can be hard to spot, even by alert parents, because it is easy for them to pass off indications as the relatively normal activity of rough-and-tumble children. The difference is in degree.

Parents should be aware of these signals—for that is what they are—particularly if they are combined with the reports of more objective observers, like teachers, who see each child in the context of many children. The youngster who repeatedly breaks windows, gets into fights, and is generally troublesome should be examined by a specialist, to seek or rule out possible brain dysfunction. The psychiatrists and neurologists at Massachusetts General's Stanley Cobb Laboratories for Psychiatric Research, headed by Dr. Ervin, begin with a detailed medical history of each patient, followed by an EEG, an examination of the visual and auditory systems, and perhaps a skull X ray.

Dr. Ervin recommends that the courts *require* a medical examination of everyone who commits a violent crime. "We should look at why a person is up before the judge," he says, as quoted by *Today's Health*. "He may be severely mentally retarded; he may be epileptic; he may have brain disease or damage; he may simply never have learned any better in the subculture he lives in. Each of these situations requires a different rehabilitative approach. Our organic theory does not account for all violent crimes, and neither does strict emphasis on environmental factors. Undoubtedly the two influences overlap." Dr. Ervin believes that from one-quarter to one-half of all those who commit violent acts or are prone to do so are diagnosable. "Some are treatable, and their acts certainly are by and large preventable," he told a group of science writers in 1970.

How many Americans suffer from brain malfunctioning? Some 10 million are believed to have severe disorders: mental retardation, epilepsy, serious illnesses. "There are probably another 10 million neglected, unrecognized cases of minor brain disorders resulting from [injuries] or infections," the *Times* quotes Dr. Ervin as saying. (A study by the Cornell

Aeronautical Laboratory found that about half of the people hurt in car accidents suffer head injuries. No one has ever examined the long-term effects, if any, of these injuries.) "I'm not saying all these 20 million people are violence-prone," Dr. Ervin continues. "But they are a reservoir of individuals with impaired central nervous systems, with impaired resources to cope with various kinds of stress."

Who are the most vulnerable?

Minor brain disorders hit children indiscriminately—all races, all income brackets. But they strike most often and most severely the city and rural poor—those children from families lacking adequate food and adequate health care. This is the nation's high-risk group, the source of most of the retarded, most of the school dropouts, most of those arrested for delinquent behavior.

But no wide-scale, comprehensive research effort into organic causes of crime has ever been attempted among this group. There are plenty of indicators that warrant a close look at these high-risk children.

The infant mortality rate among nonwhite Americans is twice that for white American infants. The death rate of nonwhite American mothers during childbirth is four times that of white American mothers. It seems reasonable to assume that the conditions responsible for the deaths of infants and mothers also could set off severe problems short of death, a variety of dysfunctions that, as far as children were concerned, might interrupt their ability to function. Early medical screening of this high-risk group for a variety of purposes, including learning impairments, would appear basic.

Large numbers of pregnant women among the city and rural poor get no prenatal care, no dietary instruction—or food assistance—and come to public hospitals just to give birth. About one-fifth of the impoverished mothers who give birth in public hospitals have complications before or during birth, but get little or no medical attention for these complications.

The rate of premature births among the poor is three times that for the middle class. Premature birth can be dangerous.

Katrina de Hirsch, director of the Pediatric Language Disorder Clinic of the Columbia-Presbyterian Medical Center, in New York, and a leading researcher into reading problems, found, in a study of first- and second-graders, that children born after a normal nine-month pregnancy were significantly ahead of prematurely born children in reading and writing. Research studies by others have revealed: (1) premature children in a poor environment have a lower average IQ than full-term children in the same environment; (2) prematurely born children are more vulnerable to neurological impairments and the harmful effects of poverty than are children carried for nine months.

Scientists grope toward an understanding of the brain. One of the instruments they use the most to try to chart it—the electroencephalograph—is a controversial and not fully understood tool. Many children who are believed to be perfectly well and normal—some scientists say as many as one out of four—show abnormal electroencephalogram tracings. Conversely, many who show signs of brain damage in the way they behave have normal EEG tracings.

Physicians who deal with EEG's take opposing positions. Some report research showing that as high as 81 per cent of the delinquents they have examined had abnormal EEG tracings. Other physicians, equally reputable, say, in effect, that "we just aren't wise enough yet about the brain and the EEG to know what all readings mean."

Some investigators claim that abnormal EEG tracings can be found in significant numbers of children with reading problems. Dr. Maurice H. Charlton, chief of neurology clinics at New York's Columbia-Presbyterian Medical Center, reports that routine use of the EEG plays an important role in diagnosis of the hyperactive child, that specific kinds of abnormal EEG patterns support other evidence of a physical—that is, nonpsychological—ailment.

Is there any likelihood that researchers will learn what makes children become antisocial, how to help them, and how *to prevent* such behavior?

To judge by the current rate of concern, the prospect is slim.

As a nation, the United States apparently worries more about tooth decay than about why boys and girls attack and steal. In 1970, more money was spent investigating tooth decay—some $18 million—than in juvenile-crime research—$14 million. Virtually no money is devoted to studies of the possible relationship between learning disabilities and delinquency.

"We are operating on alley knowledge," Dr. Joseph D. Lohman, dean of the School of Criminology at the University of California, in Berkeley, told a New York *Times* interviewer. "Until law enforcement starts conducting some real research, we're just going to go on spinning our wheels."

"Most large corporations plan ahead twenty years or more on the basis of research," Sherwood Norman, of the National Council on Crime and Delinquency, also said in the speech quoted earlier. "In law enforcement and correction, there is no competition, [so] little or no research. *Planning is in response to crisis* [emphasis added]. Everyone considers himself an expert, and use of public funds is usually guided by traditional practice and political considerations."

"Far more valid research has been done (and more money spent) on raising pigs, chickens, corn or cucumbers than on solving the problems of our troubled youth," according to Howard James's *Children in Trouble*. A reform-school official told James, "Farmers have an effective lobby. Children in trouble have no one they can count on. If they had someone, they wouldn't be in trouble."

"What are we doing about today's children?" asks a Washington, D.C., social worker, Nina Trevvett, writing in *Crime and Delinquency*. "In Washington, we are doing just about the same as we were thirty years ago. . . . Day after day and year after year . . . we grind out services and treatment that have little or no relationship *to our knowledge of the problems* the treatment is supposed to solve [emphasis added]."

No one, anywhere, demands an accounting of what happens to children in trouble. Except on a hit-or-miss basis, no hand exists to support a stumbling child or to help good families that find survival impossible without assistance. In the glut of public and private social-service agencies, children and their families are left to fall between them, because no one agency, anywhere, is responsible for anyone.

"No single agency is given continuing responsibility for a child," a U.S. Children's Bureau research team wrote, in 1967. "This responsibility may shift back and forth from courts to public or voluntary welfare agencies, state institutions, or other state departments or divisions. There may be little continuity in treatment. . . . The process is often devious and slow."

"If some of these children had been discovered and properly treated in the early grades, they could have been . . . achieving at an appropriate level and this success may have prevented their delinquent involvement," says probation officer Mulligan, in *Academic Therapy*. ". . . Unfortunately, schools . . . do not provide these children with the treatment they need. . . .

"The most difficult part of administering [a learning-disabilities screening test to delinquents] is knowing that when you find these children, the chances of working out a suitable program for them are extremely unlikely unless the parents have funds for private academic therapy. Many of the older teen-agers, while taking the screening test, have inquired, 'Will this help me?' When asked . . . what they meant, most of them indicated they were stupid, received nothing but F's in school, and couldn't do their schoolwork. It's difficult to explain to a child that we have no resources for assisting him."

What can be done? If a child has a handicap and his family cannot or will not help him, he is left "to society." This virtually always means the courts. But juvenile courts are not equipped, either by the training of their presiding judges and staffs or by the facilities backing them up, to do anything for 90 per cent of the juveniles who come before them. This 90 per cent, in the estimate of most experts, does not require jailing, but, rather, special attention of one kind or another. They are not all learning-disabled. They might be mentally retarded or emotionally disturbed, or might need nothing more than a firm, loving substitute home. The authors believe, as Milton Rector, of the National Council on Crime and Delinquency, has said, that "any community that can build jails can build treatment facilities."

Every child who is brought before a juvenile court should automatically receive intensive medical, psychological, and psychiatric examinations, to try to determine why he acts as he does. In the article quoted earlier, Dr. Sheppard, the Miami physician–juvenile jurist, says, "This should include the child's whole social, educational, and medical history. It should include [any] tests that might shed light on possible organic reasons for his or her behavioral problems."

The President's Commission on Law Enforcement and Administration of Justice, commonly called the Crime Commission, adds counterpoint when it discusses, in its report of 1967, how children are actually treated: "If pre-court services are given at all, they are generally inconsistent, haphazard, scattered among different agencies and fail to reach all children who need them. Records of serious repeating offenders show that if badly needed services had been given when the youngster was first brought to public attention, subsequent delinquencies would have been reduced if not eliminated."

The federal government's Youth Development and Delinquency Prevention Administration candidly admitted, in 1971:

"No model systems for the prevention of delinquency or the rehabilitation of delinquent youth have been developed. . . . There has been [no] feedback of knowledge gained from . . . research for use in the development of such systems.

"There is little coherent national planning or . . . priority structure among . . . programs dealing with . . . delinquency prevention. . . . There is a lack of effective national leadership."

"Whether a judge gives a kid a slap on the wrist or a harsh penalty, he'll be back—unless someone explores why he's in trouble in the first place," Dr. Benedict Mayers, a Chicago psychologist who has specialized in juvenile-crime problems, told the authors. "It [is] tragic that a program is unavailable . . . to prevent as much as possible [juveniles] from becoming chronic, dependent repeaters through their lives," writes a team of researchers, in a 1970 report on their work at the New Jersey Training School for Girls.

"There is expense involved," writes probation officer Mulligan, but "if we can prevent thousands of children from suffering fears and frustrations, if we can prevent a portion of these children from being referred to probation departments, if we can avoid locking these children up . . . at considerable expense to the . . . taxpayers . . . if we can help stabilize the lives of these children and make them productive citizens, the small amount of money spent [would] be worth while."

This is what Americans might be doing.

It contrasts with what is being done.

11 / The Future: We Are All Responsible

If we as a nation believe that free public education should be available to all children, well or damaged, then we must consider the learning-disabled child a problem for the public schools.

How many of these 7 million-plus children are being helped —right now—by the public schools? The authors asked each state department of education in the form of a questionnaire. Forty-one states replied. Used uncritically, their figures showed that 240,000 children were getting some kind of assistance in the 1970–71 school year. The aid might have been anything, down to one ineffectual half-hour tutoring session a week for a child who needed much more.

Most of the responding states didn't know how many children they were serving. New Jersey, for example, guessed somewhere between 5,000 and 10,000, a rather haphazard figure; New York, one of the best states in an undistinguished list, would not even attempt an estimate.

Two states alone, Maryland and California, accounted for half the total. In others the numbers dropped as low as: Indiana, 450 children helped out of a school population of 1,271,000; Delaware, 665 out of 133,000; Pennsylvania, 2,000 out of 2,358,000; Montana, 30 out of 104,000; New Hampshire, 200 out of 185,000.

That is about one-half of 1 per cent of all the school-age children in those forty-one states who, according to the authors' estimates, have learning disabilities. Without exception, each state total supplied was a guess. No one, anywhere, *knows.* Dr. Marianne Frostig, a California psychologist who has pioneered in the diagnosis and treatment of these children, has said flatly, "Less than 1 per cent of all children with learning disabilities in the country get help from a public school."

What's happening to all those other boys and girls?

A New Hampshire parent, in relating how his state systematically "filters out" of its public schools all but the normal child, said, "There's an awful lot of pain here." There's an awful lot of pain throughout the nation. "Most learning-disabled children are vegetating," Dr. Jerry Miller, former director of special education for the Philadelphia public schools, told the authors. "If they create problems for the teacher, they are: (1) removed to classes for the retarded or the emotionally disturbed, whichever their school district happens to offer; (2) put in state institutions for the retarded or the emotionally disturbed; (3) ejected to *sit at home.*

"If they behave [regardless of whether or not they are learning], they are allowed to remain in regular classrooms. But any way, they receive no help as their childhood slips by."

What's the problem?

Lack of commitment to this child.

No comprehensive, consistent effort is being made in any but a relatively few school districts to help children with learning disabilities. They are just another minority in the schools. Confronted with a multitude of parent and financial pressures, school districts move in the direction in which most people push them. (One middle-class, college-educated mother candidly remarked, after a stormy school-board meeting in a blue-collar New Jersey city, at which the allocation of funds for various programs had been the heated topic, "I care about *my* child. Money spent for special classes takes money away from him." Her son, fortunately, is well. Her attitude is not an isolated one.)

Thirty-five states include children with learning disabilities in their laws governing education. Only two of these states have laws that can be enforced. In Illinois, for example, where education of the learning-disabled became mandatory in 1969, fewer than half of the state's 1,400 school districts have started classes for them. "The state did not expect us to," one administrator says. "If they had, they would have given us the money."

What does this mean? That in forty-eight states any learning-disabled child *can be excluded from school* if a local school system believes it cannot handle that child.

"So we have to turn to private schools with tuitions that can range from $3,000 to $7,500 each year," one mother says. "Why? And what about the families that can't pay this, even though their hearts are breaking as they watch their bright but learning-disabled child sitting in a class with retarded youngsters?"

"Money is always available for programs that society values or finds entertaining or that reduce guilt," Dr. James Gallagher, the first chief of the Bureau of Education for the Handicapped, an agency of the U.S. Office of Education, said, in a speech at Columbia University in 1969. "If we do not have money, it is because people have not perceived our area as a high-priority one. That is the real problem—not lack of money."

Large amounts of money are commonplace in the federal budget, Dr. Gallagher continued, and so huge sums have lost their meaning. "Can we afford to go to the moon?" he asked. "Obviously yes, because we are going. It is generally accepted that about $30 billion is needed to get a man on the moon. That doesn't bring a gasp from anyone, because few can understand what $30 billion is. In more concrete terms, let's ask what $10 billion, one-third of that amount, might buy in the area of the handicapped. This will give some concept of what we talk about when we discuss a national-priority program.

"What would $10 billion buy?

"We might expand our research effort [to] $20 million, or four or five times what it is now.

"We could finance ten research and development centers, at a total of $5 million, to focus on major areas of interest and importance for education of the handicapped.

"We might spend $25 million, instead of the present $2.5 million, in a venturesome attempt to get the newest kinds of materials and skills into the hands of the teachers.

"In our colleges and universities, where we now spend $24.5 million to improve graduate and undergraduate education [to train teachers of the handicapped and trainers of those teachers], we could triple the effort, to a level of $75 million.

"We could spend $20 million, instead of the $2 million we now have, in development and dissemination of [teaching] programs for our schools.

"We could establish 100 early-education centers, at $200,000 each, to provide models for state and local programs.

"We could spend $185 million in our aid-to-states program, more than six times our current level (and we would still not be up to the authorization we have from Congress).

"One hundred million dollars would be available to help state institutions improve their educational programs, instead of the $24 million we now have.

"We could have $50 million left over for co-operative planning with other agencies inside and outside of Health, Education, and Welfare, because *nobody now has the total authority to do the job of comprehensive planning for handicapped children* [emphasis added].

"Have we spent our $10 billion? Not at all. All of this adds up to only $500 million. This hypothetical program could run for twenty years on the $10 billion I referred to.

"That is what we mean by a priority program."

Dr. Gallagher, a dedicated and talented man, subsequently left the Office of Education in protest over government policies that decimated education budgets and planning.

Not only is there still no priority program; there also is no evidence there will be any, unless national attitudes change sharply. Federal spending for the education of handicapped children—federal funds are the prime source of money for improved teacher training and the source of virtually all the money this country devotes to educational research—is running at less than 20 per cent of the amount Congress each year tells the U.S. Office of Education it will have. The difference between the amounts designated on paper for various programs and the amounts actually released by the President's Office of Management and Budget for those purposes is huge.

For example, the Bureau of Education for the Handicapped, which has acted as a superb catalyst for new services for handicapped children since it was formed in 1967, persuaded Congress, in fiscal year 1970, to designate learning disabilities as a separate category of the handicapped and to allocate for that category—on paper—$12 million. No money was released.

Twenty million dollars was set aside for 1971; $1 million was released. For 1972, and again for 1973, $31 million was authorized. In 1972, the Office of Management and Budget freed for use $2.25 million. In 1973, $3.25 million was released.

What has to be done to help children with learning disabilities?

A team headed by Katrina de Hirsch, director of the Pediatric Language Disorder Clinic of Columbia-Presbyterian Medical Center, in New York, studied fifty-three children from kindergarten through the end of the second grade in an attempt to devise a series of tests that would find those most likely to have major school problems.

The results were impressive. The tests identified as potential problems, in kindergarten, ten of the eleven children who failed reading and spelling two years later, at the end of second grade. (The tests also correctly identified the eight children who proved to be the *leaders* in school performance at the end of the second grade.)

Dr. Eric Denhoff screened a group of 240 Providence, Rhode Island, first-graders believed to be physically and intellectually normal. He found thirty-six of them to have "cerebral dysfunction." All but ten of this group went on to fail the first grade. They were the only failures in the class.

The preschool period is the time when developmental differences should be uncovered and each child started on an individual course of help. This means that someone must be on the alert to find these boys and girls.

Pasadena, Texas, began to do just that in 1964. This middle-income suburb of Houston wanted to find out if potential academic failures could be predicted at the ages of three, four, and five. If predicted, could the failures be *prevented?*

The program, supported for the first three years by the U.S. Department of Health, Education, and Welfare, and operated by the public-school system, initially found forty-eight children who, following tests of language, intelligence, perception, and co-ordination, were judged to have potential learning handicaps. The effort began with two classes. Supervision was provided by the Houston Speech and Hearing Center.

Those in the original group attended preschool classes until each child had improved enough to transfer to regular classes. Some were held until the age of seven.

A second group of youngsters, diagnosed as having disabilities comparable to those of the forty-eight, entered the Pasadena schools routinely in first grade. (Pasadena did not then have kindergarten.)

At the end of the third grade, twenty-three of the original forty-eight students (the rest had left the program, primarily because their families had moved) and the children in the comparison group were evaluated. Of those who had received preschool education, 70 per cent were performing at or above grade level in reading. Sixty-six per cent were working at or above grade level in arithmetic. Of the children who had had no preschool aid, 82 per cent were below grade level in reading, and 91 per cent were below grade level in arithmetic. The two groups of children had had similar problems when tested at the ages of three and four.

"This program works," Alfred E. Danheim, Jr., director of special services in the Pasadena schools, told the authors. "If not for the preschool preparation, virtually all of these children would have been marked as failures by the end of first or second grade, shifted off to 'slow' classes, and probably lost.

"It's expensive. It costs about $1,200 each year for each child, about twice what we spend for the average child. But for every year a youngster routinely gets left back, we have wasted $600. That doesn't count the damage to the child."

The Pasadena preschool program grew to seven classes, 120 children, and a waiting list by the 1972–73 school year. Seven teachers and a co-ordinator, supported by school psychologists, an educational diagnostician, and outside consultants, comprise the staff. The state of Texas pays about 80 per cent of the cost, Pasadena the balance.

Its success continues. "Each year, all but four or five of the 'graduates' of this preschool program go to regular classes, most of them at their proper grade level," Danheim says. "The other four or five youngsters remain in special-education classes."

What Pasadena is doing indicates a dramatic shift of emphasis, a shift from looking at a child's difficulties to an emphasis on the abilities he can develop. (*Every* child has abilities; if they are not found, society, not the child, is the culprit.)

Most school systems enroll children at the age of five or six (about half of the nation's schools still do not have kindergarten). The schools then wait until the end of the second or third grade before they *begin* to plan remedial work for a failing child. By that time additional problems, usually emotional, have begun, as the youngster has desperately attempted to deal alone with his failures and frustrations. Such secondary problems often severely complicate diagnosis and help.

It is a tragedy—and quite needless—to wait until a child has failed for a year or more before giving him help.

No facet of education today is undergoing a more intensive investigation than preschool training—the stimulation of children in the years before age five or six right down to the months just after birth. Over half a century ago, Dr. Maria Montessori, the Italian physician and educator, wrote that children as young as two and a half were curious and ready for intellectual stimulation outside the confines of their homes, however good their homes might be. Research since then has documented a growth in the intelligence of children who received varying kinds of stimulation, and a *decrease* in the intellectual ability of children confined to barren environments.

Early-learning traditionalists in the United States have studiously ignored these findings until recent years. Many educators, along with virtually every school board in the country, still ignore them.

The evidence presented by behavioral scientists is clear: children need specific kinds of stimulation well before the age of five. Dr. Benjamin S. Bloom, a University of Chicago psychologist, argued, in 1964, that half of a person's potential growth or loss in intelligence occurs between birth and the age of four, and that an additional 30 per cent takes place by the age of eight.* If Dr. Bloom is right, a child has already used up half of his capacity to raise or lower his intelligence before he reaches school—as the schools are now constituted —and 80 per cent by the time he finishes third grade. Public school as it is organized today arrives too late to play a significant role in developing a child's intelligence, in seriously influencing his potential to the extent that many researchers believe it can be influenced.

"If we want to raise the intelligence of children," psychologist Bruno Bettelheim writes, ". . . we will have to free ourselves of a few of our most widely held prejudices—that the child is the private property of his parents to do with as they please, that we are therefore powerless to change the environment he grows up in and that human beings are infinitely improvable at any age, no matter what the home environment of their childhood." Dr. Bettelheim emphasizes that planning for all children, whether from privileged or poor environments, must take Dr. Bloom's "unassailable" findings into account. Radical reforms must therefore be made in the lives of children during the most crucial years—between the ages of two and four or five. Americans are only fooling themselves, Dr. Bettelheim says, if they think children's lives can be changed after they are in school, when it is already "too late" to give them what they need most.

---

* *Stability and Change in Human Characteristics* (New York, John Wiley, 1964).

Dr. Samuel Kirk, chairman of HEW's National Advisory Committee on Handicapped Children, and one of the first researchers into the effects of early learning on children, went before a subcommittee of the United States Senate in July, 1968, to protest "the lag between research findings . . . and their implementation in practice."

"In spite of the present acceptance by social scientists, by schools and parents that amelioration of mental and physical handicaps is often possible if initiated at an early age, very little has occurred . . . ," Dr. Kirk testified.

"Social scientists have developed effective procedures by which these children can be educated.

"The reason for this lag is not that we do not know what to do with handicapped preschool children.

"Implementation of research findings in this area will not occur, as it has not occurred, without federal support and stimulation.

"Neglect of this problem further will mean an increase . . . of handicapped children at older ages and greater expense in care, education and management to local, state and national agencies."

Repeated work throughout the world has demonstrated that children, far from being born with fixed intelligence, unalterable no matter what their circumstances, are born with an intellectual range. A stimulating environment can push their abilities toward the top of that range. Barren surroundings—regardless of family wealth—can drop their abilities toward the bottom of the range. Behavioral scientists speak of intellectual normality, when measured in terms of IQ, as being the 20 points from 90 to 110. Experiments with infants and young children have shown that IQ can be changed by *more* than 20 points—in some cases, from below normal to above normal. (Keep in mind that no one as yet knows just what intelligence is. One researcher has identified 140 different components of it thus far. IQ is a highly imperfect measurement. But it is the best available tool, when properly used.)

One experiment, under the direction of Dr. Rick Heber, of the University of Wisconsin's special-education department, involved the newborn children of twenty mothers whose IQ's were less than 80. In IQ measurement, most of these mothers were mentally retarded. Each child was given intensive attention, first at home and then in school. At the end of six years *all* of the children tested above 100 in IQ, several as high as 135. A comparison group of twenty children, selected from the same kind of environment at the same time but given no special attention, tested an average of 32 IQ points lower. None of those in the second group had IQ's above 105.

What does this signify in human terms? "This could mean the difference between a life in an institution for the feeble-minded and a productive life in society," Dr. Bloom writes. "It could mean the difference between a professional career and an occupation which is at the semi-skilled or unskilled level."

"Quality preschool opportunities are essential for [children from homes devoid of stimulation] if they are ever to have the hopes of succeeding in regular classroom studies," Wilbur J. Cohen, Secretary of Health, Education, and Welfare, said, in a speech in 1968. They are just as necessary for the young child who needs a scholastic head start because he may have learning disabilities. "Early recognition . . . in the critical period of two to four years . . . could help in the prevention of irreversible patterns of learning dysfunction," a Baltimore team of doctors reported, in a study published in the *Journal of Learning Disabilities*.

The proof is there for any who will come with open minds and with concern. Unfortunately, the decisions that govern this nation—and the nation's children—are made by men who do not think much about the problems of children.

In 1968, Congress passed a law providing for the establishment and operation of experimental early-education programs for handicapped children, from which all school systems might learn. Two hundred proposals for various types of programs were submitted. Money was available for twenty-four. Enthusiasm remained high the second year; 131 proposals were written. Money was available for nineteen. The investment in fiscal year 1973: $12 million—about the cost of one F-111 fighter-bomber airplane.

Three basic major changes are necessary in the way the United States thinks about its children if it intends to combat learning disabilities.

I. *The school system must be restructured.*

"In no other species are the differences between individuals so great as in the human race . . . ," writes Julian Huxley, in *Psychology Today.* "On top of all the temperamental and anatomical differences . . . are differences in biochemical make-up and differences in general ability and special gifts—differences so great that they can almost be regarded as differences not in degree but in kind. To herd all these dissimilar creatures into one classroom and to subject them all to the same kind of intellectual, emotional, and ethical training seems, on the face of it, absurd."

Yet this is what the nation does. In every school district. If society demands that all children go to school, then it must provide an appropriate education for every child. It must accept—in fact as well as in theory—the concept of individual differences. It must identify these individual differences in learning *during the preschool period.*

Preschool programs should be available for every child beginning at the age of three. They should be free.

These classes should be in *child centers,* not traditional schools. Each incoming child would receive a comprehensive physical examination by a multidisciplinary team of professionals experienced in the many, subtle signs of learning disabilities, as well as in normal child growth and development. If necessary the examiners could schedule immediate additional tests by specialists. Right there in the same place. Not in ten different parts of town. This would be the site where educational specialists could join with physicians, psychologists, and social workers to write a "prescription" for a learning-disabled child—medical, educational, and social—and could meet periodically to evaluate his progress and make necessary changes. "Each school district must have the responsibility of providing a total assessment of each student, including medical, [so educators] can focus on strengths rather than weaknesses," said the President's Committee on Mental Retardation, in its 1967 annual report.

Three levels of services must be established:

1. Physicians in or available to the school center, to whom preschool-age children could be referred.

2. Regional medical centers containing all the facilities a child might need, regardless of his handicap.

3. Preschool classroom teachers trained in child development as well as in early education.

"Parents of children in trouble do not know where to turn for help or which organization is most likely to prove beneficial," Dr. Richard M. Silberstein, a psychiatrist, writes, in the *Journal of Learning Disabilities*. "The professional result is a huge unassembled jigsaw puzzle in which the pieces look as if they should fit but do not."

At the age of five the child would move from preschool to a primary school encompassing what are now kindergarten and the first, second, and third grades. There would be no yearly dividers. The child would work without grade levels attached to his performance. There's nothing original in this kind of system. Dr. Montessori demonstrated sixty years ago, in Rome, that it was successful with both retarded and normal children.

Each child would be allowed to stay in primary school until he had grasped the basic tools of learning: reading, writing, spelling, arithmetic. It does not really matter whether a youngster gets out of primary school at the age of eight or at ten. He should be allowed the time it will take *him* to master the basic skills.

He should have the same team of teachers during all this time, each member a specialist in a different area of study, and all trained, as well, in child development and early-childhood education.

This nongraded concept would carry through all the school years. After a child had learned the basic skills, he would move to a middle school—what are now grades four, five, and six—again working with a team of specialists. Then an intermediate school—encompassing the present seventh through ninth years—and finally high school. No grade levels anywhere.

This academic treatment would end 80 to 90 per cent of learning disabilities. Pediatrician E. Muriel Bennett goes further. "There would be no learning-handicapped children if the approaches to learning were flexible enough," she says, in an article in *Academic Therapy*.

This method automatically allows for maturational lag. Children with learning problems would continue to learn at their own pace, and with supportive help. Each child would have his uniqueness recognized *and handled appropriately.* For all but the most severely handicapped, the need for special-education classes would be eliminated.

"Insisting upon attendance of children who fail to learn and who eventually learn that they are incompetent is insisting on crippling and handicapping children, [insisting on] mental or physical illness, delinquency, economic dependency and probably another generation of parental ineptitude," psychologist Laurence Peter says in an interview in the *Journal of Learning Disabilities*.

If a child fails in school, according to Dr. Bennett's article, "it is because not enough is known about him or what is known about him has been disregarded. . . . [This] is a challenge to learn all there is to know about how he learns *before* he goes to school and then to make use of that information so his learning is . . . rewarding to him."

Most children will learn when they are able to, notes psychiatrist Donald J. Holmes. "Trying to coerce" a child of whatever age who maturationally is unable to learn to read "would yield about the same frustration, inner strain and nil result that we would expect from trying to toilet-train a three-month-old baby," he says, as quoted in *Pediatric News*. "Too often we find ourselves shoving their faces into the pool of learning and holding them there until they turn blue, only to find later that they have suffered much but swallowed nothing."

As Dr. Jeanne McCarthy, director of special education in Schaumburg Township, near Chicago, stated, in a paper

presented in 1969, "Placing children in an academic program
. . . when they are not ready to succeed . . . is inexcusable
professional negligence."

II. *Teacher training must be improved.*

Teachers must be trained for a new approach to education,
either within their own school systems or earlier, in the
teachers' colleges, where so much has yet to be done in preparing prospective teachers to understand learning disabilities,
let alone deal with them. The 1970 White House Conference
on Children recommended the "overhaul of teacher education
from top to bottom. Most of today's teachers," it noted, "are
prepared for yesterday's schools."

Teachers' colleges must break down the arbitrary partitions
between the various categories of teacher training. General
education, special education, early-childhood education, and
even reading methods are taught in separate departments.
Most regular classroom teachers are not taught the special
techniques to use with children who deviate from the teacher's expectations. One sad result: the learning-disabled child
has to get far enough behind to be referred to a special educator, who then must try to repair the mistakes that have
been made. *All* primary- and elementary-school teachers
should be trained to prevent the start of learning problems,
as well as to identify and correct disabilities that already exist.

This new kind of teacher would know that if a boy or girl,
whatever the problem, wasn't learning one way, there was
probably something out of place with the *teaching method,*
not the child. This teacher would be equipped to change, to
experiment with teaching methods for *that* child. As Dr.
Bloom said, in an interview in *Integrated Education,* "If students can't learn one way, they need to be reassured they
can learn in another."

"We must insist to general education that the basic education about learning disabilities be made available in the
teacher-training programs of *all* teachers," educator Newell
C. Kephart, formerly of the psychology department at Purdue

University, said, in a speech in 1969. ". . . We need to insist that for a teacher to be considered competent in the classroom, she know the . . . child with learning disabilities and the less technical techniques for dealing with [him]. . . . The time has come in our knowledge [when] we can insist this be made a part of the teacher's training. . . . There are also thousands of practicing teachers over the country who need this information now. . . . We need to turn our attention to . . . making [this] available to them."

There will never be enough special-education teachers to meet the present demand. The nation's public schools have 10,000 teachers working as learning-disability specialists. Perhaps 200,000 are needed. But only 1,000 new teachers enter this field each year—a smaller number than the attrition rate among these specialists. But, as was discussed in chapter 7, most children—save for the most hyperactive, emotionally disturbed, or profoundly retarded—could be handled in a regular classroom if the classroom teacher had the additional training *and the extra help in supportive staff to do so.*

III. *Schools must become comprehensive child and family centers, each school or school district containing whatever a child and his family need.*

As American families move with growing frequency and neighborhoods fragment, schools increasingly are becoming the central public buildings in a community. *They should be at least the starting point for every service a child ought to have,* health as well as educational.

Virtually every community of any size in this country has such publicly supported groups as planning boards and zoning boards. The men and women on these boards worry about where new roads should go, whether or not Mr. Jones should be allowed to enclose his front vestibule, whether to permit Mr. Smith to extend his house three feet closer to his property line than his next-door neighbor would like.

It is time the nation also had a network of planning committees on which, instead of deciding where the roads are to go over the next ten years, concerned citizens would sit to make plans for their children. Plans to provide for every kind of problem a child might have. The board of education worries about school and stops there. The recreation board considers junior-league sports as pretty much the limit of its concern. But there is no community council, anywhere, concerned with the whole child.

"Children . . . are without political clout," the 1970 White House Conference on Children noted. ". . . We recommend that top priority be given to quickly establishing a child advocacy agency financed by the federal government . . . and charged with fostering, co-ordinating and implementing all programs related to children."

The White House Conference asked for "a high level . . . network" of advocates, beginning with the Cabinet, that would co-ordinate all federal activities relating to children, from the national level, through the governor's office of each state, down to the governing body of each municipality. No one has ever tried to bring together in this manner all the work done or the money spent by the federal government for children; one researcher has estimated that the money wasted in duplicative projects runs in the millions.

Such advocates would not repeat existing services. Their primary task would be to find vacuums and see that they were filled—using the network that stretched to Washington if necessary—so that a child in need would get the right services at the proper time.

Schools must offer what Dr. Montessori called "training for life." Most children don't go to college. Only one in four graduates from college. To ignore the other three—as every state in the nation now does—is stupid. Prevocational training for the learning-disabled, and for others who will not go to college, can start at the age of twelve or thirteen, once they have the basic academic skills.

Most vocational training today is an exercise in futility. Too many schools still insist on teaching traditional woodworking and metalworking, rather than telephone installing and business-machine repair, or instead of searching their communities to learn what talents local companies need. Dr. Marland, U.S. Assistant Secretary for Education, admitted (with understatement), in his 1972 speech, "One out of four young Americans leaves school . . . utterly unprepared to find his place . . . as a productive employee." Public education, he adds, "allows 2,500,000 young people in a single year to exit our schools and colleges without marketable skills." The cost of this lost investment: $28 billion annually, about one-third of the yearly cost of running all the schools and colleges in the country.

Education should offer alternatives, what Dr. Chester Poremba, chief of the department of psychology, Denver Children's Hospital, has called "new approaches to learning and job training." The 1970 White House Conference urged "the deliberate development of experimental schools . . . seeking to redesign the entire learning environment from the curriculum through the structure of the school to completely new instructional procedures."

But what can *you* as parents do? You are just one mother and father sick with worry and anxiety about your child. You may not even know where to find diagnostic or treatment services for him.

One cold winter day about twenty years ago, the parents of a mentally retarded child, desperate with concern and with no idea what they should do to help him, placed a one-inch advertisement in their local newspaper. It went something like this: "We are the parents of a retarded boy. We plan to be home this evening from 6 to 9 P.M. We would be interested in talking with other parents of retarded children."

By five-thirty, their house was jammed. Thirty minutes later people were overflowing into the street. Everyone there was the parent of a retarded child. They came out of a deep-seated need for mutual understanding—and help. From that small advertisement, a powerful citizens' lobby on behalf of retarded children in that community was born.

The Association for Children with Learning Disabilities erupted in much the same way (see appendix B). Fifty people attended the first meeting, in Chicago, in 1964. Three years later, the Grand Ballroom of New York's Waldorf-Astoria Hotel couldn't hold everyone who wanted to attend the annual convention.

This is power.

Virtually every public-school class for learning-disabled children that exists today has resulted from parents and sympathetic professionals who educated and hectored local and state officials. There were no such classes ten years ago.

"Our ability to offer programs for the learning-disabled is *directly related to the amount of community support we have*," a director of special education in California told the authors. "We don't have the leverage inside the school system that parents do in the community. If it were not for the people on the outside, we would not be able to survive on the inside. That's why, for example, we have mandated education laws here for our handicapped." This from one of the more enlightened states.

"When parents form an organization and speak to local and state governing bodies, they speak from a position of strength—a position directly related to the number of people they have in that audience," this special educator continued. "The most politically naïve parents learn quickly where the pressure points are."

"In the entire movement . . . to bring help—in diagnosis and then in treatment—to these children, one element stands out," Dr. Gallagher has said. "The parents who influence. On a local level. On a state level. Parents who lobby. Who contact everyone who should be contacted. And when this happens, lots of other things happen."

For your children and for those in other families who will follow, begin to apply pressure. Just as the gun lobbies and the automotive lobbies do. They have far more money than you do, but you have—potentially—more voices. Put your voices together.

There are few people quite so urgent as the parents of handicapped children. They are sophisticated about the problems of their children. Many of them know as much about their children's disabilities as the professionals do.

This is why state legislation must mandate adequate classes for the learning-disabled—instead of merely leaving the matter up to individual communities. It would give parents a handle in dealing with a local district—a means of exerting force on a district that might not believe in educating the handicapped. Mandatory legislation would allow parents to turn on a searchlight, to appeal to higher authority, ultimately to sue.

Anything less than mandatory legislation is a rationalization to do less.

Local school systems have many problems. But their job, nonetheless, is to help your child. *No excuse for refusing or delaying services is valid.*

Only if parents educate their leaders—school and legislative —sufficiently will it be possible to see that every child has an equal opportunity to learn. Not the opportunity to learn *if* he can read without major assistance; not the opportunity to learn *if* he is physically unimpaired.

It is past time for the parents of handicapped children to walk day after day into the office of every man and woman who has a voice in the treatment of their children and say simply, "We will plead no more. This is what we want."

And when those people say, "But we have no money," parents must go to their state capital and to Congress—to the men they have elected—and say to them, "Send money back home now. Not in fiscal five-years-off. Cut it from defense. Cut it from highway construction. Cut it from tax loopholes [estimated to cost the U.S. Treasury $40 billion to $70 billion annually]. But we want it now, for teacher training and educational services. If we don't get it now, we promise you that every parent of every handicapped child will know precisely why his son or daughter is not getting all the help available, in this most technologically advanced nation in the world, to enable him or her to live a healthy, successful life."

The parents of learning-disabled children need far more than the seminars and panels and specialty journals they now sponsor to bring information to professionals and parents— vital as each one of these things is.

Parents need power. Power comes only from strength and pressure, intelligently applied. *Until* parents achieve power in their legislatures—local, state, and national—they will not get the significant, *sustained* supply of money learning-disabled boys and girls must have.

These parents are not asking for charity. They are demanding that America's tax money be spent on its children, a more vital resource for the nation's future than, say, another generation of bombers. The Association for Children with Learning Disabilities has begun this fight. All parents must help.

In attempting to get public-school services for learning-disabled boys and girls, parents—and the professionals behind them—face a major barrier unlike any confronting the parents of children with other handicaps: there are so many of these boys and girls.

"Legislators are led to believe that too many children will be included in the category of learning disabilities if [that group] is added to the existing legal definition of handicapped children," writes Dr. Corrine E. Kass, a University of Arizona special educator, in the *Journal of Learning Disabilities*. The U.S. Office of Education knows approximately how many children have some form of learning disability. "But we had to tell Congress just 1 per cent," a ranking staff member admitted privately, "just to get learning disabilities on the books. Else they would have gone through the ceiling and thrown us the hell out." In addition, as Dr. Kass's article notes, "Parents of other kinds of handicapped children . . . fear that some of the benefits and [money] will be taken . . . from their youngsters if a new category is inserted in the definition of handicapped children."

This is another job parents must undertake: the start that has been made with other organizations for handicapped children to work together, to lobby, must be continued. Few efforts can have more tragic results than to argue for money for the learning-disabled at the expense of the budget for retarded children. Yet something like this is done whenever government money is doled out.

Parents have friends at the Bureau of Education for the

Handicapped (see appendix C). For the first time in the history of federal concern for disabled children, a group of dedicated men and women are working for your children in Washington. The bureau's efforts are a principal reason why federal spending for all categories of handicapped children has jumped from $50 million to over $200 million since 1967. Go to the bureau and say, "We want to help. Tell us how."

At a meeting of the American Academy of Pediatrics in 1969, psychiatrist Leon Eisenberg, discussing student unrest, noted somewhat obliquely, "Perhaps we should be asking not why the student unrest, but why is there no adult unrest." The point is applicable to the learning-disabled.

"Congress," as consumer advocate Ralph Nader has written in the New York *Times,* "has been a continuous underachiever. It would be difficult to overstate the extent of abdication to which Congress has been driven by external and internal forces. Contrary to its constitutional authority and constitutional stature as the branch of government closest to the people, it has been reduced to a puny twig through which flows the allocation of a massive taxpayer treasure chest of over $200 billion in appropriations, largely at the beck and call of the Executive branch and *special-interest advocacy and pressure* [emphasis added]. It reacts to the Executive far more than it initiates. . . . There is, to be sure, a widespread cynicism about 'politicians' along with a feeling that nothing can be done about them beyond mere endurance, [but] nothing remotely compares with the Congress as the hope of reclaiming America."

The emperor is naked where treatment of handicapped youngsters in the United States is concerned. Unfortunately, not enough people are pointing at the exposure. It is undignified, as psychiatrist Benjamin Pasamanick said bitterly, in a speech to the American Orthopsychiatric Association, "for an intellectual or a researcher in the professions to scream in the streets. You would lose your effectiveness, said my colleagues; you would lose your job and your place at the table, said the inner voices." Not enough as yet are screaming in the streets.

The attitudes that today threaten the potential of each learning-disabled child to function, to live well, threaten virtually all children in virtually all schools. And that is all this chapter is really talking about—attitudes.

By any definition one cares to select, in this country, at this time, we as a nation are destroying our children.

Not openly and pridefully on the gallows, as England once hanged children as thieves. But silently and with a large degree of cowardliness.

Destroying because, while most of these children do live, they live as the misfits and institution-bound of this society. Cowardliness because we know what is happening—and choose to ignore what we know.

Consider:

• "Two-thirds of the nation's children under 15 get anything from zero to inadequate health care," Dr. William B. Weil, Jr., past president of the Society for Pediatric Research, told a Senate subcommittee in 1971, and this "highly variable care [affects] even those who can pay for it." According to the White House Conference on Children, "When health problems are discovered through school examinations and screening programs, community agencies often lack the resources to provide treatment." "At least one-third of [all] handicapping conditions could be prevented or corrected by comprehensive care prior to age six," pediatricians Julius B. Richmond and Howard L. Weinberger write, in the *American Journal of Public Health*. Continuing comprehensive care up to the age of eighteen would prevent or correct as much as 60 per cent of these conditions, the two doctors claim.

• The United States is thirteenth among comparable nations in infant mortality. A most revealing statistic: while the death rate among white children dropped in 1970, the rate among black infants rose. Almost twice as high a percentage of black infants—and three times as high a percentage of Indian infants—died in 1970 in relation to the white infant death rate. (One researcher has estimated that this meant there were 15,000 unnecessary infant deaths—of all races—in 1970.) The nonwhite infant death rate is not the sole reason for the abysmal international standing. Ten nations have a better infant-mortality rate than the United States toll for *white* children alone. "By applying techniques and information we already have, we can make a significant impact on [this] mortality," says pediatrician Marvin Cornblath, of the University of Maryland, as reported in *Pediatric News.*

• But the infant death rate is "not the most important part of the picture . . . ," writes physician Edward S. Quilligan, of Yale, in an article in *Yale News.* "The submerged portion of the iceberg, which can sink families or even societies, is those individuals who do not die at birth but who, through damage during pregnancy, labor, delivery or the neonatal period, are never able to achieve their full potential as productive citizens. We have absolutely no idea of the magnitude of this problem."

One million children are born each year to mothers who have received inadequate or no care during pregnancy and inadequate care during delivery. These mothers have premature deliveries at a rate two and a half times the national average. Premature birth accounts for two-thirds of all infant deaths. These low-weight babies are much more likely to have permanent neurological disorders. Lack of prenatal care is believed to be the single most important factor leading to major illness in low-birth-weight infants.

"Without question, the most serious disabling conditions in our society result from brain dysfunctions originating at or prior to birth," says Dr. Richard L. Masland, former chief of the National Institute of Neurological Diseases and Stroke, in the *Journal of Learning Disabilities.* "For example, of the increasing number of individuals who receive Social Security benefits for lifetime disabilities occurring before age eighteen, 94 per cent have a neurological origin. . . . The role of subtle factors and their relationship to lesser degrees of brain dysfunction which are observed in . . . learning disabilities have hardly been explored."

• Close to half of all American children are not adequately immunized. The number of young children fully immunized against polio, for example, dropped from 87.6 per cent in

1964 to 67.7 per cent in 1969. In poverty areas, rural or urban, only 54 per cent of children aged one through four have been immunized. One major reason: the federal government in 1969 stopped giving the states money specifically for inoculations. When Congress became alarmed the following year and offered the Department of Health, Education, and Welfare $75 million to give to the states for immunization programs, it was turned down. HEW's explanation? The money was not necessary or desirable, because it ran counter to the administration's revenue-sharing program, of giving the states money in lump sums to use as they wanted. Half the states do not require preschool immunization for diseases like polio and measles. "The financial cost of a single measles epidemic?" Dr. Masland's article asks. ". . . Between $1 billion and $2 billion. The social costs are incalculable."

• Half of all American children under the age of fifteen have never been to a dentist.

• Health care is nonexistent for most children of the poor. "If the developing regions [of the world] are those in which the population cannot satisfy its critical needs," one physician said, in testifying before a Senate subcommittee on migratory labor, "then we would have to talk of pockets of underdevelopment in the United States."

The subcommittee also heard testimony from a team of doctors who had gone into Hidalgo County, Texas, to investigate health conditions among migrant farmworkers and came back to ask, "How can you justify the endless words and the devious political maneuvers which have delayed and withheld meaningful aid to children who don't have enough to eat, children whose parents have no jobs and no money for food or medical care?

"The children we saw have no future in our society. Malnutrition since birth has already impaired them physically, mentally and emotionally."

What happens when a child is malnourished?

"Malnutrition is now widely accepted as a cause of brain damage and central nervous system malfunction in the fetus, the infant, and the schoolchild, including all types of behavior problems," Dr. Pasamanick said, in the speech previously cited. The President's Committee on Mental Retardation said, in its 1967 report, "Neurologic and mental abnormalities caused by poor nutrition that occur at . . . early, rapid stages of development have been found to be permanent, even when physical signs of poor nutrition have been corrected. . . . Children with physical signs of earlier malnutrition rated consistently and significantly low in tests for neurological functioning."

• Some 6 million Americans are believed to be irreversibly mentally retarded. About 125,000 children are added each year. In its report of 1964, the President's Committee on Mental Retardation estimated that 75 per cent of the total, an incredible three out of four, were not born handicapped. *They were born with healthy minds.* They were made irreversibly retarded by the failure of society to provide what they needed to survive. "If I wanted to draw a master plan to develop mentally retarded people," one physician told the authors, "I couldn't do better than propose the conditions that exist where so many of the poor live." The President's Committee on Mental Retardation adds, "Much of the underperformance being diagnosed in children as mild mental retardation is *preventable and reversible* if attacked early [emphasis added]."

• Some 10 million children and adults under the age of twenty-five have varying degrees of emotional disturbance serious enough to require immediate aid, the nongovernmental Joint Commission on Mental Health of Children estimated, in a report issued in 1969. These include the psychotic and severely disturbed. Many children, 25 per cent in some poverty areas, demonstrate "crippled . . . emotional development by the age of four."

In 1930, the White House Conference on Child Health and Protection proclaimed, "The emotionally disturbed child has a right to grow up in a world which does not set him apart, which looks at him not with scorn or pity or ridicule—but which welcomes him exactly as it welcomes every child, which offers him identical privileges and identical responsibilities."

How far has the nation come since then? Not one "community in the U.S. [today] has the facilities for the care, education, guidance and treatment of mentally ill and emotionally disturbed children," the Joint Commission's report stated. No one co-ordinates the $13.5 billion in services estimated to be available annually for this purpose.

"What happens to emotionally sick children for whom there are no services?" the Joint Commission asks.

"Each year, increasing numbers of [children] are expelled from the community and confined in large state hospitals so understaffed that they have few, if any, professionals trained in child psychiatry and related disciplines. It is not unusual . . . to tour one of these massive warehouses for the mentally ill and come upon a child, aged nine or ten, confined to a ward with 80 or 90 sick adults. . . . Thousands upon thousands of elderly patients now confined on the back wards of these state institutions were first admitted as children 30, 40, and even 50 years ago. . . . One state estimates that one in every four children admitted to its mental hospitals can anticipate being . . . hospitalized for the next 50 years of his life.

"[Yet] we have the knowledge and the riches to remedy many of the conditions," the Joint Commission concludes.

These are "the kinds of kids that [Lee Harvey] Oswald and [Sirhan] Sirhan were," sociologist Thomas S. Langner told the New York *Times.* "They have the worst potential in the country."

• Of the estimated 7 million handicapped children in this country—all handicaps except learning disabilities—the public schools say they help 40 per cent to some degree. This means that more than 4 million children who could profit from appropriate education sit in catchall classes in which they cannot learn.

"We commissioned a survey of school districts . . . and had responses from more than 15,000 [of some 19,000]," Dr. Edwin W. Martin, the head of the Bureau of Education for the Handicapped, told the authors. "Of these, about 11,500 offered special education classes. . . . The . . . majority offered only classes for the educable retarded and/or speech and hearing therapy—by no means a full range of services for handicapped children. We have states by their own admission that help perhaps 10 per cent of their handicapped children."

Less than a century ago children were considered of little value in this country. The homeless were paid scant notice as they wandered the streets. Today, however, Americans boast of their concern and consider mistreatment of children the most heinous of crimes.

But "if you look at our [national] actions . . . the answer is clear: . . . We as a nation [do not] give a high priority to children," writes Dr. Ralph J. Wedgwood, professor of pediatrics at the University of Washington School of Medicine, in the *American Journal of Public Health.*

"This nation, the richest of all world powers, has no unified national commitment to its children and youth," the Joint Commission on Mental Health of Children reported. "The claim that we are a child-centered society, that we look to our young as tomorrow's leaders, is a myth.

"This nation, which looks to the family to nurture its young, gives no real help with child-rearing until a child is badly disturbed or disruptive to the community. . . . The family cannot be allowed to withstand alone the enormous pressures of an increasingly technological world. Within the community some mechanism must be created which will assume the responsibility for insuring the necessary supports for the child and family.

"Our lack of commitment is a national tragedy. . . . Most children, regardless of class or race, whether in the ghetto or suburbia, do not receive the needed support and assistance from our society. *But it is the damaged, the vulnerable and the poor who are given the least from our health, welfare and educational services. Those who are the most helpless are the most neglected* [emphasis added]."

This is the attitude that governs the care of all children in this country today. Unless parents are aware of it, attempts to help the handicapped, and all children who have learning disabilities, will suffer through naïveté. For the same citizen and leadership attitude that allows children to go hungry and ill is precisely the attitude that lets children with handicaps of any kind go undetected and untreated in school and in the community. It is an attitude that has permeated *every* federal administration and virtually all government at local and state levels. It's an attitude for which we, as citizens, are all responsible.

No one even knows how many handicapped children there are in this country.

No comprehensive census of the handicapped has ever been made. Conservatively, it is estimated that 10 per cent of the 75 million boys and girls in the United States of high-school age and younger have some kind of disability that demands special attention. Add the 10 per cent estimated to have learning disabilities on top of this, and the total is 15 million children.

What is the quality of the special-education programs that do exist in public schools?

"Nationally, we have no idea," Dr. Martin has said. "We know many school districts where the quality is superb. We know others that are atrocious—or totally nonexistent. The rest fall somewhere in the middle—and no one knows exactly where.

"Until we can develop sophisticated local and state programs with federal help, we will not know answers—numbers, quality, anything."

"The lesson of history is that hardly any disease of major significance has ever been effectively controlled by attacking it only after symptoms have occurred," Dr. George James, former dean of Mt. Sinai School of Medicine, in New York, said in an interview.

The failure of one-quarter of the country's students to learn to read is a disease. "Until the early 1960's . . . Washington tried to repair the damage [with vocational rehabilitation] years after it had been done," Harold Howe II, the head of the U.S. Office of Education, said, in a speech in 1967. "Now, poked and prodded by citizens, legislators and scientists, the federal government has at last recognized the simple truth that handicapped adults were once handicapped children and that the early years—not the teens or the twenties—are the years to identify and treat handicaps."

This wisdom is still without much practical effect. "We cannot as educators and parents rid our consciences of the haunting presence of . . . 20 to 25 per cent whom [education] simply has not reached . . . who so long were in the shadows of education," according to a speech by Dr. Marland in 1971. "There is no longer a place for this. As teachers and responsible citizens, we must face former students now trapped in dead-end jobs, early unhappy marriages, on welfare, ridden by drugs. We in this land known as the world's first example of equal educational opportunity have among us more than 8 million adult functional illiterates."

Who gets a large share of blame for the failure of the schools to do what is necessary for children?

The schools themselves.

Why, asked U.S. Commissioner of Education James E. Allen, Jr., in a speech in 1969, when the nation needs "a vigorous, widespread program of research and development do we not yet have it? . . . The basic reason is lack of support —the support of sufficient money and the support of philosophical commitment. [But] why have we not been able to secure the necessary support?"

Dr. Allen then answered his own question:

"Too many of those . . . *in the field of education* . . . who play a part in determining the support for research and development are not sufficiently sold on its value to give it full and enthusiastic backing.

"A national survey . . . asking school administrators . . . to identify recent educational research and development results or products that have had or will have widespread influence on school practices throughout the nation found two-thirds of the respondents *unable to identify even one such advance.* The vast majority of school systems surveyed had had no experience with nongraded sequences, programmed instruction, modular scheduling, instructional television or team teaching —all of which are now familiar, well-tried parts of instructional practice [emphases added]."

"It would seem," Dr. Allen continued, "that much of what we have so laboriously learned about educational theory and practice has been—to say the least—under advertised, poorly packaged and thinly distributed."

"Our biggest need is to get acceptance," Dr. Jerry Miller, the former director of special education in Philadelphia, told the authors. "And you know from whom the most? The . . . educators. We have principals who won't allow classes for retarded children in their schools. We have teachers who tell their students to 'stay away from those sick kids.' And we wonder why a so-called normal child will walk by a learning-disabled boy and shout, 'Hey, retard.'"

"There is a school district that forced physically handicapped children to stay home because these boys and girls couldn't lift their feet to the bottom step of the school bus," Dr. James Gallagher said. "A school superintendent in a town of 60,000 looked me right in the eye and said, 'We have no hearing problems here.'" "Most states, most local school boards and most teachers just don't care," added special educator Frank Wawrzaszek, of Eastern Michigan University. "Too many say, 'I'm willing to help the handicapped as long as it doesn't handicap me.'"

"School spending decisions are made locally," an official in the Department of Health, Education, and Welfare told the authors. "Their desire to do the greatest good for the greatest number plus the general pessimism about what can be done with a handicapped child generally results in a decision that somebody ought to take care of them, but not us. Send them to a state institution, a hospital, send them somewhere. It's not our responsibility. . . .

"That's why federal money has to demonstrate that it can be done, that virtually every child, no matter what his handicap, can learn. So if someone says it can't be done, we can say, 'You go to such and such a school and then come back and tell me why you can't do the same thing here.'

"The difference between the skills we know and what we're doing with them is substantial."

"The gaps are extraordinary. There is not enough fabric to

dignify it by calling it a system," Dr. Robert Henderson, of the University of Illinois special-education department, said in an interview. "Even where a good school program exists, it is usually unrelated to the whole of a kid's problems; for example, if school takes him through vocational training, he's on his own when he tries to get a job. We operate at a primitive level in services we offer, in getting diagnosis to a child. Most children rarely need just one kind of service. In addition to the handicap, slight as it might be, there are health problems, social adjustment problems. The poor parent is chasing around trying to find all this. That's the parent who is savvy enough to be able to do it. What about all the poor families who are trying just to survive? Can they also take a non-system, a school district that wishes they would go away?"

"Some states will pay up to 75 per cent of the cost for some disabilities," according to Wawrzaszek. "They want local school districts to have at least a 25-per-cent commitment, but even this doesn't work. When money is low, that 25 per cent is the first to go."

The problem, of course, is money—and the will to use it properly.

"We do, each year, provide some aid for others," John Kenneth Galbraith writes, in *The Affluent Society*. "But first we have a prayerful discussion of whether or not we can afford the sacrifice. . . . The nineteenth-century plutocrat who devoted his energies to expanding his already considerable income; who was led by his competitive position . . . to live on a suitably ostentatious scale; who found, as a result, that his income was never entirely adequate . . . came to the aid of the poor only after careful consideration of their worth, his ability to spare from his needs and the realistic likelihood of revolt and disorder if he abstained. . . . Thus with nations."

Do you recall the comment from Dr. Gallagher, earlier in this chapter, about what might be done with $500 million a year? President Richard M. Nixon, in 1972, granted—secretly, and in possible violation of the Constitution—$435 million in economic aid to the dictatorial regime in Portugal, in return for U.S. use of port and air-refueling facilities there. The

Department of Defense has been developing some 140 new weapons systems estimated to cost $162 billion. The United States has been building eighty-one C5A cargo planes for $4.6 billion (an increase of some $1.2 billion over the original estimate). The nation could save $1 billion each year if political pressures did not keep unneeded military bases open, says former Deputy Secretary of Defense David Packard. The Air Force is planning to spend $20 billion (by congressional estimate) for a fleet of supersonic bombers. One independent study, made at Princeton, estimated this cost could go to $80 billion. And in India, in 1971, the U.S. military-aid mission incurred $375,000 in administrative costs to dispense $234,000 in assistance.

The Department of Defense has not been the only profligate government spender. The President has ordered the National Aeronautics and Space Administration to develop a space shuttle. The estimated cost of two test vehicles was over $2 billion. The federal government has been spending $5 billion each year for highway construction, and $5.5 billion annually on farm subsidies. It spent $900,000 to build a toilet on Interstate Highway 29, in Iowa (the engineers had picked a scenic but swampy site). And it has been paying $16.06 to subsidize the average meal in the Department of Transportation executive dining room. The diner paid a regulated $1.51.

Shortage of money?

How much money can be saved by helping learning-disabled children at the right time?

Each child put into an institution—whether an institution for the mentally ill or the retarded or a prison—costs $3,000 to $12,000 per year. A child warehoused for life costs, conservatively, $150,000 over his lifetime.

"If a child with a potentially normal mind and a learning disability is identified early—at age three or four, say—treating his disability so he can take his place in a regular classroom can require as much as three years," Harold Howe II said, in the speech cited earlier. "The [total] cost of this care in a typical case will run an average of $6,000."

So: 7.5 million children at $2,000 each, less the $900 the

average school district spends annually for each boy and girl, adds up to $8.25 billion annually. That is less than 1 per cent of the gross national product, and 3 per cent of the annual federal budget. *But if only one schoolchild in every twenty in this country was not promoted each year, that annual cost would be $2.25 billion.*

The $8.25 billion estimate calls for *maximum* assistance for all learning-disabled boys and girls. As has been pointed out, most of these children don't need that much. They could be helped in the regular classroom if classroom teachers were adequately trained and supported. This would reduce the amount required sharply below $8.25 billion.

The United States government spent $160.5 million in 1970 for research into heart disease, the leading killer in this country. During the same year it spent $3.9 billion in the space-exploration program.

The United States is spending some $400 million during 1973 in research against cancer, the second leading cause of death. But it has set aside $2.3 billion during the same period for development and testing of missiles and related equipment.

The United States spent $111 million in 1970 for research on mental illness, a problem that affects some 20 million Americans. In the same year it spent $254 million for agricultural research, $285 million in forest programs, $187.5 million for outdoor recreation.

"If you want to persuade someone to do something," a politician once told the authors, "you've got to convince him that it's in his own self-interest."

"Once we turn that corner," Dr. Martin, of the Bureau of Education for the Handicapped, says, "from 'let's be good fellows and help our fellow man' to 'these guys are going to make it cheaper for me in the long run,' we will have taken a hell of a step."

"We must realize that many of our social programs do not depend for their essential force *on notions of charity or of shedding a tear for the handicapped,* whether their handicap be of mind or limb or color of skin [emphasis added]," Harold Howe's speech continues. "At bottom, we are talking about investment, about economics, about the sensible allocation of our national resources. . . . We are, in crude but accurate terms, talking about gain, about profit, about interest on our national investment."

Parents of the learning-disabled will never get the money their children need from local school districts. The pressure must be placed on state and federal legislatures. No longer for catalytic, pump-priming money, as is now the case (in 1973, some 7 per cent of all money for schools came from Washington, down from 9 per cent in 1967), but for block grants, directly to school districts, marked for specified disabilities. This earmarked money must be backed up by laws that will force recalcitrant school districts to use it as directed.

Most local districts, dependent primarily on local property taxes, can no longer afford to maintain their schools properly. Aid for the "special" child, the youngster who needs more than the healthy boy or girl, will be lost.

A national survey of public-school financing, conducted under the direction of the U.S. Office of Education, certified what parents and teachers had always known: "great inequities exist" in the money raised and spent by individual school districts in all states but one, Hawaii. This results in "unequal" education.

According to the survey report, released in 1971, some districts spend four times as much per student as other districts in the same state, "primarily the result of the tremendous differences in the abilities of local districts to finance education and the methods used" in distributing state aid. In New York State, the richest school district has 10.5 times the wealth of the poorest district. It is frequently true that proportionately more state money for education goes to the suburban districts that need it least.

The five states with the highest per-capita net income spent an average of $1,000 per pupil in 1970–71, the survey reported. The five poorest states spent an average of $574 per pupil.

"We believe the education . . . of every individual should be a function of the total taxable wealth *of the state* and should not be limited to the taxing ability of a local school district [emphasis added]," says the survey. "The time has come to seek new directions . . . in raising and allocating revenues if we are to achieve equality in education."

The survey urged that the federal share of school financing jump to between 22 and 30 per cent of the present $39-billion-a-year national bill for kindergarten through high school. States should increase their share from the present 41 per cent to 55 per cent. Local districts, which now pay an average 52 per cent of their own school bills, should pay a maximum of 15 per cent.

This would increase federal spending for schools from $2.8 billion to about $12 billion.

These are just recommendations, and meaningless at this point.

However, they closely follow a rash of state-court decisions saying that differences in public-school spending based on the comparative wealth of school districts violate state constitutions. Reliance on the local property tax (source of 98 per cent of a school district's locally raised funds, in most cases) "invidiously discriminates against the poor because it makes the quality of a child's education a function of the wealth of his parents and neighbors," California's Superior Court has ruled. Although the United States Supreme Court has voided one federal-court ruling, that decision is not likely to affect verdicts based on state constitutions.

These court moves are only one start toward a drastic overhaul of public-school financing for all children in the United States, not just the handicapped. The immediate answer is direct contributions by federal and state governments for specific purposes.

Parents of the learning-disabled must work through their state legislatures and Congress toward this goal.

Or parents must go, more forcefully than ever, to the courts.

These court decisions—and two others, in Washington, D.C., and in Pennsylvania—give hope that solutions may come more quickly through litigation.

In 1972, a federal judge in Washington, D.C., ruled that

handicapped children in the District of Columbia have a constitutional right to a public education. He is believed to be the first jurist to say that handicapped youngsters have the same claim to public-school education under the Constitution that healthy children do. When school officials argued that they faced a number of obstacles in helping handicapped boys and girls, the judge said no obstacle mattered.

In 1971, a panel of federal judges in Philadelphia ordered the state of Pennsylvania to provide free education to all retarded children in the state. The action came in a suit brought by the Pennsylvania Association for Retarded Children, in part for a number of children from twelve school districts, with IQ's ranging from 20 to 75, who had been refused admission to the public schools. (No one, incidentally, can measure the intelligence of a five-year-old child so precisely as to report that it is 75 and not, say, 85, which is just below borderline normality.) The judges' decision was spurred by experts who testified in court that most retarded children can become self-sufficient through education.

"There is a fundamental difference between the way European countries finance their school programs for handicapped children and how we finance ours," a friend recently told the authors. "I visited one school in the Netherlands where they have small units of six or seven children, each unit divided according to the kinds of learning needs the boys and girls have. A teacher plus two attendants for each three children. That means, of course, one adult for each child in the unit. All free. I asked my guide, 'How do you afford this?' He replied, 'They have to give it to us. It's in the national constitution.' I said, 'What do you mean, it's in the constitution?' He said, 'The constitution says every child should be educated to the limit of his ability, and so when we tell the government what we plan for *this* youngster, *they have to give it to us.*'"

"How much research is necessary to demonstrate that [lack of money] can kill and maim . . . and degrade?" Dr. Pasamanick's speech asks. ". . . The eternal cry that we must have more facts, more research before we can institute programs is a hateful disservice of investigators of society. . . . Where do we stand as a society . . . maiming hundreds of thousands of children each year in full knowledge of what we have done and continue to do?" His attention was directed to hunger, but his words serve all forms of crippling.

As parents, all of us must invade the schoolrooms. Not with hostility, but with curiosity—and the determination to remain. For the first time in our nation's history, the United States has a generation of parents who are as well educated as their children's teachers. We must make use of this.

Questioning, prodding parents can be a nuisance to school personnel—administrators, directors of special education, and teachers. Even if these professionals acknowledge privately that their programs for the learning-disabled leave something to be desired, they don't want parents to get into the act too much. If parents start to poke around and express dissatisfaction, some educators get uncomfortable.

It is clear that *all* children can learn. When they don't, something is interfering. If your child cannot learn to read, it is the job of his teacher to tell you why. If she cannot, then something is wrong with her—and the school system supporting her. It is not your task to diagnose the ailment. But you must make it your task to find out why that teacher—or that school—does not know why he can't read or how to help him.

It is far too late for schools to say or imply—as most do every day—that their job is to teach only those who are "ready to learn." It is the task of the schools to teach.

With millions of children the schools need help desperately. With the child who is hungry, who is ashamed of the way he looks, who is troubled by the kind of home he lives in, who cannot understand why he can't read—as simple a task for a healthy child as learning to walk—the schools need help beyond their *present* scope. The best and most conscientious teacher can do little when the budget parers hire only one psychologist for three elementary schools. But the schools must speak up for the rights of their children. And this failure may be their biggest shame. Remember Mike's mother: "No one gave us any help."

There is a magic in the lives of all of us in spite of what

the most "adult" and cynical of us believe. It is the magic called truth. If we admit to ourselves—the hardest admission—that we are all at fault because children are being crushed and families destroyed, if enough of us go to city hall, to the statehouse, to Congress, and say, "This is the truth," a marvelous thing may very well happen.

Money may be "found."

Let no one tell you there is none. The money is in hand, from present federal tax revenues that are being diverted to other purposes. Let no one tell you that your property tax or your income tax or your sales tax must go up.

Ultimately we are all responsible for the way our children are treated. We elect the legislators. We pay the educators. If they do not serve us well, it may be because we have not told them loudly enough and clearly enough what we want done with our tax dollars. Many of them are doing what they believe our society wants. "We are putting our money where our values are," says one director of special education. "Until we can push [a program for handicapped children] to where our national conscience should be, we won't do very much for these children."

Our survival as a civilized country depends upon the well-being of the weakest of us. If we as a nation count as unimportant the future of the child who needs help in reading, of the vision-impaired child, of the familyless child, then we admit something terrible about ourselves.

"I cannot say that I am in the slightest impressed by your bigness or your material resources . . . ," T. H. Huxley said, at Johns Hopkins University, in 1876. "Size is not grandeur and territory does not make a nation. The great issue . . . is what are you going to do with these things."

"The greatest discovery of my generation," wrote William James, "is that human beings can alter their lives by altering their attitudes of mind."

This is magic—and we can make it happen.

There is a madness in our land. It is a madness that allows us to acknowledge facts—and then to ignore them. It is a madness that allows us to boast of our dedication to children

—and then, surely and competently, to destroy everyone who is not well and has not been pulled out of the line of fire by his family. For this is the truth: in this country, few troubled children get help when it is beyond the reach of their family.

And that is our insanity.

Appendix A. Sources of Help: University-Affiliated Facilities for the Developmentally Disabled

University-affiliated facilities (UAF) that provide an interdisciplinary team approach to the diagnosis and evaluation of developmental disorders in children are listed here. Although policies vary somewhat, most of these facilities accompany their evaluations with recommendations for a course of treatment and education, within the facility or elsewhere in the community. Follow-up care is provided when necessary.

Some of the centers accept patients directly. Most, however, prefer to have them referred by physicians or by social or health agencies. There are no geographical limitations on the acceptance of patients. Although the words *mental retardation* appear in some of the titles, all these institutions deal with every kind of child-development disorder.

New institutions are added periodically. For up-to-date lists and other information, contact the Association of University Affiliated Facilities, Suite 1114, The Watergate, 2600 Virginia Avenue N.W., Washington, D.C. 20037.

University of Alabama at Birmingham
Center for Developmental and Learning Disorders
1919 Seventh Avenue, South
Birmingham, Alabama 35223
    Director: Andrew C. Lorincz, M.D.
    Administrator: Charles L. Davis   205–934–5471

University of Alabama at Tuscaloosa
Center for Developmental and Learning Disorders
Tuscaloosa, Alabama 35401
    Director: Alfred A. Baumeister, Ph.D.
    Associate Director: Joseph Gallagher   205–348–4550

University of California–Irvine
Department of Pediatrics
Irvine, California 92664
    Director: Kenneth W. Dumars, Jr., M.D.   714–833–5011

University of California at Los Angeles
Mental Retardation Research Center
760 Westwood Plaza
Los Angeles, California 90024
    Director: George Tarjan, M.D.   213–825–0121
    Associate Director, Administration:
      Charles V. Keeran, Jr.   213–825–0321

University of Southern California
UAF Training Project
4650 Sunset Boulevard
Los Angeles, California 90027   213–663–3341
    Director: Wylda Hammond, M.D.   ext. 788

University of Colorado Medical Center
JFK Child Development Center
4200 East 9th Avenue
Denver, Colorado 80220
    Director: John H. Meier, Ph.D.   303–394–7224
    Administrator: William Fitzsimmons

University of Miami
Child Development Center
Box 6, Biscayne Annex
Miami, Florida 33152
    Associate Director for Administration:
      Henry Lord   305–350–6631
    Assistant to Director: Edmond Onorati

University of Georgia
Georgia Retardation Center
Athens Unit
850 College Station Road
Athens, Georgia 30601
    Acting Director: Andrew Shotick, Ph.D.   404–549–6423
    Assistant Director for UAF:
      Roy E. Fossett   404–458–5111

University of Georgia
Georgia Retardation Center
Atlanta Unit
4770 North Peachtree Road
Atlanta, Georgia 30341   404–458–5111
    Director: James Clement, M.D.   ext. 321

University of Indiana
UAF
2853 East 10th Street
Bloomington, Indiana 47401
    Director: Henry J. Schroeder, Ed.D.   812–332–0211

University of Indiana–Indianapolis
Medical Center
1100 West Michigan Street
Indianapolis, Indiana 46202
    Director: Morris Green, M.D.   317–635–8431

University of Iowa
University Hospital School
Iowa City, Iowa 52240
    Director: Raymond Remboldt   319–388–0525

University of Kansas Medical Center
Children's Rehabilitation Unit
University of Kansas
Kansas City, Kansas 66103
    Director: John Spaulding, M.D.   913–236–5252

University of Kansas
UAF Central Office
223 Haworth Street
Lawrence, Kansas 66044
    Director: Richard L. Schiefelbusch, Ph.D.
    Associate Director: Ross H. Copeland   913–864–4295

University of Kansas
Kansas Center for the Mentally Retarded
Haworth Hall, Room 233
Lawrence, Kansas 66044
    Director: John M. Throne, Ph.D.   913–864–4950

Parsons State College Hospital and Training
    Center
UAF
Parsons, Kansas 67357
    Director: Sidney De Briere, M.D.   316–421–6550

University of Kentucky
University Center for the Handicapped
University of Kentucky Medical Center
Lexington, Kentucky 40506
    Director: Vernon L. James, M.D.   606–233–6141
    Assistant Director: Walter Lindley   606–233–5249

Johns Hopkins University
John F. Kennedy Institute
707 North Broadway
Baltimore, Maryland 21205
    Director: Robert H. Haslam, M.D.   301–955–4001
    Administrator: Albert R. Hartgrove   301–955–4004

Children's Hospital Medical Center
Development Evaluation Clinic
300 Longwood Avenue
Boston, Massachusetts 02115   617–734–6000
    Director: Allen C. Crocker, M.D.   ext. 2116
    Associate Director: Bruce Cushna, Ph.D.   ext. 2106

Walter E. Fernald State School
Eunice Kennedy Shriver Center
200 Trapelo Road
Waltham, Massachusetts 02154
    Director: Hugo W. Moser, M.D.   617–899–3072
    Administrator: Donald E. McNamee   617–893–0740
    Director of Outpatient Facilities:
      Robert E. Flynn, M.D.   617–899–8135

University of Michigan
Institute for the Study of Mental Retardation and
    Related Disabilities
611 Church Street
Ann Arbor, Michigan 48104
    Director: William Cruickshank, Ph.D.   313–763–3171
    Assistant Director for Administration:
      Norman Thoburn, Ph.D.   313–763–3171
    Associate Director: Julius S. Cohen, Ph.D.   313–763–3171
    Associate Director and Co-ordinator for
      Clinical Services: Arthur Fleming   313–763–4150

St. Louis University
221 North Grand Boulevard   314–535–3300
St. Louis, Missouri 63103   *or*
    Director: Allen Barclay, M.D.   314–772–7990

University of Nebraska
Meyer Children's Rehabilitation Institute
University of Nebraska Medical Center
Omaha, Nebraska 68105
    Director: Paul Pearson, M.D.   402–541–4730
    Administrative Assistant: Dale Duncan   402–536–4000
    Dean of College of Medicine:
      Robert Kugel, M.D.   402–536–4000

New York Medical College
Mental Retardation Institute
1249 Fifth Avenue
New York, New York 10029
    Director: Margaret J. Giannini, M.D., F.A.A.P.   212–876–7724
    Administrator: Seymour Klass   212–876–2112

University of North Carolina
Division for Disorders of Development and
    Learning
Box 523, North Carolina Memorial Hospital
Chapel Hill, North Carolina 27514
    Director: Harrie R. Chamberlin, M.D.   919–966–4417
    Administrator: J. Robert Gray   919–966–5171

University of Cincinnati
UAF
295 Erkenbrecher Avenue
Cincinnati, Ohio 45229
    Director: Jack H. Rubinstein, M.D.   513–221–8282
    Administrator: Joseph J. Kroger

Ohio State University
Nisonger Center
Mental Retardation Training Program
9 West Buttles Avenue
Columbus, Ohio 43215
    Director: William M. Gibson, M.D.   614–422–8365
    Administrator: Vern Reynolds
    Chief of Pediatrics: Geoffrey Woo-Ming, M.D.

University of Oregon at Eugene
Clinical Services Building
College of Education
Eugene, Oregon 97403
    Director of Clinical Services:
      Robert H. Schwartz, Ph.D.   503–686–3111

University of Oregon at Portland
University of Oregon Medical School
Portland, Oregon 97201
    Director: Richard L. Sleeter, M.D.   503–228–9181
    Project Director: Leroy O. Carlson, M.D.

Pennsylvania State University
Rackley Building
University Park, Pennsylvania 16802
    Head of Department of Special Education:
      Joseph L. French, Ph.D.   814–865–6072
    Associate Director: G. Phillip Cartwright   814–865–0471

St. Christopher's Hospital
Handicapped Children's Unit
2603 North Fifth Street
Philadelphia, Pennsylvania 19133   215–426–5600
   Director: John Bartram, M.D.   ext. 211

University of Tennessee
Child Development Center
711 Jefferson Avenue
Memphis, Tennessee 38105
   Director: Robert G. Jordan, M.D.   901–525–2592
   Administrator: Melvin D. Peters

Utah State University
UAF Exceptional Child Center
Logan, Utah 84321
   Director: Marvin F. Fifield, Ph.D.   801–752–4100
   Educational Director: DeVoe Rickert, Ph.D.
   Medical Director: Joseph Kessler, M.D.

University of Washington
Child Development and Mental Retardation
   Center
Seattle, Washington 98105
   Director: Charles R. Strother, Ph.D.   206–543–3224
   Director of Clinical Training Unit:
     Robert Deisher, M.D.   206–543–8791
   Administrator: Henry G. Schulte   206–543–3224

Georgetown University Medical Center
University Affiliated Program for Child
   Development
3800 Reservoir Road N.W.
Washington, D.C. 20007
   Director: Robert J. Clayton, M.D.   202–625–7675
   Administrator: Walter Weiss

University of Wisconsin
Mental Retardation Center
415 West Gilman Street
Madison, Wisconsin 53706
   Directors: Rick F. Heber, Ph.D.   608–262–1728
         Ann Clark, Ph.D.   608–263–1656

Appendix B. The Association for Children with Learning Disabilities

A national nonprofit organization of parents and sympathetic professionals, the Association for Children with Learning Disabilities (ACLD) has been primarily responsible for the gains made for learning-disabled children in this nation. It is a parent's biggest ally. Join it.

Through state affiliates, the ACLD disseminates the best current information concerning help for learning-disabled children. Although the association cannot endorse sources of diagnosis or treatment, it does alert families to the professionals or facilities closest to their homes where other parents have had favorable experiences. It provides information about federal and state laws, court rulings, and various private facilities, ranging from preschools to camps to vocational-training centers.

The ACLD sponsors national, state, and local meetings. These sessions attract speakers in the disciplines related to learning disabilities. The association publishes or distributes a variety of books, articles, and service directories. They are invaluable.

Members are enrolled through state affiliates. If the address of your state affiliate is not available, apply directly to the national office. Send name, address, and annual dues of $5 to:

> Association for Children with Learning Disabilities
> 2200 Brownsville Road
> Pittsburgh, Pennsylvania 15210

That office will forward the membership and dues to the proper state affiliate. If there is none, the applicant will be enrolled as an independent member, and kept informed of available materials and activities through the national office.

Every parent of a learning-disabled child should become active in a local ACLD unit, or should help form one if none exists. The national office will provide guidance.

Appendix C. Other Sources of Information

There are several child-care organizations that, while not exclusively concerned with learning disabilities, can supply useful information on various aspects of the problem.

1. Closer Look is a government information service intended to help parents find services for children with all forms of handicaps. It is administered by the Bureau of Education for the Handicapped, in the U.S. Office of Education.

This service will send, without charge, listings of facilities in your state that work with learning-disabled children. It does not endorse any of these facilities. Parents or other interested parties must make their own evaluations.

Closer Look also publishes a newsletter and other material directed to parents of handicapped children. The address:

Closer Look
Box 1492
Washington, D.C. 20013

2. The Bureau of Education for the Handicapped, an agency of the U.S. Office of Education, in the Department of Health, Education, and Welfare, is the key federal agency concerned with the education of all handicapped children. It will supply reports of current federal activity on behalf of learning-disabled children. Write to:

Dr. Edwin W. Martin
Associate Commissioner
Bureau of Education for the Handicapped
Office of Education
Seventh and D Streets S.W.
Washington, D.C. 20202

3. The Council for Exceptional Children is a private agency concerned with both handicapped and intellectually gifted children. It provides valuable information principally in the area of state and federal laws and rulings concerning the education of exceptional children. The council also monitors current litigation throughout the country involving children who have been excluded from appropriate public education. Write to:

Council for Exceptional Children
1411 South Jefferson Davis Highway
Arlington, Virginia 22202

4. A parents' organization called the Co-ordinating Council for Handicapped Children has compiled a detailed booklet entitled *How to Organize an Effective Parent Group and Move Bureaucracies.* It is excellent. The cost is $1.

This council also publishes two other booklets, *Your Rights as Parents of a Handicapped Child* (25 cents) and *Your Guide to Services for Handicapped Children* ($1.50). Although the first is concerned only with the state of Illinois and the second with services only in the Chicago area, both are excellent models for other parent organizations to emulate. To obtain copies, send to:

Co-ordinating Council for Handicapped Children
Room 950
407 South Dearborn Street
Chicago, Illinois 60615

Appendix D. National Organizations in Related Fields

The following organizations work in areas closely related to or overlapping learning disabilities.

Alexander Graham Bell
Association for the Deaf
1537 35th Street N.W.
Washington, D.C. 20007

Allergy Foundation of America
801 Second Avenue
New York, New York 10017

American Academy of Child
Psychiatry
100 Memorial Drive, Suite 2–9B
Cambridge, Massachusetts
02142

American Academy of
Neurology
4005 West 65th Street
Minneapolis, Minnesota 55435

American Academy of
Pediatrics
1801 Hinman Avenue
Evanston, Illinois 60204

American Association for
Rehabilitation
614 Ivygate Drive
St. Louis, Missouri 63129

American Association of
Ophthalmology
1100 17th Street N.W.
Washington, D.C. 20036

American Association of
Psychiatric Services for
Children
250 West 57th Street
New York, New York 10019

American Optometric
Association
7000 Chippewa Street
St. Louis, Missouri 63119

American Orthopsychiatric
Association
1790 Broadway
New York, New York 10019

American Psychiatric
Association
1700 18th Street N.W.
Washington, D.C. 20009

American Psychological
Association
Division 22—Psychological
Aspects of Disability
1200 17th Street N.W.
Washington, D.C. 20036

American Rehabilitation
Counselors Association
431 Erickson Hall
Michigan State University
East Lansing, Michigan 48823

American Speech and Hearing Association
9030 Old Georgetown Road
Washington, D.C. 20014

Epilepsy Foundation of America
733 15th Street N.W.,
Suite 1116
Washington, D.C. 20005

International Reading Association
6 Tyre Avenue
Newark, Delaware 19711

National Association of Social Workers, Inc.
2 Park Avenue
New York, New York 10016

National Easter Seal Society for Crippled Children and Adults
2023 West Ogden Avenue
Chicago, Illinois 60612

National Rehabilitation Association
1522 K Street N.W.
Washington, D.C. 20005

Orton Society, Inc.
Box 153
Pomfret, Connecticut 06258

United Cerebral Palsy Association, Inc.
66 East 34th Street
New York, New York 10016

Recommended Reading

The first two items in this listing are newsletters published by, respectively, the Association for Children with Learning Disabilities and the California Association for Neurologically Handicapped Children. The others are journals that contain worth-while information concerning learning-disabled children.

ACLD Items of Interest
2200 Brownsville Road
Pittsburgh, Pennsylvania 15210

CANHC–Gram
11291 McNab Street
Garden Grove, California
    92640

Academic Therapy (quarterly)
Academic Therapy Publications
1539 Fourth Street
San Rafael, California 94901

American Journal of
    Orthopsychiatry
AOC Publications Sales Office
49 Sheridan Avenue
Albany, New York 12210

Exceptional Children
Council for Exceptional Children
1411 Jefferson Davis Highway
Jefferson Plaza, Suite 900
Arlington, Virginia 22202

Journal of Learning Disabilities
Professional Press, Inc.
5 North Wabash Avenue
Chicago, Illinois 60602

Teaching Exceptional Children
    (quarterly)
Council for Exceptional Children
1411 Jefferson Davis Highway
Jefferson Plaza, Suite 900
Arlington, Virginia 22202

The following directories offer information about various services for children with learning disabilities.

Annual Directory of Facilities
    for the Learning Disabled
Academic Therapy Publications
1539 Fourth Street
San Rafael, California 94901

Directory for Exceptional
    Children
Porter Sargent, Publisher
11 Beacon Street
Boston, Massachusetts 02108

*Directory of Day and
Residential Schools for
Minimal Brain Dysfunction*
Canadian ACLD
Suite 318, Eglington Avenue
East
Toronto 12, Ontario, Canada

*A Guide to Agencies and
Organizations Concerned
with Exceptional Children*
Council for Exceptional Children
1411 Jefferson Davis Highway
Jefferson Plaza, Suite 900
Arlington, Virginia 22202

*Directory of Schools, Agencies,
and Institutions for Children
and Youth with Special
Needs*
Ohio Youth Commission
2880 West Broad Street
Columbus, Ohio 43223

*National Directory of Clinic
Facilities for Diagnosis and
Treatment of Epilepsy*
Epilepsy Foundation of America
733 15th Street N.W.
Washington, D.C. 20004

Many books and journal articles have been written concerning learning disabilities and the learning process in general. A selected reading list follows.

Anderson, Camilla M. *Society Pays.* New York: Walker & Co., 1972.

Anderson, Lauriel E., ed. *Helping the Adolescent with the Hidden Handicap.* San Rafael, Calif.: Academic Therapy Publications, 1970.

Arena, John I., ed. *Teaching Educationally Handicapped Children.* San Rafael, Calif.: Academic Therapy Publications, 1967.

Baird, Henry W. *The Child with Convulsions: A Guide for Parents, Teachers, Counselors, and Medical Personnel.* New York: Grune and Stratton, 1972.

Beadle, Muriel. *A Child's Mind: How Children Learn during the Critical Years from Birth to Age Five.* Garden City, N.Y.: Doubleday and Co., 1971.

Becker, Wesley C. *Parents Are Teachers: A Child Management Program.* Champaign, Ill.: Research Press Company, 1971.

Beecher, Marguerite, and Beecher, Willard. *Parents on the Run.* New York: Julian Press, 1955.

Behrmann, Polly, and Willman, Joan. *Excel: Experience for Children in Learning.* Cambridge, Mass.: Educators Publishing Service, 1968.

Bernstein, Bebe. *Everyday Problems and the Child with Learning Difficulties.* New York: John Day, 1967.

Birch, Herbert G., ed. *Brain Damage in Children*. Baltimore: Williams and Wilkins, 1964.

Bloom, Benjamin S. *Stability and Change in Human Characteristics*. New York: John Wiley, 1964.

Bricklin, Barry, and Bricklin, Patricia M. *Bright Child—Poor Grades: The Psychology of Underachievement*. New York: Delacorte Press, 1967.

————. *Strong Family—Strong Child*. New York: Delacorte Press, 1970.

Brown, George W. "Suggestions for Parents." *Journal of Learning Disabilities*, vol. 2, no. 2, February 1969.

Chalfant, James C., and Scheffelin, Margaret A. *Central Processing Dysfunction in Children: A Review of Research*. Monograph No. 9. Washington: U.S. National Institute of Neurological Diseases and Stroke, 1969.

Chess, Stella, et al. *Your Child Is a Person: A Psychological Approach to Parenthood without Guilt*. New York: Viking Press, 1965.

Clements, Sam D. *Minimal Brain Dysfunction in Children: Terminology and Identification*. Public Health Service Publication No. 1415. Washington: U.S. National Institute of Neurological Diseases and Stroke, 1966.

Crawford, John E. *Children with Subtle Perceptual-Motor Difficulties*. Pittsburgh: Stanwix House, 1966.

Critchley, Macdonald. *Developmental Dyslexia*. Springfield, Ill.: Charles C. Thomas, 1964.

Crosby, R. M. N., and Liston, Robert A. *The Waysiders: A New Approach to Reading and the Dyslexic Child*. New York: Delacorte Press, 1968.

Cruikshank, William M. *The Brain-Injured Child in Home, School, and Community*. Syracuse: Syracuse University Press, 1967.

————. *The Teacher of Brain-Injured Children: A Discussion of the Base for Competency*. Syracuse: Syracuse University Press, 1966.

Cruikshank, William M., and Johnson, Orville, eds. *Education of Exceptional Children and Youth*. Englewood Cliffs, N.J.: Prentice-Hall, 1958.

Dreikurs, Rudolf. *Children: The Challenge*. New York: Duell, Sloan and Pearce, 1964.

Edgington, Ruth. *Helping Children with Reading Disability*. Chicago: Developmental Learning Material, 1967.

Edgington, Ruth, and Clements, Sam D. *Indexed Bibliography on the Educational Management of Children with Learning Disabilities.* Chicago: Argus Communications, 1967.

Fraiberg, Selma H. *The Magic Years: Understanding and Handling the Problems of Early Childhood.* New York: Charles Scribner's Sons, 1959.

Frierson, Edward C., and Barbe, Walter B. *Educating Children with Learning Disabilities.* New York: Appleton-Century-Crofts, 1967.

Gersh, Marvin J. *How to Raise Children at Home in Your Spare Time.* Greenwich, Conn.: Fawcett Publications, 1969.

Gesell, Arnold, and Ilg, Frances. *Infant and Child in the Culture of Today.* New York: Harper and Row, 1943.

Ginott, Haim G. *Between Parent and Child.* New York: Avon Books, 1969.

Golick, Margaret. *Learning Disability.* Toronto: CBC Publications, Box 500, Station A, 1969.

————. *A Parents' Guide to Learning Problems.* Montreal: Quebec Association for Children with Learning Disabilities, 6338 Victoria Avenue, 1970.

Gordon, Sol. *Facts about Sex: A Basic Guide.* New York: John Day, 1968.

Gordon, Sol, and Golob, Risa S., eds. *Recreation and Socialization for the Brain-Injured Child.* East Orange, N.J.: New Jersey Association for Brain-Injured Children, 1966.

Hainstock, Elizabeth G. *Teaching Montessori in the Home.* New York: Random House, 1968.

Hart, Jane, and Jones, Beverly. *Where's Hannah? A Handbook for Parents and Teachers of Children with Learning Disorders.* New York: Hart Publishing Co., 1968.

Hellmuth, Jerome, ed. *Learning Disorders.* Vols. 1–3. Seattle: Special Child Publications, 1965.

Holt, John. *How Children Fail.* New York: Pitman Publishing Co., 1964.

————. *How Children Learn.* New York: Pitman Publishing Co., 1967.

Johnson, Doris J., and Myklebust, Helmer R. *Learning Disabilities: Educational Principles and Practices.* New York: Grune and Stratton, 1967.

Kephart, Newell C. *Learning Disability, an Educational Adventure.* Danville, Ill.: Interstate Printers and Publishers, 1968.

————. *The Slow Learner in the Classroom.* Columbus, Ohio: Charles E. Merrill Co., 1960.

Kirk, Samuel A. *Educating Exceptional Children.* Boston: Houghton Mifflin, 1962.

Kronick, Doreen. *They Too Can Succeed: A Practical Guide for Parents of Learning Disabled Children.* San Rafael, Calif.: Academic Therapy Publications, 1969.

Kronick, Doreen, ed. *Learning Disabilities: Its Implications to a Responsible Society.* Chicago: Developmental Learning Materials, 1969.

Le Shan, Eda J. *Natural Parenthood: Raising Your Child without a Script.* New York: New American Library, 1970.

Lewis, Richard S.; Lehtinen, Laura E.; and Strauss, Alfred A. *The Other Child: A Book for Parents and Laymen.* New York: Grune and Stratton, 1960.

Lidz, Theodore. *The Person: His Development Throughout the Life Cycle.* New York: Basic Books, 1968.

McCarthy, James J., and McCarthy, Joan F. *Learning Disabilities.* Boston: Allyn and Bacon, 1969.

Madsen, Clifford K., and Madsen, Charles H. *Parents/Children/Discipline.* Boston: Allyn and Bacon, 1972.

Mallison, Ruth. *Education as Therapy: Suggestions for Work with Neurologically Impaired Children.* Seattle: Special Child Publications, 1968.

Minde, K. *A Parents' Guide to Hyperactivity in Children.* Montreal: Quebec Association for Children with Learning Disabilities, 6338 Victoria Avenue, 1970.

Money, John, ed. *The Disabled Reader: Education of the Dyslexic Child.* Baltimore: Johns Hopkins Press, 1966.

Montessori, Maria. *Dr. Montessori's Own Handbook.* New York: Schocken Books, 1965.

————. *The Montessori Method.* New York: Schocken Books, 1964.

————. *Spontaneous Activity in Education.* New York: Schocken Books, 1965.

Myers, Patricia I., and Hammill, Donald D. *Methods for Learning Disorders.* New York: John Wiley and Sons, 1969.

Myklebust, Helmer R., ed. *Progress in Learning Disabilities.* Vol. 1. New York: Grune and Stratton, 1968.

National Advisory Committee on Dyslexia and Related Reading Disorders. *Reading Disorders in the United States.* Washington: U.S. Department of Health, Education, and Welfare, 1969.

Neurological and Sensory Disease Control Program. *Minimal Brain Dysfunction. Phase Two: Educational, Medical, and Health-Related Services.* Washington: U.S. Public Health Service, 1969.

Orton, Samuel T. *Reading, Writing, and Speech Problems in Children: A Presentation of Certain Types of Disorders in the Development of the Language Faculty.* New York: W. W. Norton, 1937.

Patterson, Gerald R., and Gullion, M. Elizabeth. *Living with Children: New Methods for Parents and Teachers.* Champaign, Ill.: Research Press Company, 1971.

Radler, D. H., and Kephart, N. C. *Success Through Play.* New York: Harper and Row, 1960.

Rappaport, Sheldon. *Public Education for Children with Brain Dysfunction.* Syracuse: Syracuse University Press, 1969.

Rawson, Margaret B. *Developmental Language Disability: Adult Accomplishments of Dyslexic Boys.* Baltimore: Johns Hopkins Press, 1968.

Robinson, Mary E. "New Ways of Looking at the Social Adaptation of the Specific-Learning-Disability Child." Mimeographed. Department of Psychology, Children's Hospital of D.C., Washington, D.C., 20202, 1970.

Ross, Alan O. *The Exceptional Child in the Family.* New York: Grune and Stratton, 1964.

Sharp, Evelyn. *Thinking Is Child's Play.* New York: Avon Books, 1969.

Siegel, Ernest. *Helping the Brain-Injured Child: A Handbook for Parents.* New York: New York Association for Brain-Injured Children, 1962.

———. *Special Education in the Regular Classroom.* New York: John Day, 1969.

Silva, Willetta. *The School Daze of the Learning Disability Child: A Resource and Information Booklet for Parents of Children with Learning Disabilities.* Radnor, Pa.: Alpern Communications, 220 Gulph Hills Road, 1971.

Smith, Bert Kruger. *Your Nonlearning Child: His World of Upside Down.* Boston: Beacon Press, 1968.

Spock, Benjamin, and Lerrigo, Marion O. *Caring for Your Disabled Child.* New York: The Macmillan Company, 1965.

Strauss, Alfred A., and Kephart, Newell C. *Psychopathology and Education of the Brain-Injured Child.* Vol. 2. New York: Grune and Stratton, 1955.

Strauss, Alfred A., and Lehtinen, Laura E. *Psychopathology and*

Education of the Brain-Injured Child. Vol. 1. New York: Grune and Stratton, 1947.

Tarnapol, Lester, ed. *Learning Disabilities: Introduction to Educational and Medical Management.* Springfield, Ill.: Charles C. Thomas, 1969.

Thompson, Alice C. "How to Do It—A Baker's Dozen of Suggestions to Teachers." Mimeographed. Carbondale, Ill.: Southern Illinois University, Department of Special Education, 1971.

Valett, Robert E. *Modifying Children's Behavior: A Guide for Parents and Professionals.* Palo Alto, Calif.: Fearon Publishing Company, 1971.

————. *The Remediation of Learning Disabilities.* Palo Alto, Calif.: Fearon Publishing Company, 1967.

Wender, Paul H. *Minimal Brain Dysfunction in Children.* New York: Wiley-Interscience, 1971.

Woods, Nancy E. *Delayed Speech and Language Development.* Englewood Cliffs, N.J.: Prentice-Hall, 1964.

Acknowledgments

For the encouragement and assistance so willingly and generously given them by many during the planning and writing of this book, the authors are grateful. Limitations of space prevent a listing of each helpful individual and the nature of his or her contribution, but the absence of such a list does not limit our gratitude to all of them. A few must be cited for particular devotion and most special aid:

To the hundreds of parents of learning-disabled children who patiently filled out detailed questionnaires, and the dozens of parents who allowed the authors to visit their homes for interviews. Their cumulative insight made this a far better book.

To the Association for Children with Learning Disabilities, for its co-operation during our research, and for its encouragement. To the Bureau of Education for the Handicapped and to the Council for Exceptional Children, for research assistance. To Dr. Samuel Kirk, for his counsel. To Judith Quirus, for her research assistance.

To Joseph and Dorothy Hirt, dedicated teachers, who provided inestimable support and counsel from their experience.

To Kay Marshall, dear friend, who typed and retyped without losing her graciousness.

To Irving Wallace and Betsy Nolan, for their belief and enthusiasm.

To Catherine Fauver, our manuscript editor, who made the results immeasurably better.

To Julian Muller, Vice President and Director of the Trade Department of Harcourt Brace Jovanovich, who guided us over the rough terrain.

Most of all, to Helen, Bobbie, and Bill, who deserve equal billing with us.

M.B., S.R., C.M.

Index

Marcia Henry - Stanford
415 - 497 - 9532 -
Lives in Los Gatos.
358 - 2453

Charles Armstrong school
Menlo Park

415   - 854 - 0888

South Valley Learning &
Language Clinic
* Barbara Stephen (marvello
448 - 1923